THE WOMEN BONAPARTES

PAULINE BONAPARTE
FROM THE PAINTING BY LEFÈVRE AT VERSAILLES

THE WOMEN BONAPARTES

THE MOTHER AND THREE SISTERS OF NAPOLEON I.

BY

H. NOEL WILLIAMS

AUTHOR OF "FIVE FAIR SISTERS," ETC.

WITH ILLUSTRATIONS

VOLUME I

NEW YORK
CHARLES SCRIBNER'S SONS
1909

TO
MY WIFE

PREFACE

GREAT men, it has been said, are like great mountains, of whose altitude we can form no just conception until we view them from a distance. Certain it is that, with the flight of time, interest in all that relates to the Man of Destiny, so far from showing any signs of decline, seems only to increase ; and during the past two decades English and American readers have not only been invited to study in detail almost every phase of that amazing career, but also those of the Empress Joséphine, the Duke of Reichstadt, Queen Hortense, Jérôme Bonaparte, Eugène de Beauharnais, Talleyrand, and others who played a more or less important part in the life of Napoleon.

Yet, strangely enough, though Napoleon has been presented to them, in turn, as military cadet, soldier, conqueror, statesman, lover, husband, father, exile, and captive, as a son and a brother he is still comparatively unknown ; and, with the single exception of a translation of a monograph on Letizia Bonaparte by the Norwegian historian, Madame Tschudi, there is not, so far as I am aware, any work in our language which professes to deal in an adequate manner with his mother or either of his three sisters—Élisa, Pauline, and Caroline.

Such neglect is the more singular, since all four women were, in their several ways, striking personalities, and the strange vicissitudes which they underwent, and the momentous events with which their names are associated, make the story of their lives one of the greatest possible interest.

That this has been fully recognised by French writers is evident from the attention which has been devoted to them of recent years. Baron Larrey, son of the celebrated surgeon-in-chief of the Grand Army, has written the life of *Madame Mère*, in two bulky volumes of the highest interest and value, though the panegyrical tone adopted by the author detracts not a little from the pleasure of their perusal. M. Paul Marmottan is responsible for two works on Élisa; the first (*Élisa Bonaparte*), a narrative of her life up to the establishment of the Empire; the second (*les Arts en Toscane sous Napoléon: la Princesse Élisa*), a sumptuously-illustrated quarto dealing with her patronage of the arts during her rule at Lucca and Florence; while M. E. Rodocanachi, in his *Élisa Napoléon* (*Baciocchi*) *en Italie*, describes the same period of her career, from a more general point of view. Pauline has found a biographer, though it must be confessed, a somewhat credulous one, in M. Henri d'Alméras (*Une Amoureuse: Pauline Bonaparte*); and Caroline, in company with her sisters, has provided M. Joseph Turquan with material for another of his entertaining, if not very discriminating, chronicles (*les Sœurs de Napoléon*). Finally, M. Frédéric Masson, in his great, though as yet unfinished, work (*Napoléon et sa famille*) deals exhaustively, and with rigid impartiality, with both mother and daughters, and clears away much previous misconception concerning them.

It will therefore, I think, be admitted that the present volumes, in which I have endeavoured to give a full and unprejudiced history of the Women Bonapartes, call for no apology; and I may even venture to believe that, whatever their shortcomings, they will be welcomed by the English and American public as an attempt to fill a place in our Napoleonic literature which has been too long vacant.

In conclusion, I must take this opportunity of acknowledging my obligations to the works above mentioned—particularly to those of M. Frédéric Masson and Baron Larrey—as well as to M. Colonna de Cesari Rocca's *le Nid de l'Aigle*, Mr. Oscar Browning's *Napoleon: The First Phase*, and MM. Jules Chavanon and

Georges Saint-Yves's *Joachim Murat*. Most of the other authorities, both contemporary and modern, which I have had occasion to consult are mentioned either in the text or the foot-notes.

I must also tender my thanks to Mr. Whitman and other officials of the British Museum Print Room, for their kind assistance in the selection of several of the illustrations.

H. NOEL WILLIAMS

London
October, 1908

CONTENTS

CONTENTS

CHAPTER VIII

CHAPTER IX

CHAPTER X

CHAPTER XI

CHAPTER XIV

CHAPTER XV

LIST OF ILLUSTRATIONS

THE WOMEN BONAPARTES

THE
WOMEN BONAPARTES

CHAPTER I

Letizia Ramolino—History of the Bonapartes of Corsica—Carlo
Bonaparte—His marriage with Letizia Ramolino—Birth of
Joseph Bonaparte — Letizia and the confessor at Bastia —
Enthusiasm of Carlo Bonaparte for Paoli and the cause of
Corsican independence—Cession of the island to France—
The Bonapartes at Corte—Outbreak of the war between the
Corsican patriots and France—Courage of Letizia, who follows
her husband throughout the war—Adventures of the Bona-
partes after the battle of Ponte-Nuovo — Carlo Bonaparte
makes his submission to France.

AT the beginning of the fifth decade of the
eighteenth century, there was living at
Ajaccio, in Corsica, a young man named
Gian Geronimo Ramolino. He came of a family
of Lombard origin, branches of which had settled
at Florence, Naples, and Genoa, and it was
from the last-named city that his ancestors had
emigrated to Corsica, towards the end of the
fifteenth century. Since the treaty of Cateau-
Cambresis, in 1559, the island had belonged to
Genoa, and Gian Ramolino obtained a commission
in the army of that republic. He proved himself
an excellent officer, and the ability he displayed

as an engineer impressed his superiors so favourably that, in May 1750, he received the post of
inspector-general of roads and bridges in Corsica.

Four years earlier, on February 2, 1745,[1] the
young soldier had taken unto himself a wife, one
Angela Maria Pietra - Santa, a member of an
old Corsican family, originally of Sartine, near
Ajaccio. Of this marriage, three children were
born : two girls and a boy. The elder daughter
died in infancy, and of the son little or nothing
seems to be known ; but the younger daughter,
Maria Letizia, the date of whose birth was long
a matter of dispute, but is now generally given
as 1750,[2] was destined to achieve immortality as
the mother of the greatest military genius that
the world has seen.

In 1755, when his little daughter was five years
old, Gian Ramolino died, and, five years later, his
widow married Franz Fesch, a member of a
Swiss family and a captain of Genoese marines,
who had abjured Protestantism in order to obtain
her hand. The children of this marriage were a
girl, who became the wife of a compatriot of her
father named Bürkly, and a boy, Joseph, celebrated
in after years as Cardinal Fesch.

In the South, girls mature early ; at thirteen,
Letizia Ramolino seems to have been, by common
consent, one of the most beautiful maidens in

---

[1] And not on May 20, 1743, as several historians state.
[2] According to the *Almanach impérial* for 1815, she was born
on August 4, 1750.

Corsica; and her mother and stepfather had already begun to look about them for a suitable husband. She had a wealth of sunny chestnut hair, dark eyes, a well-formed, though rather long nose, a beautiful mouth and pretty white teeth, small and exquisitely modelled ears, hands and feet, and a slightly prominent chin, which indicated firmness of character. Her figure, though somewhat below middle height, was perfect and her carriage easy and graceful. Altogether, a most alluring damsel.

The young lady's education had been sadly neglected; but what of that? One did not cultivate blue-stockings in Corsica. She could read and write; she knew a little—a very little—Latin; that was all. Of any modern tongue but her own, of music or of art, her ignorance was profound. For the rest, she was devout, at least outwardly, as were all Corsican women, though not extravagantly so; a little superstitious, believing in the power of the evil eye, fairies, and so forth, and a good—that is to say, a submissive—daughter.

A suitor for the hand of the fair Letizia was not long in presenting himself. About the year 1490,[1] an Italian mercenary named Francesco di Bonaparte[2] had come to the recently founded

---

[1] And not in 1529, which is the date given by several writers. His name appears in the list of the town-guard for the year 1490 preserved in the Archives of Genoa.

[2] The correct orthography is, of course, Buonaparte, but we propose to use the gallicized form of the name adopted by Napoleon in 1796.

Genose colony of Ajaccio, not in the quality of
"captain-commandant of the Genoese troops," as
several genealogists have stated, but as a simple
cross-bowman of the town-guard. This Francesco
di Bonaparte was a descendant of a family which
came, like the Ramolini, from Lombardy, whence
they removed to Tuscany, and branches of them
subsequently settled at San Miniato, Genoa, Pisa,
Florence, and Sarzana. Francesco himself belonged to the Sarzana branch, and his father
Giovanni di Bonaparte had been syndic of that
town.

Francesco, who is styled in official documents
"the Moor of Sarzana" or "Francesco Bonaparte,
called the Moor," either on account of an unusually
swarthy complexion, or because he had served
under Ludovico the Moor, Duke of Milan,
resolved to settle in Corsica, and obtained a
grant of land on the confines of the Genoese
colony of Saulo della Pieve, in the district of
San Giovanni. Some years before migrating to
Corsica, he had married a certain Caterina di
Castelletto, the daughter of an official of the
Bank of San Giorgio, who bore him two children,
a daughter, Antonia, and a son, Gabriele. This
Gabriele was the ancestor in the ninth degree of
Napoleon Bonaparte.

During the sixteenth century, most of the
Corsican Bonapartes of whom any record remains
seem to have been soldiers. Gabriele followed
his father's profession in his youth, though in his

later years he entered the priesthood, and in
1582, when it is calculated he must have reached
the patriarchal age of ninety-seven years, became
arch-priest and canon of Ajaccio. We read also
of an Antonio Bonaparte, likewise in the Genoese
service, who was killed in an encounter with the
Corsicans, who, having tied his dead body on his
horse, with the head towards the crupper, drove
the animal back to Ajaccio ; of an Anzio Bonaparte, who, in 1560, was despatched on an
expedition to Cauro in pursuit of some banditti ;
and of one Luca Bonaparte, a natural son of
Francesco's younger brother, Cesare, a corporal
of the garrison of Ajaccio, concerning whom a
tragic anecdote is related.

In 1572, a certain Antonio Ornano quarrelled
with and struck Luca in the street at Ajaccio.
The latter laid his hand on his sword, but the
companions of Ornano threw themselves upon
him, and he was compelled to stomach the affront.
Time passed, and the episode had been forgotten,
when, one fine morning, Ornano was found mor-
tally wounded on the threshold of his house, with
his right hand pinned to the door-post by a
poniard. From subsequent inquiries, there appears to have been little doubt that his assassin
was the man whom he had insulted several years
before.

After the close of the sixteenth century, the
history of the Bonapartes of Corsica seems to
have been, on the whole, very uneventful. In

that land of unrest, in the midst of a turbulent and quarrelsome population, at a time when it was computed that two-thirds of the male inhabitants perished by violent deaths, they lived a tranquil and peaceful existence, giving offence to none whom it was dangerous to offend, making prudent marriages,[1] educating their children with a care which showed that they had inherited, to some extent, the cultured taste of their Italian ancestors, and labouring incessantly for the increase of their patrimonies. They farmed their lands, traded in wine and oil, followed the professions of advocate or notary, and filled various public offices in Ajaccio. Prudent and peaceable, they took no active part in any political movement, but they frequently rendered good service to their adopted country ; and we find one Agostino Bonaparte, grandson of Francesco, erecting, at his own expense, a watch-tower on the coast near Ajaccio, to give warning of the approach of the dreaded Barbary corsairs. This tower long preserved the name of the "Tower of Bonaparte."

In 1763, the head of the family was one Carlo Maria Bonaparte, a strikingly handsome youth of eighteen,[2] of courtly manners and quite unusual

[1] Among these alliances, the family was especially proud of the marriage of Giuseppe di Bonaparte, great-grandfather of Carlo Bonaparte, Napoleon's father, with Maria Bozzi, the daughter of Guglielmo, lord of Bozzi, whose wife was a member of the Ornano family. Through this marriage, some of the oldest blood in Corsica runs in the veins of the Bonapartes.—Rocca, *le Nid de l' Aigle*.

[2] The date of Carlo Bonaparte's birth, like that of Letizia Ramolino, has been much disputed, and is impossible to fix with

culture, with "a pretty taste for verse-making."[1]
His father, Giuseppe Maria Bonaparte, had died
some years before,[2] since which event the boy had
been brought up by an uncle, Luciano Bonaparte,
who had entered the priesthood and was at this
time archdeacon of Ajaccio. After studying for
a year or two at the so-called University of
Corte, Carlo was sent to complete his education
at the University of Pisa, where he eventually
obtained the degree of Doctor of Laws. While
at Pisa, he made the acquaintance of a well-to-do
family named Alberti. The eldest daughter was
pretty, and, it was understood, likely to receive a
considerable *dot*. The young Corsican fell in love
with the girl, or the prospective dowry, or both,
and proposed for her hand. But Signor Alberti,
having caused inquiries to be made in regard to
Carlo's prospects, which were somewhat uncertain
(since Giuseppe Bonaparte had left to his brother
the entire control of the family property, and

certainty, owing to the loss of the official registers of Ajaccio at
the time of the Revolution. According to his eldest son, Joseph,
who instituted careful researches into the history of his family, he
was born in 1740. Several writers place his birth four years
later, in 1744; while others again, among whom are Baron
Larrey, M. Frédéric Masson, and M. Rocca, incline to the
belief that he was born in 1746. This last date appears the
most probable.

[1] "A superb man," writes the Abbé de Chardon, who saw him
in 1779, when he brought his sons Joseph and Napoleon to France.
His wife describes him as *"un bel homme, grand comme Murat"*
(Joachim Murat, King of Naples).

[2] The name of his mother, who was still living, was Maria
Saveria Paravicini, a member of a family of Ligurian origin.

during his uncle's lifetime the youth would only have what the archdeacon chose to allow him), and into his manner of life, which seems to have been decidedly extravagant, came to the conclusion that his daughter might do very much better for herself elsewhere, and refused his consent to the match.

While Carlo was still smarting under this blow to his self-esteem, for he always entertained a most exalted opinion of his own merits, he received a letter from Uncle Luciano, urging him to return home, since he had discovered a *signorina* possessed of all the charms and all the virtues that the heart of man could desire and—what, we fear, the worthy archdeacon considered of more importance than either—a little fortune of her own.

Carlo lost no time in obeying the avuncular summons, and speedily forgot all about his Pisan inamorata in contemplating the perfections of the lovely Letizia. Signora Fesch, as became a lady whose present and departed husbands had both eaten the bread of Genoa, had some scruples about allowing her daughter to enter a family which made no secret of its sympathies with Pasquale di Paoli, the "Washington of Corsica," and the Party of Independence. But, since the young man was in other respects an eligible suitor—the standard of eligibility in Corsica, of course, differed very widely from that which prevailed at Pisa—and Letizia seemed to be as much

in love with Carlo as he was with her, she decided to overlook the latter's political predilections, and, on June 2, 1764,[1] the archdeacon pronounced the blessing of the Church on the young
couple.

Corsican women are proud of their fecundity; it
is almost a disgrace for them to have no children.
Signora Bonaparte had no reason to reproach
herself on that score, for in her nineteen years
of married life she presented her husband with
twelve tokens of her affection. However, Carlo
Bonaparte was not destined to see quite so many
olive-branches round about his table. Nature invariably exacts retribution from those who violate
her laws, and of the first six children born of this
premature marriage, four were either stillborn or
died in early infancy. Since all of the remaining
six survived to grow up, the loss of these four in-
fants was perhaps a fortunate circumstance for
Carlo Bonaparte's mother, who, in a rash moment,
which she must surely have regretted later, had
made a vow that she would attend a mass every
day for each grandchild with whom her daughter-
in-law presented her. Even as matters were, the
good lady must have spent a considerable portion
of her days upon her knees.

The first of Letizia's children destined to sur-

---

[1] The record of the marriage of Carlo Bonaparte, like the record
of his birth and that of his wife, has disappeared from the official
registers of Ajaccio ; but the above-mentioned date is the one given
by Lucien Bonaparte in his *Mémoires*, and accepted by most
historians.

vive was born on January 7, 1768, at Corte, at
the house of Tomaso Arrighi di Cazanova, an
uncle of Carlo Bonaparte. The child—a fine,
healthy boy—was called Giuseppe, after his paternal grandfather, though his name, like that of
his brothers and sisters, was afterwards gallicized.
Tomaso Arrighi and his wife stood sponsors,
and the register in which his baptism is recorded is still preserved in the archives of the
mairie at Corte. This, as Baron Larrey points
out, effectually disposes of the story that Napoleon,
and not the future King of Spain, was really the
eldest son.[1]

Some three months after the birth of her son,
an incident occurred which, we are assured, greatly
enhanced the high esteem in which Signora Bonaparte was already held by all who possessed
the privilege of her acquaintance. During Holy
Week, she happened to be visiting some friends
at Bastia, and, together with a number of other
ladies in the town, was the recipient of a request
from the bishop of the diocese to set a good example to the poorer classes by confessing before
Easter. Letizia, a devout Catholic, so far as
forms and ceremonies went, hastened to comply
with the episcopal wish, and presented herself, in
all humility, at the confessional of the cathedral.
But what was her astonishment and indignation
when the confessor before whom she knelt, carried away by the contemplation of so much love-

[1] *Madame Mère.*

liness, proceeded to address to her questions which, it is to be sincerely hoped, are seldom heard at the tribunal of penitence! At first, the lady refused to reply, but, as the priest persisted in his sacrilegious interrogatory, she rose up, in all the majesty of offended virtue, and, raising her voice, exclaimed in the Corsican dialect: "Father, you are forgetting what is seemly!" The angry divine threatened to refuse her absolution, to which she scornfully replied : " You are at liberty to withhold it, but, if you do so, I will put you to shame before all the congregation." The church was crowded, and the confessor, ashamed and humiliated, lost no time in pronouncing the desired absolution. However, some scraps of the conversation between him and his offended penitent had been overheard by those present, with the result that he was shortly afterwards dismissed by his superiors, while the conduct of the virtuous Letizia seems to have been the subject of universal admiration.[1]

The desire that his wife's confinement should take place amid the bracing air of Corte was not the only reason which had induced Carlo Bonaparte to remove temporarily from Ajaccio. A grave crisis in the history of the island was rapidly approaching, and young Bonaparte, who had become a very ardent patriot, was determined

[1] Baron Larrey, *Madame Mère*. This anecdote was related to him by M. Ornano, at one time French Consul at Tangier, who had it from the lady's own lips.

to play a part in it. " He was," says a contemporary, " terribly impassioned for his country, which he desired should be free and independent, and for Paoli. This enthusiasm had caused him to abandon his native town, and to remove to Corte, where Paoli had his headquarters, with his wife, his uncle Napoleone, and Geltruda, his sister." [1]

The Corsicans had bitterly resented the article in the treaty of Cateau-Cambresis by which the island had been ceded to Genoa, and for several years they waged a fierce and sanguinary struggle against their masters, under the leadership of Sampiero Corso, who had served with distinction in the French army. Finally, Sampiero was assassinated,[2] and his followers submitted.

For more than a century and a half after the death of Sampiero, Corsica enjoyed comparative peace, though little else, since the Genoese ruled with an iron hand, and so mercilessly pillaged the wretched inhabitants that it became customary for a new official to inquire jestingly of a retiring one: " Have you left anything to take?" At length, in 1730, the people rose in revolt against their oppressors, and for thirty-four years the unhappy land was given over to anarchy and bloodshed. French, Sardinians, English, and Austrians lent

[1] Ambrogio Rossi, *Osservazioni storiche sopra la Corsica*, cited by Rocca, *le Nid de l'Aigle.*

[2] One of his assassins was that same Antonio Ornano, who afterwards fell a victim to the vengeance of Luca Bonaparte.

their assistance to one side or the other, and marched up and down the country, burning and pillaging.   It was during this period that Gaffori, Rivarola, and Giacinto Paoli and his two sons, Clemente and Pasquale, sprang into fame.   It was during this period, also, that there appeared that strange adventurer Theodore von Neuhof, who exercised a brief period of sovereignty, under the title of King Theodore I, but was soon compelled to vacate his kingdom, and died in London, in 1756, a pensioner on the bounty of Horace Walpole.   Finally, in 1764, the Genoese finding that the insurgents, under the able leadership of Pasquale Paoli, were beginning to carry all before them, perceived that, unless they had once more recourse to the assistance of France, which had rendered them powerful aid in several campaigns since the beginning of the insurrection, they would be compelled to abdicate all pretensions over Corsica.   During the Seven Years' War, which had terminated so disastrously for France in the previous year, she had been compelled to borrow several million livres from Genoa, and, on August 7, a treaty was concluded at Compiègne, whereby it was agreed that this debt should be liquidated by French troops garrisoning the fortresses of Ajaccio, Calvi, Bastia, Saint-Florent, and Algajola for four years.

Paoli, who had no suspicion of the real design of the French Minister, Choiseul, which was, of course, the annexation of the island, was willing enough to recognise the French protectorate, with certain guarantees, and until early in 1768 the peace to which Corsica had been so long a stranger reigned once more. Then the imprudence of the Genoese in offering the exiled Spanish Jesuits an asylum in the towns occupied by the French, gave France a pretext for withdrawing her troops; the Paolists immediately seized upon Ajaccio and Algajola, and Genoa, convinced of the hopelessness of attempting the reconquest of her turbulent colony, ceded Corsica to France, in exchange for a sum of two million livres.

Paoli, however, was very far from disposed to accept with equanimity this change of masters, although most of the abuses which had provoked the insurrection of 1730 had been removed by the recent treaty. He summoned a meeting of the principal inhabitants of the island at Corte, drew up a manifesto, sent appeals for aid to every Court in Europe, declaring that the Corsicans were being treated "like a flock of sheep sold in the market-place," and prepared for a desperate resistance.

After the birth of her son, Letizia went to stay at a little country-house belonging to her husband's family, called the Villa Milelli, situated in an olive-garden on the sea-coast, about seven miles from Ajaccio. In the mountains close at hand was a rocky grotto, which was converted into a summer-house by the Bonapartes, and, in after years, became the favourite retreat of Napoleon when he came to spend his furloughs with his family.   While his wife was recruiting her health in this delightful spot, Carlo Bonaparte made a journey to Rome, presumably to seek financial assistance for the Corsicans in the impending struggle, but he soon returned, and Letizia rejoined him at Corte, where he had been lodged, by Paoli's orders, in a house which had formerly belonged to the Corsican patriot, Gaffori.

This house had a tragic history.   In 1750, during the absence of Gaffori from Corte, the Genoese determined to seize his wife and hold her as a hostage.   The lady, however, warned of their intentions, barricaded the house, and, with the assistance of her friends and servants, held out for several days.   At length, as further resistance seemed impossible, some of the besieged proposed that they should surrender, whereupon Signora Gaffori, descending, with a lighted match in her hand, to the cellar, where several barrels of gunpowder had been stored, vowed that she would blow herself and them to the skies, if any one so much as spoke of surrender.   Her courage was rewarded, for, shortly afterwards, her husband returned and compelled the Genoese to raise the siege.[1]

[1] An historian of Napoleon, Dr. Emile Bégin, relates that the Genoese, on another occasion, succeeded in capturing the infant

Some time later, Gaffori was assassinated, with the complicity of his own brother, surnamed the Cain of Corsica. But his death did not long remain unavenged. In the fond belief that no suspicion attached to him, the traitor came to offer his condolences to the widow, bringing with him his two young children. The infuriated woman, taking him unawares, beat out his brains with a club, after which she rushed upon the hapless children and flung them from an upper window into the street, killing them instantly. Finally, she left the house, having first laid a train to fire the gunpowder in the cellar. The house, however, was saved from destruction by the neighbours, who had hastened to the spot on seeing the children fall, and "preserves to this day the traces of the sieges and assaults which it has sustained."

Here Carlo Bonaparte, who had been elected a member of Paoli's council and appointed private secretary to the Corsican general, seems to have considered it incumbent upon him to dispense an hospitality out of all proportion to his means, and to have kept open house for the insurgent leaders. His extravagance was a sore trial to poor Letizia, who, however, did not dare to remonstrate. She endeavoured to counteract it,

---

son of the Corsican chief, and placed him in the breach of the citadel of Corte, which his father was besieging. "Soldiers," cried the general, "advance and continue to fire. I am a Corsican citizen first, a father afterwards." The insurgents redoubled their efforts, the citadel was taken, and the child saved by a miracle.

to some extent, by exercising the most rigid economy wherever possible; and this was no doubt the origin of that parsimony which eventually became a kind of second nature, and was a reproach to her to the end of her days.

Although she was even thus early in her married life entirely absorbed in her household duties and cared little for the pleasures of society, her husband, proud of her beauty, which added not a little to his own importance, desired her to appear in public as often as possible. Thus, she attended a splendid fête given by Paoli in honour of an embassy from the Bey of Tunis, with whom he was endeavouring to negotiate an alliance. Although the most beautiful women in the island had been invited to this fête, it was the unanimous opinion of those present that the palm must be awarded to Signora Bonaparte.

At the end of July 1768, hostilities between the French and the Corsican patriots began, and, in spite of the superior discipline and numbers of the invaders, the operations during the remainder of the year were altogether favourable to the latter. The French, who had some 10,000 men in the field, under the command of the Marquis de Chauvelin, took Furiani and Casina—after a desperate resistance on the part of the defenders—and several other places. But the necessity of distributing their forces over a wide area, in order to preserve the conquests they had made, gave the Corsicans an advantage of which Paoli was not slow to avail himself; the captured towns, attacked one after the other by the whole strength of the patriot army, were speedily retaken, and the campaign closed with a veritable triumph at Borgo, where Paoli repulsed the relieving force and compelled the French garrison of over five hundred men to capitulate.

Throughout the whole of this campaign, Carlo Bonaparte accompanied Paoli, at the head of a little band of relatives, friends, and servants, mounted on the hardy little native horses.   His intrepid and devoted wife insisted on sharing the dangers and privations of her husband, and followed him everywhere, fording swift rivers, traversing mountain defiles, woods, and morasses, suffering hunger, thirst, and fatigue, but never losing her courage and enthusiasm.   " Often in his expeditions," writes an historian of Napoleon, in tracing the career of the Emperor's father, " one saw, riding on horseback by his side, his young wife, Letizia Ramolino.   Letizia's beauty, her sweet expression, her refined and delicate features, seemed but little in harmony with this adventurous ardour which dragged her at the heels of a robust combatant.   But the bold and regular lines of her aquiline nose, the compressed angles of her disdainful mouth, the sudden fire which at times lighted her eyes, revealed an obstinate courage, and under that splendid forehead masculine thoughts were concealed." [1]   And

[1] Élias Regnault, *Histoire de Napoléon*, cited by Larrey.

MARIA LETIZIA BONAPARTE
FROM A PAINTING IN THE MUSEUM OF AJACCIO

Napoleon, himself, wrote of his mother: "She endured privations and fatigues, braving everything; she had a man's head on a woman's body."

Hostilities were resumed in the spring, Chauvelin having in the interim been superseded by the Comte de Vaux, while large reinforcements had arrived from France. Burning to avenge the reverses they had sustained, the invaders at once assumed the aggressive, and, before their superior numbers, Paoli was forced to evacuate Murato, where he had fixed his headquarters, and fall back beyond the Golo. The patriots flocked to his assistance from all sides and fought with the most desperate valour, " bounding like the chamois from rock to rock, vengeance in their hearts, threats in their mouths, and guns in their hands," while "the mountains echoed with the bellowing of their great hunting-horns."[1] But all their courage, all their devotion, was in vain, and, after gaining a slight success near Monte-Borgo, they were utterly crushed in the sanguinary combat of Ponte-Nuovo (May 9, 1769).

In this fatal campaign, as in that of the previous year, Letizia accompanied her husband, notwithstanding that she was enceinte some four months with the future hero of the century. "I carried my Napoleon in my womb," she observed, "with the same joy, the same calm happiness, the same serenity, that I experienced

---

[1] Ménard, *Souvenirs de la Conquête corse.* The author served with the French troops during the war.

later, when I held him in my arms and fed him at my breast. My mind was entirely occupied by the dangers of his father and those of Corsica. To gather news of the army, I quitted the safe retreat of our steep rocks, to which the women had been consigned, and ventured on to the very fields of battle. I heard the bullets whistling about my ears, but I knew no fear, since I trusted in the protection of the Holy Virgin, to whom I had dedicated my Napoleon."[1] On the day of the combat at Monte-Borgo, and also on that of the disaster at Ponte-Nuovo, Letizia followed her countrymen, animating them by her presence to still further exertions, and crying out to those who wavered : "Let us fight to the last man, and conquer or die ! "

After the latter engagement, all hope of further resistance was at an end, and nothing remained to the vanquished but surrender or flight. Carlo Bonaparte and his wife, who bore her little son Joseph in her arms, found a refuge, along with several other families, in a grotto, which still bears the name of the "Fugitives' Grotto," amid the almost inaccessible rocks of Monte-Rotondo, the highest mountain in Corsica, about half a day's journey to the north of Corte. Here, almost without food, and without sufficient clothing to protect them from the piercing mountain air, their situation was pitiable, and death seemed to stare them in the face. Happily,

[1] Beauterne, *l'Enfance de Napoléon*.

however, they had not long to remain in this
desolate region, as, a day or two later, a French
officer appeared bearing a flag of truce, with the
intelligence that the patriot leaders had offered
their submission, that Paoli himself had decided
to embark for England, and that they might
return to their homes without fear of being
molested.   Acting under instructions from Choiseul, the French general had resolved to adopt
a policy as generous as it was wise.   A complete
amnesty was to be extended to all who had taken
up arms;   Paoli, "whose capture," de Vaux
observed, "would be more embarrassing than
useful," was to be allowed to depart in peace,
and everything possible was to be done to eradi-
cate the bitterness engendered by the struggle
which had just terminated, and to reconcile the
inhabitants to the rule of France.

The Bonapartes immediately quitted the "Fugitives' Grotto," and, accompanied by most of
their companions in misfortune, began to descend
the mountain, in order to regain the road to
Ajaccio. It was a difficult and dangerous journey,
and it was not accomplished without a perilous
adventure.   In fording the river Liamone, the
mule upon which Letizia was riding lost its foot-
ing amidst the strong current which was running, and was carried rapidly down the stream.
The danger was great, but the young woman
preserved her presence of mind, and, though
hampered by the little Joseph, whom she carried

in her arms, succeeded in keeping her saddle and in guiding the terrified animal safely to the bank.

For a moment, Carlo Bonaparte seems to have had some idea of following Paoli into exile ; but his uncle Luciano strongly dissuaded him from such a step, and Letizia added her entreaties to the archdeacon's counsels. Carlo, supple, intriguing, and not over-scrupulous, was scarcely the man to remain heroically attached to a vanquished cause, from which no profit could be expected, and his loyalty to his chief did not remain proof against the pressure brought to bear upon him. A day or two after his return to Ajaccio, he headed a deputation which waited on the Comte de Vaux to negotiate the peace, on which occasion he received such flattering promises, that any lingering scruples he might still have entertained speedily vanished, and, on May 23, he made his formal submission to the French Government.

CHAPTER II

IT was noon on August 15, 1769, the Feast of the Assumption of the Virgin, and a general holiday throughout Corsica. All the bells of the town had been ringing since early dawn ; the churches were decorated with flowers, and the houses with flags and green boughs, and the narrow streets were crowded with the townsfolk and peasants from the surrounding country, dressed in their best clothes, all on their way to Mass. Holding her little half-brother Joseph Fesch—then six years old— by the hand, and followed by her sister-in-law Geltruda Paravicini, and her uncle Luciano, Letizia Bonaparte proceeded to the cathedral, the crowd making way for her with deference, for the courage and devotion she had displayed during the War of Independence had raised her to the position of a public heroine. Scarcely, however, had the service begun, when she found herself seized with the pains of labour. Rising from her knees, she made her way out of the building and, supported by her sister-in-law, regained her house, which was fortunately only a short distance from the cathedral ; and here, on a couch in the salon[1]—for there was no time to reach her bedroom—with the assistance of Geltruda and a maid-servant, Mammucia Caterina, she was delivered of her fourth child—a boy, with a big head and a very intelligent face, who screamed loudly, and soon began sucking his thumb, which was considered a good augury among the peasants of Corsica.

The baptism of the little boy was deferred for nearly two years, during which Letizia's family was further increased by the arrival of a daughter (July 14, 1771). The delicate state of the newcomer's health necessitated her being received into the Church without delay, and accordingly both children were baptised together on the 21st of that month, the boy being christened Napoleone, gallicized in after years into Napoleon, and the girl, who, unhappily, died not long afterwards, Maria Anna.[2]

---

[1] There is a well-known legend to the effect that, since no preparations had been made for the reception of the new arrival, he was wrapped up in some hangings on which were roughly embroidered scenes from the Iliad and the Odyssey, or, according to some writers, scenes depicting the conquests of Alexander the Great and Julius Cæsar. When, in later years, Letizia was interrogated on this matter, she smiled and answered : "In our house in Corsica we had no tapestries, not even in winter; therefore, certainly not in summer."

[2] The name Napoleone, spelt, also, Napollone, Napolione,

THE HOUSE OF THE BONAPARTES AT AJACCIO

It is related that Napoleon, whose behaviour had been all that could be desired during the preliminary prayers, began to manifest signs of restlessness when he saw the holy water being sprinkled over his sister's head, and when the priest approached to perform the same office for him, he struggled fiercely and actually struck the good man, as well as his god-parents, Lorenzo Giubega and his aunt Geltruda. Indeed, from early infancy, the Man of Destiny evinced a decidedly masterful disposition, which increased as he grew older, and his mother was the only person who appears to have had any control over him. "When I was quite little," he remarked while at St. Helena, "I was terribly quarrelsome ; I feared nobody, and fought and scratched continually."

The house of the Bonapartes at Ajaccio, which dated from the beginning of the seventeenth century, was situated in the Rue Saint-Charles, almost in the centre of the town, facing a little square, now called the Place Letizia. As it stands to-day, it is a modest three-storeyed building, painted a greyish yellow, with a flat roof. Over the portico is a marble tablet, with the following inscription :

NAPOLÉON.
EST NÉ DANS CETTE MAISON.
LE XV AOÛT MDCCLXIX.

Napulione, and Nabulione, is, according to M. Rocca, probably a Corsican form of the old Genoese name Nebulone. Napoleon was named after his great-uncle, who was killed at Ponte-Nuovo.

In 1793, it was pillaged and partly burned by the partisans of Paoli, and remained in a half-ruined state for three years. In October 1797, Napoleon, who was then in Italy, sent directions to Joseph Bonaparte to have it restored as " he desired to see it in a proper condition and fit for habitation." The future Emperor's evident intention was to see his old home reconstituted in all its primitive simplicity; " *il faut la remettre comme elle était*," he writes. But Joseph, whose tastes were more luxurious than his brother's, and who evidently considered that it was only fitting that the family residence should correspond, in some degree, to the increased importance of the family, instead of following his brother's directions, added a new storey and a long gallery, lighted on both sides by numerous windows.

As for the various objects of interest in the interior of the house which are shown to visitors, none of these, in M. Rocca's opinion, are authentic,[1] for, though many pieces of furniture which had been carried off by the Paolists in 1793 were subsequently recovered, they were again dispersed after the fall of the Empire. " A relative of the Bonapartes, M. Napoléon Levie, mayor of Ajaccio," he writes, " under the pretext of restoring the house, renovated it completely, and caused all the old

---

[1] With the exception of a little *crèche* in ebony and mahogany, presented by Napoleon to his mother, on his return from Egypt in 1799, which he allows to be beyond dispute the genuine article.

furniture which he judged unworthy to adorn the 'Eagle's nest' to be removed. It was reserved for a member of the Orléans family, the Prince de Joinville, to collect religiously these relics, which he carried off to the Continent. As for the present furniture, it is said that some really authentic pieces were replaced in the house by the care of Napoleon III. Nevertheless, however modest these commodes and chests ornamented with marquetry and incrustations may appear, they seem rather to have belonged to Joseph than to have been in the possession of the needy author of the Imperial Family." [1]

The Bonapartes only occupied the ground and first floors of this house; the second storey being occupied by the *ménage* of Antonio Pozzo di Borgo and his wife, Maria Giustina Bozzi, a second cousin of Carlo Bonaparte. This arrangement was not without its inconveniences, as the following incident will show.

In those days, sanitary arrangements were still in a very primitive state, and it was the custom for people to empty the contents of their slop-pails into the street. For the protection of passers-by, an ordinance had been enacted strictly prohibiting the throwing of water or refuse from the windows, but it appears to have remained a dead letter. Any way, one fine evening in 1784, Carlo Bonaparte happened to be taking the air at the door of his house, when a pailful of greasy water was

[1] Colonna de Cesari Rocca, *le Nid de l'Aigle.*

suddenly emptied over him from the second floor, to the no small detriment of an elegant costume that he had lately ordered from a Parisian tailor.

His wrath was great, and, failing to obtain reparation from the offender, he summoned her before the *podestà* of Ajaccio, who, after hearing the evidence on both sides, and taking the opinion of various sartorial experts as to the amount of damage done, made an order for Signora Pozzo di Borgo to pay for the coat, "according to the estimate of the experts."

At Ajaccio, the Bonapartes spent the greater part of the year, but, during the heat of summer, it was their custom to remove to their little country-house at Milelli, of which we have already spoken.   In this tranquil spot, which commanded one of the finest prospects in Corsica, it is probable that Letizia passed some of the happiest hours of her busy life, though, save in the early morning and at night, when her noisy, high-spirited brood were asleep, she must have had few moments of leisure to contemplate the beauties of Nature.

For her family was steadily increasing, and, as her family increased,[1] her domestic cares multi-

---

[1] The following is the list of her children who survived, with the dates of their birth :

(1) Giuseppe (Joseph), born January 7, 1768. (2) Napoleone (Napoléon), born August 15, 1769. (3) Luciano (Lucien), born May 25, 1775. (4) Maria Anna (Élisa), born January 3, 1777. (5) Luigi (Louis), born September 2, 1778. (6) Maria Paoletta

plied also, until they absorbed her entire thoughts,
and sometimes threatened to overwhelm her
altogether, since to feed and clothe so many
children—to say nothing of her little half-brother
Joseph Fesch, whom she had taken to live with
her on her marriage—would have taxed the resources of people of ample means, and the Bonapartes were very far from rich, even for Corsica.
Letizia, who passed for being an heiress in a
small way, possessed property valued at some
7,000 livres, represented by part of a house in
Ajaccio, which was let to a baker, a vineyard
called "La Sposata," in which Napoleon tells us
the grapes were of a peculiarly fine quality, and
"three parcels of land situated at Campolauro."
The rent which Letizia received from the baker,
joined to the produce of her land, seems to have
constituted, for the first few years of her married
life, the principal source of revenue to the household; for Carlo Bonaparte's practice as an advocate
was worth but little, while, for some time, his
two principal vineyards, situated at Salines and
Bacciochi, brought him in nothing whatever,
from want of money to cultivate them.   Later,
thanks to the assiduous court which he paid to
the two French Commissioners, Marbeuf and
Boucheporn, his income improved.   He was
appointed assessor of the Royal Jurisdiction

(Pauline), born October 20, 1780. (7) Maria Annunziata (Caroline),
born March 25, 1782. (8) Geronimo (Jérôme), born November 15, 1784.

of Ajaccio;[1] was nominated a member of the Nobili Dodici, a commission of twelve nobles who exercised a kind of authority when the Estates were not in session,[2] and one of whom was always attached to the suite of the royal commissioners; and he seems to have received other marks of favour.

He was now able to cultivate his neglected vines, and, had he only been content to live as a simple bourgeois, he and his wife might have found themselves, notwithstanding their ever-increasing family, in comparatively easy circumstances. But, unhappily, he was by nature ambitious and discontented; perhaps he already suffered from that internal affection to which he was to succumb in his thirty-ninth year, and his restless character and unquiet life were in some degree attributable to this cause. " He finds nothing to his taste in any of the places where he resides; he is satisfied with none of the offices which he obtains; he dreams continually of something else : of enterprises which will enrich him, of missions which will bring him glory or profit, of employments which will procure his sons an assured future and mutual support. He wants everything at once; he is importunate, meddlesome; he brings to his desires

---

[1] The judicial administration of the island was in the hands of a Conseil Supérieur, a kind of French *parlement* in miniature, which sat at Bastia, and of eleven royal jurisdictions.

[2] Corsica was now a *pays d'état*, with three Orders : clergy, nobles, and Third Estate. They met at Bastia.

an anxiety which frustrates them. When he has secured the favours he seeks, he is already tired of them, and neglects what he has for what he may be able to have."[1]

Moreover, he was vain, ostentatious, and recklessly extravagant, and, though he frequently displayed considerable ingenuity in obtaining money, it was only to squander it immediately. In 1769, when he was admitted to the degree of Doctor of Laws at the University of Pisa, he gave a banquet in celebration of the event, which is said to have cost 6,000 livres—probably about double his income at this period—and actually contemplated selling his wife's vineyard in order to pay for it. In 1777, on his return from a political mission to Paris, he wrote in his register of expenses : " I started for the Court of France, deputy noble of the Estates of Corsica, taking with me one hundred louis. I received while in Paris four thousand francs in *gratifications* from the King, and one thousand écus in fees ; and I returned without a sou." From the same interesting document, we learn that, two years later, he had made in Paris at the world-famous establishment of M. Labille, of the Rue Saint-Honoré, twelve costumes, in the composition of which silk, velvet, and other costly fabrics figured prominently, to say nothing of elegant *robes de chambre* for summer and winter wear, and other garments indispensable for a man of fashion. All

[1] M. Frédéric Masson, *Napoléon et sa famille.*

of which must have considerably astonished the worthy folk of Ajaccio.

Although he appears to have been a kind and affectionate husband, he was far from a faithful one. Women, we are told, possessed for him "an irresistible attraction." Scarcely more than a year after his marriage, he paid a visit to Italy, and was compelled to fly precipitately from Rome, leaving behind him all his belongings, save the clothes which he happened to be wearing, in order to escape the vengeance of the relatives of a lady to whose charms he had succumbed. On his return journey, he stopped at Bastia, at the house of a certain Signor Franceschi, and, in due course, a very pretty handmaiden of his host gave birth to a son, "concerning whose origin," wrote Signor Franceschi, "I have never had any doubt."[1]

Retiring, modest, and contented, virtuous, practical, and thrifty, Letizia Bonaparte was the exact antithesis of Carlo, and well indeed it was for her children that she was! The customs of a country where the wife is merely the servant of her husband interdicted to her all criticism, all reflection even on the conduct of the 'master,' but, on the other hand, gave her an almost unlimited authority over the household, her children, and all domestic matters. And surely seldom in history shall we find an instance of such entire self-abnegation, of such whole-hearted devotion to duty! Not for her the joys of aping the

---

[1] Letter to the Comte de Cerdi, published by Rocca.

fashions of the Rue Saint-Honoré and the Faubourg Saint-Germain, of exhibiting her beauty at social functions, of flirtation with elegant French officials. Her household duties, the care of her children, absorbed every moment of her time, and for years she scarcely set foot over the threshold of her home, except when she went to attend Mass on Sundays. "When I became the mother of a family," she says, "I consecrated myself entirely to its proper direction, and I did not leave my house except to attend Mass. I am aware that one of the obligations of the true Christian should be to go to church every day, and indispensably on festivals. Nevertheless, I do not believe that the Church insists that, during the week, persons who are at the head of affairs, and particularly mothers of families, should spend the greater part of the day away from home. That would be to interrupt the regular course of affairs, and to render them guilty in the sight of God for the serious inconveniences which might arise in families during the absence of the head. Besides, my presence at home was necessary to keep my children in check, as they were so young."[1]

She kept only one servant, the woman Mammuccia Caterina, who had received Napoleon on his entry into the world, and who lived with her,

---

[1] *Souvenirs de Madame Mère, dictés par elle-même, dans les derniers temps de sa vie*, published by Baron Larrey, *Madame Mère*.

without wages, as a friend, almost as a relative, and quarrelled persistently with Carlo's mother. Mammuccia's duties seem to have been confined to looking after the children, and Letizia performed almost all the household duties herself.

And what a housekeeper she was! Giving her attention to the smallest details, eking out every sou which passed through her hands with the most infinite care, haggling incessantly over the smallest purchase, denying herself every luxury, every comfort, often, we may well believe, necessaries also, and, while giving her children everything that was necessary for their welfare, allowing them only such pleasures as cost nothing. These habits of rigid economy, which she continued to practise long after there was apparently any necessity for them, might well pass for avarice, were it not that, as we shall see hereafter, she was ready to sacrifice, without hesitation or regret, all the savings so laboriously accumulated when the honour, liberty, or happiness of her family were at stake.

Possessing little education herself, knowing no French nor even Italian correctly, she was unable to give her children any personal instruction, nor even to teach them to read. She sought, however, to inculcate certain lessons which she herself had been taught : to yield an unquestioning obedience to their parents, to show respect for their elders, to speak the truth, to avoid gluttony, and to accustom themselves to a cleanliness of body unusual in that age and in that country.

Although she was a strict observer of the ritual of her Church, so far as her multifarious duties permitted, and consecrated each of her three daughters to the Virgin (Maria Anna, Maria Paoletta, Maria Annunziata), she would appear to have given her family little religious instruction, and that of the most formal character. The little Bonapartes attended Mass with praiseworthy regularity, and were accustomed, like all Corsicans, to make the sign of the Cross at moments of great astonishment, joy, and grief; but they grew up pagans at heart, although they would doubtless have been highly indignant had they heard themselves thus described. It is related that, on being asked in her declining years how it had been possible for her to support all the trials she had undergone, Letizia replied : " I bore all, because it was sent me by God." At the time when she said this, her religion was undoubtedly sincere enough ; but in early and middle life it would appear to have been very much on the surface, and to have been confined to the formal duties which she taught her children. As M. Masson points out, she showed no surprise when her sons, and even her daughters, contracted purely civil marriages, nor does she seem to have been at all shocked when her half-brother Joseph Fesch took the oath to the Civil Constitution of the Clergy, unfrocked himself temporarily, and engaged in occupations which had nothing sacerdotal about them. This neglect of what is rightly regarded as one of the first duties of a mother was no doubt, in a great degree, responsible for the indifference shown by her sons to religion, except so far as it was necessary to take it into account as a political factor, and for the circumstance that her daughters, when transported to France and into an environment totally different from that to which they had been accustomed, at an age, too, when the mind is particularly susceptible to new impressions, speedily forgot the lessons of their childhood, and, ignoring the admirable example their mother had set them, became as frivolous, as extravagant, and as lax in their morals as any women of their time.

But, in all other respects, Letizia was indeed, as her eldest son Joseph once observed, "a model among mothers." Her children loved as well as respected her, and, she tells us, "even after they had grown up, always showed for her, at all times, the same respect and affection." Her husband and her mother-in-law, who lived with her son, were foolishly indulgent, and would have spoiled the children, if she had not interfered. "At the least cry, at the least reprimand, they rushed to their aid, lavishing upon them a thousand caresses." But Letizia knew how to be "severe or indulgent as the occasion required," and ruled with an exceedingly firm hand.

The precept of Solomon with regard to the

use of the rod was religiously observed by the
Corsican mother of those days, and corporal
punishment occupied a conspicuous place in the
education of both girls and boys. Letizia was
not one to spare this time-honoured form of
correction when she considered it well-deserved,
and many stories are told of her chastisement
of her children, of which Napoleon, who was by
far the most unruly of the boys, seems to have
enjoyed the lion's share.

One day, during the temporary absence of his
mother, he made a raid upon a particularly fine
fig-tree in the garden, which the children had
been expressly forbidden to touch, and, when on
the point of beating a retreat with his booty, was
surprised by the gardener. However, he succeeded in coaxing the man not to betray him,
and went off to enjoy the contents of his bulging
pockets, imagining himself secure from punishment. As ill-luck would have it, however, his
mother happened to visit the tree the next morning, and, finding it almost as barren as the one in
the Scriptures, sent for the gardener and demanded an explanation of the phenomenon.
The man reluctantly admitted the truth, and
Napoleon's back ached for some days afterwards.

On another occasion, shortly before Napoleon
left Corsica to enter the military school at
Brienne, he so far forgot what was due to his
elders as to make game of his grandmother,
Maria Saveria Bonaparte, who was in the habit

of leaning on a stick when she walked, and even to allude to her as a witch. Letizia, who happened to overhear the remark, gave him a threatening look, which made the boy decide to keep out of her way till evening, by which time he hoped her anger might have abated. The moment he reappeared, however, Letizia pounced upon him, with the intention of administering condign punishment; but he contrived to escape from her grasp. Not wishing to expose herself to the mortification of a second defeat, his mother resolved to wait for an occasion when escape would be impossible. It came the following day, when Napoleon, having received an invitation to dine with some friends in the town, went to his room to change his clothes. Letizia followed, and finding him half undressed, locked the door behind her, and administered a sound thrashing.

But, if she seldom overlooked a fault, she could be all love and tenderness when circumstances demanded it; unwearying in her solicitude for a child who was ill, cheerfully sacrificing her own hard-earned night's rest to soothe the little sufferer's pillow, and ready to extend to her children the fullest and most generous sympathy in all their troubles. "You are very good to me," said Napoleon to his physician at St. Helena, "and you spare no effort to alleviate my sufferings; but this is nothing compared with a mother's tenderness."

Madame Bonaparte seems to have early dis-

cerned the exceptional character of her second
son, and, while sternly checking his unruly inclinations, to have done everything possible to encourage his taste for study and the strong desire he
expressed, while still a child, for a military career.
She bought him a toy drum and a wooden sabre,
and tells us that, when his brothers were drawing
grotesque figures on the walls of a large empty
room which she had set apart for them to play
in, Napoleon drew only soldiers ranged in order
of battle. A little later, when his remarkable
aptitude for figures began to manifest itself, she
had a little shed built on the terrace in front of
the house, to which he might retire every day
to work undisturbed by his brothers. She
relates how, when he was a pupil in the school
in Ajaccio formerly kept by the Jesuits, she
was informed that he had been met several
times in the street munching the coarse brown
bread supplied to the French soldiers, "a thing
which was not becoming for a child of his
station," and that when she questioned him on
the matter, he replied that he exchanged every
morning the piece of white bread which she gave
him for his lunch for that of a soldier, "since,
as he was also to be a soldier, it was expedient
that he should accustom himself to eat this kind
of bread, besides which he preferred it to white
bread; how one evening he remained out of
doors during a terrific thunderstorm until he
was soaked to the skin, declaring, in answer to

his mother's remonstrances, that one who was to become a soldier ought to inure himself to all kinds of weather; and how he so astonished the family bailiff by the intelligent questions he asked him in regard to the working of a mill that the man told her that, 'if God granted the little gentleman a long life, he could not fail to become the greatest man in the world.'"[1]

It is pleasant to know that Letizia's intense affection for her extraordinary son was abundantly returned. Indeed, their devotion for each other throughout life has evoked the unstinted admiration of even the most hostile critics of the Bonapartes.

[1] *Souvenirs de Madame Mère.*

CHAPTER III

ALTHOUGH he had embraced with enthusiasm the cause of Paoli and had fought with courage during the War of Independence, Carlo Bonaparte was quick to recognise the advantages which Corsica—and incidentally he himself—would derive from a union with France, and he lost no opportunity of proclaiming his adhesion to the new Government and of ingratiating himself with its representatives. Intelligent, specious, and insinuating, and speaking and writing French with a facility which few of his countrymen were able to emulate, he placed no limits to his hopes of advancement, and if he failed to realise his dreams, it must be admitted that it was certainly not for lack of enterprise. He was the most indefatigable, the most audacious, the most ingenious beggar, it is possible to conceive. If he exchanged so much as a dozen words with a person of influence, he henceforth considered himself his *protégé*, and did not hesitate to solicit his good offices on his behalf. He would wait all day in a Minister's ante-chamber on the chance of being accorded a two minutes' interview, and, if he failed to obtain it, would return again on the morrow. He became the terror of all officialdom from commissioners and Ministers to junior clerks and doorkeepers, for he would take no denial, he was proof against every rebuff. And when distance, or some other reason, made a personal solicitation impossible, he had recourse to his pen. He wrote letter after letter, petition after petition, servile to the last degree when he was seeking a favour, reproachful or even indignant when he desired to create the impression that he was demanding a right. Now, he is seeking compensation for some wrong, real or imaginary; now, some advantageous concession; anon, a *bourse* (free scholarship) for one of his children. Everywhere where there was anything to be obtained, the name of Carlo Bonaparte was to be found. " I am the father of seven children, Monseigneur; the eighth is on the way," he writes to Calonne, in 1784; "and almost without fortune, for the reasons detailed . . . and I have the honour to implore your protection and your justice in favour of my poor family." [1]

To the Comte de Marbeuf,[2] the military com-

---

[1] Published by Rocca.
[2] Louis Charles René, Comte de Marbeuf; born, at Rennes,

mandant of Corsica, he paid the most assiduous
court, and with highly satisfactory results. The
commandant was a courtly, easy-going old gentleman, by no means unsusceptible to flattery ; and
in flattery Carlo Bonaparte was an adept. He
eulogised his private and public acts, in prose and
in verse, in Latin and in Italian ; he hung his
portrait in the place of honour in the salon of his
house ; he invited him to stand godfather to his
son Louis, and he gave sometimes admirably-
cooked little dinners in his honour—dinners which
meant weeks of stern retrenchment for poor
Letizia, who had, besides, to borrow furniture,
plate, and linen for the occasion from her relatives
and friends, in order that the great man might
not suspect the straits to which his hosts were
reduced.

But these sacrifices were cheerfully made, for
they promised an abundant return ; while an

October 4, 1712 ; died, at Bastia, September 20, 1786. He
entered the army as an ensign in the Régiment de Bourbonnais in
1728, and attained the rank of *mestre de camp* in 1762. Two years
later, he was sent to Corsica, in command of the troops who
garrisoned the citadels of Ajaccio, Calvi, Bastia, Saint-Florent, and
Algajola. He took part in the War of Independence, and held the
chief command of the French forces between the recall of Chauvelin and the arrival of the Comte de Vaux. After the pacification
of the island, he was promoted to the rank of lieutenant-general
and made military commandant of Corsica. Many historians speak
of him as governor of the country, but, though he exercised most
of the functions of that office, he never held the title, which was
bestowed, in 1772, on the Marquis de Monteynard, then Secretary
of State for War, who, however, never resided in Corsica.
Marbeuf was extremely popular with the inhabitants, and, by his
liberality, kindness and tact, did much to reconcile them to French
rule.

event which occurred in 1777 made Marbeuf
their friend for life.

After the death of Louis XV, in 1774, Marbeuf had been summoned to Court, and temporarily superseded in his government of Corsica
by the Vicomte de Narbonne-Pelet.[1] The
viscount found the post so much to his liking
that he resolved to retain it, and, with this object
in view, sent very unfavourable reports of the
condition of affairs in the island to Versailles,
and severely censured the laxity shown by his
predecessor in his dealings with the inhabitants.
The Government, anxious to ascertain the facts
of the matter, offered to receive a deputation
from the Estates of Corsica. Carlo Bonaparte
succeeded in getting himself appointed a member
of this deputation, and, on his arrival in Paris,
pleaded the cause of his patron with such eloquence and ability that it was decided that
Marbeuf should be restored to his office.

The count was not long in giving his *protégé*
substantial proofs of his gratitude. The Genoese,
who had done everything in their power to
debase the Corsican aristocracy, had steadily
refused to recognise a nobility. But France, in
the belief that an hereditary caste would make

[1] Jean François, Comte de Narbonne-Pelet (1725–1804). He
had greatly distinguished himself in 1762, during the Seven Years'
War, by his heroic defence of the post of Fritzlar, which saved
the French army under the Duc de Broglie, which had got itself
into a very perilous situation, from destruction. He was made
lieutenant-general in 1784.

CARLO MARIA BONAPARTE

FROM THE PAINTING BY GIRODET-TRIOSON AT VERSAILLES

for stability, had pursued a different policy, and, after the restoration of order in 1769, had invited all families who claimed to be of noble descent to submit such proofs as they possessed to the Government, in order that an aristocracy might be established. Carlo Bonaparte lost not a moment in instituting researches into his family history, and, thanks to the assistance he received from the Grand-Duke of Tuscany and the Archbishop of Pisa, had no difficulty in proving eleven generations of nobility, and his right to assume a count's coronet and a coat of arms: " Gules two bends argent between two estoiles of the second."[1]

In establishing his claims to nobility, Carlo had been actuated by a more practical motive than that of satisfying his vanity. Those fortunate persons who possessed the right of placing the all-important particle before their names were eligible for numerous posts and favours which were closed to those of middle-class origin. Among these, one of the most coveted was the privilege of free admission for their sons—in cases where the parents were too poor to defray the cost of their education—to the military schools recently established by Louis XVI, on the advice of the War Minister, the Comte de Saint-Germain,[2] as well as to several other institutions;

[1] Mr. Oscar Browning, *Napoleon: The First Phase.*
[2] These were twelve in number, and, singularly enough, were all managed by monks. The most important were : Pont-à-Mousson, Sorèze, Tiron, Tournon, and Brienne. Each accommodated about fifty pupils.

and, in 1778, the grateful Marbeuf promised to procure for Napoleon a nomination to one of the military schools, and to secure, through the good offices of his nephew, the Archbishop of Aix, a benefice for Joseph, of whom Carlo had decided to make a priest. In the meanwhile, the archbishop promised to arrange to have them both placed at the college of Autun, and also to send Joseph Fesch, who was now fourteen, and was likewise destined for an ecclesiastical career, to complete his theological studies at the seminary at Aix.

The favour shown by Marbeuf to the Bonaparte family seems to have occasioned a good deal of comment, and the evil-minded did not hesitate to declare that it was prompted by admiration for the *beaux yeux* of Letizia, rather than by gratitude for the services of Carlo ; while libellous pamphleteers and chroniclers hostile to the Bonapartes have even cast suspicion upon the legitimacy of Napoleon and others of his brothers and sisters.

As regards Napoleon, this charge is too monstrous to merit a moment's consideration. There is no evidence that the Bonapartes were even acquainted with Marbeuf until after the close of the War of Independence ; while, even if they were, during the year which preceded Napoleon's birth, Carlo and his wife were with the patriot army, and Marbeuf with the French troops, and nothing could be more unlikely than that the count and Letizia were ever in each other's company.

Very much the same may be said in regard to his brothers and sisters. "Letizia's children," remarks M. Masson, "all bear, to an equal degree, the imprint, physical and moral, of the double atavism from which they spring; in themselves, in their descendants, they reproduce, in a striking manner, a type which, undoubtedly after generations, intermarriages have been able to alter from the point of view of beauty, but which is found, nevertheless, among the least favoured in such a degree that it is impossible to mistake it. And it is the same in regard to character, turn of mind, personal habits, temperament, and diseases. Her children are then certainly—that is to say, all the eight who survived—the issue of Charles Bonaparte."[1]

Moreover Letizia's devotion to her husband,[2] the stern sense of duty which she evinced throughout her life, her entire absence of sentimentality or imagination, the ceaseless round of household tasks in which she passed her time, her frequent pregnancy, the presence of her children, and, finally, the great disparity in age between her supposed lover and herself—all go to show that the accusation is as absurd as it is odious.

[1] *Napoléon et sa famille.*
[2] "How," she observed, on one occasion, in speaking of her husband, "could I fail to be happy and proud to belong to him? He is good, he is handsome, he is celebrated, and he loves me."

On December 15, 1778, Joseph and Napoleon bade farewell to their mother, for whom the parting from her children seems to have been a sore trial, and set out with their father for France. They were accompanied by Joseph Fesch, whom they left at Aix, and by a cousin of Carlo, Aurelio Varese, who had been appointed sub-deacon to the Archbishop of Autun.

The little party reached Autun on New Year's Day 1779, where Carlo Bonaparte, who had again been appointed a member of a Corsican deputation, left his two sons and proceeded to Paris, to join his colleagues and to complete the arrangements for entering Napoleon at one of the military schools. The school for which the boy received a nomination was Tiron, but this was subsequently cancelled, for what reason does not appear to be known, and he was sent to Brienne, in Champagne.

Carlo's persuasive tongue obtained for the Corsican deputation an indemnity from the Government for the expense and loss of time occasioned by their journey to Paris. Nevertheless, he himself must have been considerably out of pocket by his visit, since it was on this occasion that he ordered from Labille the twelve elegant costumes already mentioned, and he presumably lived in a manner befitting the splendour of his apparel. No doubt, however, he considered that his presentation to the King, which took place on March 16, fully justified such extravagance.

Napoleon remained at Autun until April 23, when he left for Brienne. His time had been mainly occupied in learning French, of which language, until then, he appears to have known little or nothing; but he had made such rapid progress that he already spoke it fluently, though with a strong Corsican accent. The brothers, who were deeply attached to each other in early life, were in despair at their separation; Joseph cried bitterly, but Napoleon, though not less moved, succeeded in controlling his grief and shed, we are told, but a single tear, which he hurriedly wiped away.

Napoleon passed five and a half years at Brienne, that is to say, from the beginning of May 1779 to the end of October 1784, when he was one of five candidates chosen to enter the École Militaire of Paris, as gentlemen cadets. For the first part of the time, at least, he appears to have been very unhappy. His fellow-pupils made jest of his Italian accent, his Christian name, his studious habits, and his meagre wardrobe, while his teachers were harsh and unsympathetic. Once, for some breach of discipline, he was ordered to do penance by dining on his knees, at the door of the refectory. He replied that he would dine standing up if required, but that he had been taught never to kneel, except to God. The teacher, however, insisted and seized him, in order to force him on to his knees, upon which he exclaimed: *"N'est-ce pas, maman, devant Dieu!*

devant Dieu !" turned deadly pale, and trembled
so violently that it was deemed advisable to
remit his punishment. Eventually, however,
he appears to have become quite popular at
Brienne, and he always retained grateful memo-
ries of the place, as the favours bestowed upon
many of his old schoolfellows in after years
testify ; while, in his will, he bequeathed a million
francs to the town.

In the spring of 1780, Carlo Bonaparte obtained for his third son, Lucien, admission to
Autun, with a promise that he should, in due
course, proceed to Brienne.

Notwithstanding the relief afforded to the
Bonapartes' exchequer by the departure of
Joseph, Napoleon, and young Fesch, the financial outlook was anything but promising, added
to which Carlo had just received another addition
to his family, in the person of a daughter, Maria
Paoletta, the future Princess Borghese. Nevertheless, Letizia could not resist the temptation of
seeing her two sons again, salving her conscience
with the reflection that the cost of her journey
would be more than neutralized by the check
which her presence would impose upon her husband's expenditure. Accordingly, it was arranged
that when Carlo Bonaparte took Lucien to
Autun, his wife should accompany him ; and,
towards the end of April, they set out for
France.

After leaving Autun, the Bonapartes proceeded

to Brienne, where Letizia seems to have been much shocked by the change in the appearance of her son, who had become so thin that she scarcely recognised him. " I was in fact very much altered," said Napoleon to the Comte de Montholon, many years later, in speaking of this circumstance. " My nights were often passed in meditating on the lessons of the day. From the very beginning, I, naturally, could not bear the idea of not being the first in my class." And he added : " My mother was then twenty-nine ; she was *belle comme les amours.*" [1]

Madame Bonaparte indeed, in spite of her life of domestic drudgery, her constant anxiety over money matters, and her frequent pregnancy, was still as beautiful as ever, and during her stay in France excited universal admiration wherever she went. With a modesty that was habitual to her, however, she merely smiled at the compliments she received, and observed : " The women of my country who are really beautiful are still at Ajaccio."

According to Baron Larrey, Letizia's visit to Brienne was responsible for an all-important decision in regard to Napoleon's future. Carlo Bonaparte seems to have been strongly in favour of Napoleon entering the Navy, in preference to the Army, and the boy himself was not averse to this arrangement, which, if he happened to be employed on the southern

[1] Montholon, *Mémoires.*

coast of France, would afford him many opportunities of visiting his native land.   At Brienne,
pupils were prepared for both services, though
the chief difference in the education of the young
gentlemen who aspired to the marshal's *bâton*,
and of those who hoped to emulate the deeds
of Duquesne and Jean Bart, seems to have been
that the latter slept in hammocks, instead of in
beds.   Napoleon was accordingly placed in the
so-called naval class, and no doubt suffered not a
little from the temptation which a hammock offers
to practical jokers.   However, Madame Bonaparte,
who was naturally averse to exposing her son to
the dangers of more than one element at the same
time, and moreover considered that a military
career would afford him far greater scope for
his talents, did everything possible to dissuade
him from becoming a sailor, and succeeded
in bringing her husband round to her views.
Representations were therefore made to the
authorities at Brienne ; the report of the boy's
professors, which declared " *M. de Buonaparte-
Napoléon apté à devenir un excellent officier de
marine*," was cancelled, and all idea of the Navy
definitely abandoned.

About eighteen months after the return of
the Bonapartes to Ajaccio, Letizia gave birth
(October 8, 1782) to her youngest daughter
Maria Annunziata, afterwards called Caroline,
the future Queen of Naples.   Towards the end
of the same year, Carlo Bonaparte, thanks to

the good offices of Marbeuf, was successful in
obtaining a nomination for his eldest daughter,
Maria Anna, or Marianna, to the school of
Saint-Cyr, the celebrated institution for young
girls founded by Madame de Maintenon. As,
however, the little girl was not yet six years old,
and the earliest age for admission to Saint-Cyr
was seven, she was not required to leave home
for more than twelve months.

This was a great piece of good fortune for the
impoverished family, for not only was Marianna's
education assured, but she would receive, on
leaving the school, a trousseau and a *dot* of 3,000
livres. But alas! when the time came for her
departure, Carlo and Letizia found themselves
in a serious predicament, for, although when a
pupil had completed her education, the expenses
of her journey home were paid by the school, her
parents were expected to defray the cost of her
journey to Saint-Cyr; and matters had now come
to such a pass with them that they were at their
wits' end to find the money. The harvest that
year had failed, both the little property at Milelli
and the vineyard at Salines were mortgaged up
to the hilt, and a lawsuit in which Carlo had
been for some time past engaged with the Jesuits,
over some property which had been bequeathed
to the Order by one of his ancestors, "*enivré d'un
faux principe de religion*," was involving him in
endless expense. At length, the difficulty was
overcome, through the kindness of the deputy-

governor of the island, the Comte Rosel de Beaumanoir, who lent Carlo five hundred francs, and, early in June 1784,[1] he set out for France, taking with him Marianna and another little Corsican girl, Mlle. Cattineo, who had also received a nomination to Saint-Cyr.

Before taking his charges to Saint-Cyr, Carlo Bonaparte visited Autun, to inquire as to Joseph's progress and to conduct Lucien, who was now nine years old and had completed his preparations for Brienne, to Champagne. Then he proceeded to Brienne, where Napoleon's course was now drawing to an end, and saw Lucien duly installed there, although until the elder brother had left, the younger could not become a free scholar of the establishment, it being contrary to the rules to elect two scholars from the same family. Presumably, however, Marbeuf or the good-natured Bishop of Autun had offered to defray the cost of Lucien's education until that time arrived.

In a letter to one of his uncles, probably Joseph Fesch, Napoleon speaks of his father's visit and describes Lucien as "three feet eleven inches in height, healthy, fat, lively, and mischievous," and adds that "he knows French well and has entirely forgotten Italian."[2]

---

[1] And not in June 1783, which is the date given by M. Turquan, in his *Sœurs de Napoléon*, and by several other writers.

[2] This letter, which is of great interest, is given at length by Mr. Oscar Browning, in his *Napoleon: The First Phase*. The author observes that the visit of Carlo Bonaparte in June 1784 was the only one which Napoleon received from any of his family

In the same letter, Napoleon mentions that one of the objects of his father's visit to France was the hope that the change might restore him to health. Carlo's health, indeed, had, for some time past, been occasioning his family grave anxiety. The affection of the stomach, "of which," says Letizia, " he always complained, particularly after dinner,"[1] had first become serious, at Ajaccio, in the course of the previous year, though, thanks to the unremitting care of his wife and the more regular life he led while at home, the progress of the disease had been temporarily arrested.

After taking his daughter to Saint-Cyr and spending some time in Paris, where he endeavoured to induce the Comptroller-General of Finance to entrust him with a contract for the draining of the salt marshes of Corsica, Carlo went to take the waters—presumably at Bourbon-les-Bains, which he had visited with his wife in 1780. Towards the end of the summer, he returned to Ajaccio, bringing with him Joseph, who, to the great disappointment of h's family, had abandoned his intention of entering the Church, in which, according to Napoleon, a fat benefice and eventually a bishopric awaited him, and had begged his father to procure him a commission in the army.

during his stay at Brienne. He has apparently overlooked the visit which he received from both his parents in the late spring of 1780.   [1] *Souvenirs de Madame Mère.*

Scarcely, however, had Carlo arrived home, than the alarming symptoms which had manifested themselves in the previous year returned with redoubled violence, and he determined to set out again for France, to place himself under the care of a Paris physician. As he was too ill to travel alone, it was arranged that Joseph Bonaparte and Fesch, who had now taken Holy Orders and was known as the Abbé Fesch, should accompany him, and in October they left Corsica, which Carlo was never to see again.

A stormy passage aggravated the unfortunate man's complaint, and he was unable to travel farther than Montpellier. A doctor who was called in pronounced him to be suffering from an ulcer in the stomach and held out no hope of his recovery, though of opinion that his life might, with care, be prolonged for some time. As his wife was again enceinte—she gave birth to their youngest son, Jérôme, on November 9—Carlo strictly forbade her to be informed of his condition and wrote her reassuring letters. Happily, a countryman and friend of Madame Bonaparte, the beautiful Madame Pernon, mother of the future Duchesse d'Abrantès, was then residing with her husband at Montpellier, and offered the sick man, who was lodged at a second-rate inn in the town, the shelter of her roof. Under the care of these good people, his health so far improved that he began to entertain hopes of ultimate recovery ; but this improvement was not long maintained, and, after several weeks of acute suffering, he died at seven o'clock in the evening of February 24, 1785. Allowing him to have been born in 1746, the date which, as we have mentioned elsewhere, is that given by the best-informed writers, he was between thirty-eight and thirty-nine years of age.

Shortly before his death, he advised Joseph to abandon all thoughts of a military career, and to remain in Corsica, in order to assist his mother in watching over the interests of his younger brothers and sisters. He spoke frequently of Napoleon: "I greatly wish that I could have seen my dear little Napoleon again. I feel that his caresses would have soothed my last moments, but God has not permitted it." He seems to have had some presentiment of the future greatness of his second son, for, during his last moments, he repeatedly murmured his name; and the last words he was heard to utter before lapsing into unconsciousness were: "Where is Napoleon? Why does he not come, with his big sword, to defend his father?"

Carlo Bonaparte was buried very quietly in the crypt of the Franciscan convent at Montpellier,[1] after which Joseph and Fesch set out for Ajaccio to break the sad news to Letizia.

[1] His body was subsequently removed to the crypt of the church of Saint-Lieu.

ALTHOUGH Carlo Bonaparte had been
a far from satisfactory husband, he had
always been a kind and affectionate one,
and Letizia grieved for him sincerely. His
children felt his death severely, too, and, in after
years, always spoke and wrote of him in terms
of esteem and affection. His good-nature, his
handsome face, his elegant dress, and his reputation for personal courage, had all appealed to
their youthful imaginations, and they were not
old enough to understand the ceaseless labour
and anxiety which his vanity and extravagance
had imposed upon their devoted mother.

Some of Madame Bonaparte's friends urged
her to marry again, and, as she was still a very
lovely woman, suitors were not lacking. But the

experiences of her married life were not of a
nature to encourage her to embark upon a second
matrimonial venture, and she felt, moreover, that
the care of her children would require every
moment of her time.   Carlo had left his affairs in
the most hopeless confusion, but, with the aid of
his uncle, the archdeacon, who was chosen by the
family council as guardian to the children, she
eventually succeeded in restoring them to some
degree of order, though the income which the
heavily mortgaged and neglected property produced was pitiably small.   On this and a small
State pension, which Marbeuf succeeded in obtaining for her, she contrived to maintain herself
and her family.

But the task was one which required the most
complete self-sacrifice, the most unceasing drudgery.   She laboured from morning until night :
cooking, sewing, washing, ironing.   She made
every article of her younger children's clothes
and all her elder children's linen with her own
hands, until a sore on her finger, which "prevented
her from sewing a stitch," compelled her to
engage a woman from Tuscany at three francs
a month.   This was the devoted Saveria, who
followed her mistress everywhere and died in
her house in Rome, in 1825.   In 1813, she received a pension of 1,200 francs from Napoleon.

It would be difficult to conceive the rigorous
economy she was compelled to practise and the
scarcity of money, observes M. Masson, were it

not for the family correspondence.   In one letter,
Napoleon complains that his mother has not
returned six écus he has lent her ; in another, he
mentions that she owes him three.   Although, as
we have said, she made all her elder children's
linen, she could not afford to pay the carriage of
even the smallest parcel to Paris, Brienne, or
Pisa—where Joseph, who had resolved to follow
his father's profession, was pursuing his studies—
and had therefore to wait until her sons sent her
the money before forwarding it.   On one occasion, when the family removed from Ajaccio to
Ucciani, the children took their mattresses with
them, as they only possessed one apiece.

And, while Letizia laboured for the family in
Corsica, Napoleon, who, at the end of October
1785, had passed out of the École Militaire and
had received a commission in the artillery regiment
of La Fère, then stationed at Valence, worked for
it in France.   In the midst of his military duties,
in the midst of his philosophical and social studies,
and of "all the ideas which were bubbling in his
brain," never for a moment did he forget his
impoverished relatives and his duty towards them.
For them he was ready to deny himself everything.   He lived in the simplest possible manner ;
he never contracted a debt ; he never permitted
himself the smallest extravagance, and, out of his
miserable pittance as a second lieutenant, he contrived, as we have seen, to send occasionally small
sums to his mother.   He charged himself, too,

with the conduct of the family's foreign affairs, drawing up petitions importuning the Government for *bourses* for his brothers, for the arrears of his mother's pension, for the balance of a grant which had been promised Carlo Bonaparte for the establishment of a nursery of mulberry trees in Corsica.[1] And, if he were not very successful, like his father before him, he certainly lost nothing for the asking.

In September 1786, Napoleon returned to Ajaccio on furlough, after an absence of seven years. He found many changes. His father was dead, and the house, which in Carlo's lifetime had been the resort of a good deal of company, and had occasionally worn an almost festive air, was now conducted with the regularity and simplicity of a monastery or a school. "Prayer, sleep, meals, amusements, and exercise, all were calculated and measured out."[2] Marbeuf was dead, too, in his eighty-fourth year, "*entouré de l'estime publique,*" leaving behind him a young wife, whom he had married two years before his death,[3] and a little son, six months old.[4] And,

[1] The Government had promised 8,500 livres, and one sol per tree for grafting, but in May 1786, after between five and six thousand livres had been paid, it refused to advance any more money.

[2] Nasica, *Mémoires sur l'enfance et la jeunesse de Napoléon.*

[3] Catherine Antoinette Salinguera Gayardon de Fenoyl, daughter of a *maréchal de camp* in the French army. In 1805, Napoleon bestowed upon her a pension of 6,000 francs, "in consideration of the services rendered to Corsica by her husband during his government."

[4] Laurent François Marie, Baron de Marbeuf. He entered the

finally, he found a little brother, Luigi (Louis), born just before his departure for France, and three little ones who had come into the world since he left home: Maria Paoletta (Pauline), Maria Annunziata (Caroline) and Geronimo (Jérôme).

The two elder ones, and particularly Pauline, captivated his heart at once. Already giving promise of those charms which she was one day to employ with such fatal effect, merry, affectionate, and a veritable imp of mischief, she was the joy and despair of the whole Bonaparte family. Nothing—not even the fear of Letizia's rod—could restrain her. Clambering over tables and chairs, playing with fragile ornaments which even her elders handled with religious respect, running downstairs at breakneck speed, climbing trees in quest of forbidden fruit, chasing poultry and sheep, crawling through prickly hedges, and returning home tattered and dirty, to receive a well-merited castigation, to promise amendment, and to resume her pranks on the morrow!

And Napoleon—this grave young officer—who already carried the head of a man of mature years on his youthful shoulders, became a boy again in the company of this little madcap, and romped with her as merrily as though those

army, and, after serving with distinction in several of Napoleon's campaigns, became, in October, 1811, colonel of the 6th regiment of Chevau-Légers; but died the following year, of wounds received during the disastrous invasion of Russia.

seven years at Brienne and the École Militaire
and Valence had never been. For, in the privacy
of his family circle, he always remained young;
indeed, his exuberant playfulness was occasionally found somewhat trying by certain of his
relatives, his two wives in particular.

Poverty-stricken though were his surroundings,
Napoleon seems to have been perfectly happy
in Corsica, for never was there a man more im-
pregnated with the love of home and country.
He read and studied, worked at his *Histoire
de la liberté corse*, which he had begun in 1786,
and of which he read passages to his mother,
discussed literature, philosophy, and politics with
Joseph, and business matters with Letizia and
the archdeacon, taught little Louis mathematics,
and romped with Pauline ; and when, after a
stay of twelve months, his furlough, which had
been extended to December 1, 1787, owing to
an attack of fever, was cut short by the fear of
a war with Prussia, which caused all officers on
leave to be recalled to their regiments, he quitted
the island with regret.

On reaching Marseilles, he found that the
alarm had subsided and that his recall had been
countermanded. He did not, however, return to
Corsica, but proceeded to Paris, with which he
was still unacquainted, for during his course at
the École Militaire, he had been kept strictly
within its walls. Here he passed six months,
bombarding the Comptroller - General with de-

mands for the settlement of his mother's claim in the matter of the mulberry trees, though, unhappily, without result. Here, too, by his own confession, he seems to have indulged in his first *passade*, with a woman of the town whom he met in the Palais-Royal, though one of his most recent biographers, Mr. Oscar Browning, in contradiction to M. Masson, charitably refuses to believe that the young officer "deviated on this occasion from the stern principles of virtuous conduct which he both taught and practised at this period."[1]

He also appears to have gone to Saint-Cyr, to visit his sister Marianna; for it is no doubt in connection with a visit paid about this time that the Duchesse d'Abrantès relates the following anecdote.

"One day, my mother [Madame Permon] and some other members of my family went to pay a visit to Saint-Cyr, and Bonaparte accompanied them. When Marianna came into the parlour, she appeared very melancholy, and at the first word that was addressed to her, she burst into tears. My mother embraced her and endeavoured to console her, but it was some time before Marianna would inform her of the cause of her distress. At length, my mother ascertained that one of the young ladies (Mlle. Montluc) was to leave the school in a week,

---

[1] See, in regard to this incident, M. Masson, *Napoléon et les femmes*, and Mr. Oscar Browning, *Napoleon: The First Phase*.

and that the pupils of her class intended to give her a little entertainment on her departure. Every one had contributed, but Marianna could give nothing, because her allowance was nearly exhausted, and she had only six francs left. 'If I give the six francs,' said she, 'I shall have nothing left, and I shall not receive my allowance for some weeks to come; besides, six francs are not enough.' Napoleon's first movement, as my mother told me, when relating this anecdote, was to put his hand into his pocket. However, a moment's reflection showed him that he would find nothing there. He checked himself, coloured a little, and stamped his foot. . . . My mother asked Marianna how much she required. The sum was small: ten or twelve francs. My mother gave her the money, and her distress was at an end. When they got into the carriage, Napoleon, who had restrained his feelings, burst forth into violent invectives against the detestable system of such establishments as Saint-Cyr and the military schools. It was evident that he felt deeply the humiliation of his sister."[1]

Napoleon had suffered at the École Militaire from the same want of money for unnecessary expenses as his sister was suffering from at Saint-Cyr. The "detestable system" against which he inveighed, was that which permitted the few children of wealthy parents which these institutions

[1] Duchess d'Abrantès, *Mémoires.*

contained to set the tone to the school and in-
volve their schoolfellows, the great majority of
whom were pensioners of the State, in an expenditure out of all proportion to their slender means,
with the humiliating alternative of having their
poverty continually cast in their teeth.

On New Year's Day 1788, Napoleon returned
to Ajaccio—leave was very easy to obtain in
those days—where he remained six months, leading much the same life as he had in the previous
year, and doing everything possible to assist his
mother, who, crippled by the fees which she had
to pay for Joseph at the University of Pisa and for
Lucien, who had quitted Brienne eighteen months
after Napoleon and was now at the seminary at
Aix,[1] was in worse straits than ever.

Both Madame Bonaparte and Napoleon were
exceedingly anxious to secure the admission of
little Louis to one of the military schools; but,
though they both appear to have made repeated
applications and to have indited the most touching
letters, they met with no success. In an epistle
which the former addressed to the Minister for
War on June 18, 1788, she thus concludes:

Charged with the education of eight children,
widow of a man who always served the King and
the administration of the affairs of the Island of

---

[1] Lucien had been sent to Aix in the hope that he would obtain
one of the free scholarships reserved for young Corsican gentlemen
who intended to enter the priesthood; but alas! in spite of the im-
portunities of Napoleon, the *bourse* did not arrive.

Corsica, who sacrificed considerable sums in order to further the views of the Government, deprived of resources, it is at the foot of the Throne and in your sensitive and virtuous heart that she hopes to find them.

Eight children, Monseigneur, shall be the organ of the prayers which she will address to Heaven for your preservation.[1]

At the beginning of June 1788, Napoleon quitted Corsica and rejoined his regiment, which since the end of the previous year had been stationed at Auxonne. He lived in a single, barely furnished room, studied incessantly, and restricted himself to one meal a day, either from motives of economy or from the belief that an empty stomach sharpens the intellect. In July, he wrote to his mother:

I have nothing to do here except to work. I only put on my uniform once a week. I sleep very little since my illness; it is incredible. I go to bed at ten o'clock and rise at four in the morning. I have only one meal a day, at three o'clock, which makes me very well in health.

Some months after Napoleon's departure from Corsica, Lucien Bonaparte, who, although he had spent two years at the seminary at Aix, had failed to evince any vocation for the ecclesiastical state, and was, besides, in somewhat delicate health, was removed by Letizia, and returned to Ajaccio. In his *Mémoires*, he has left us the following

[1] Published by Baron Larrey, *Madame Mère*.

sketch of the Bonaparte family at the moment of his arrival :

" My mother, left a widow in the prime of life, devoted herself to the care of her numerous family. Joseph, the eldest of her children, who was twenty-three years of age, seconded her zealously and showed towards us a father's affection.   Napoleon, two years younger[1] than Joseph, had not yet been to the royal school at Saint-Cyr to fetch their sister, Marianna (Élisa).   Louis, Jérôme, Pauline, and Caroline were still children.

" A brother of my father, the Archdeacon Lucien, had become the head of the family. Although gouty and bedridden for some time past, he maintained an unceasing watch over our interests.   If Providence had struck us the heaviest of blows in depriving us so soon of our father, it atoned for this blow as much as possible by leaving us for some time longer this excellent uncle.   It endowed also the best of mothers with that spirit of constancy and that strength of mind of which the future which was opening before us furnished her with the opportunity of giving so many proofs.   A brother of our mother, the Abbé Fesch, completed our family."

When Napoleon next visited his family, at the end of September 1789, the Revolution had begun, and great events were preparing in Corsica.   Although social conditions in the island were very different from those which prevailed in France,

---

[1] He was only thirteen months younger.

the tyranny of the French officials and the restricted powers possessed by the Corsican Estates
had provided a naturally turbulent and discontented people with ample pretext for disorder,
and riots had already broken out at Ajaccio,
Corte, and Bastia. Generally speaking, the populace of the towns, the peasantry, and the middle-
classes—or, at least, the younger generation
among them—welcomed the Revolution with
enthusiasm, while the nobility and the clergy were
opposed to it. But the situation of affairs was
complicated by family quarrels and individual
jealousies. Napoleon, burning with enthusiasm
for the Revolution, plunged eagerly into the fray,
and drew up an address to the National Assembly,
entreating it "to restore to the Corsicans the
rights which Nature had given to every man."
It is probable that this address, which received
an immense number of signatures, had no small
influence on the passing of the decree of November 30, 1789, declaring Corsica an integral part
of France, and placing it under the same laws as
the rest of the kingdom.

In an excess of generosity, the National Assembly next proceeded to recall Paoli, who, since
his departure from Corsica, in 1769, had been
living in England, where George II had granted
him a pension of £1,500 a year. Mirabeau proposed his recall, "to expiate an unjust conquest,"
and the motion was carried with acclamation.
Paoli came to Paris to salute the Assembly, and

was presented by Lafayette to the King, and
when he set out for Corsica, he carried with him
the title of lieutenant-general and military commandant of the island. His journey through
France was a prolonged ovation, and he was
received everywhere with cries of "*Vive Paoli!*"

At Lyons, a deputation from Ajaccio, of which
Joseph Bonaparte formed part, met him and
accompanied him to Bastia, where he arrived on
July 17, 1790, to be greeted with frantic enthusiasm. Both Joseph and Napoleon attached
themselves closely to the aged chief, and
Napoleon, with the idea of securing the latter's
favourable attention, wrote in his defence an
open letter to Matteo Buttafuoco, a Corsican
deputy who had attacked Paoli in the National
Assembly, couched in the most violent language.

At the end of January 1799, Napoleon returned
to his regiment at Auxonne, accompanied by his
little brother Louis, whose education he had
resolved to undertake himself. The education
and maintenance of a child of twelve was a
heavy responsibility, but the *bourses* hitherto
reserved for the sons of noble parents had
now been suppressed, and the family could not
afford to pay for Louis's schooling; and he did
not hesitate. And so he shared with his little
brother his meagre pay, occupying a single room
with a tiny closet attached, which served for
Louis's bedroom, watching over him with almost
paternal tenderness, teaching him mathematics,

PASQUALE PAOLI

FROM A LITHOGRAPH BY DELPECH

geography, and history, and depriving himself for
his sake of all those little pleasures which make
garrison life endurable, and sometimes—or so, at
least, he reminded Louis, in after years, when, as
King of Holland, he refused to comply with his
suzerain's wishes—even of bread.

In the following spring, a change in the
organisation of the artillery led to Napoleon
being promoted to the rank of first lieutenant
and transferred to the Regiment of Grenoble,
stationed at Valence. He did not remain long
here, however, as towards the end of September,
the illness of his uncle Luciano necessitated his
return to Corsica. The archdeacon died on
October 16, 1791, surrounded by all the family.
A few hours before his death, he turned to
Joseph and said: "You are the eldest of the
family, but Napoleon is the head of it. Take
care to remember that!"[1]

Uncle Luciano had been a very thrifty old
gentleman—so thrifty, indeed, that ill-natured
people called him a miser. Not only did he
hoard his own money, but the meagre revenues
of the family property, of which he was adminis-
trator, as well. Poor Letizia might have been
spared many an anxious hour, had the good man
consented to dip his hand a little more frequently

[1] *Souvenirs de Sainte-Hélène.* According to Joseph, the words
were: "You are the eldest of the family, but here"—and he pointed
to Napoleon—"is he who will be its head, for he will become a
great man."—*Mémoires du Roi Joseph.*

into the bag containing his treasure, which he
kept under the mattress of his bed. One day,
little Pauline, who was no respecter of arch-
deacons, made a raid, and before any one suspected her purpose, had drawn the precious bag
from its hiding-place and emptied its contents in
a glittering stream on to the floor, the gold and
silver rolling in all directions. What must have
been the feelings of those poverty-stricken children as they ran dutifully to pick up the scattered
treasure, the while Uncle Luciano swore "by all
the saints in Paradise" that not so much as a sol
of it was his or theirs; that all belonged to a
third party, who had constituted him his banker!

But now at length they were to reap the
reward of the archdeacon's thrifty habits; the
treasure was theirs, and small though the amount
probably was, when judged by a Continental
standard, it was sufficient to place them, if not
among the wealthy families of the island, at least
among those who were in comfortable circumstances—those who would have to be reckoned
with in the coming political crisis.

For Joseph, Lucien, even, to a certain extent,
the prudent, thrifty, unimaginative Letizia herself, had all become infected by the restless spirit
of the time, which had already laid so powerful a
hold on Napoleon, and proposed to devote no
small part of the archdeacon's savings—it was
surely enough to make the poor old gentleman
turn in his grave!—not to liquidating the mort-

gages on Salines and Milelli, not to improving their neglected property, but to promoting the candidature of the aspiring lieutenant of artillery for the lieutenant-colonelcy of the battalion of the "National Volunteers of Ajaccio and Talano," one of four similar battalions to be raised in Corsica, the officers of which were to be elected by their men. What appreciable advantages the Bonapartes expected to derive from Napoleon's occupation of this post are not quite clear, but "the confidence that they had in him was unbounded,"[1] and they were prepared to make any sacrifices to ensure his success.

The Corsican of those days dearly loved an election of any kind, which not only afforded a welcome break in the monotony of his life, but presented unique opportunities for the payment of old scores, under cover of the turmoil which it invariably aroused—which payment did not take the form of a broken head, as in more northern latitudes, but of a stiletto in the back—and, as this contest promised to be an unusually strenuous one, the excitement was intense. There were five candidates, of whom the most formidable were one Quenza, a *protégé* of Paoli, and Carlo Pozzo di Borgo. Napoleon and Quenza came to an agreement, whereby they were to unite their forces against Pozzo, in order to secure the election of Quenza as first lieutenant-colonel of the battalion, and Napoleon as second. Pozzo

[1] Nasica, *Mémoires sur l'enfance et la jeunesse de Napoléon.*

was supported by the powerful Peraldi family, to
the head of which, Marius Peraldi, Napoleon
sent a challenge to a duel, which, however, was
prudently declined.

The expenditure of the Bonapartes was "enormous, in comparison with their fortune." The
archdeacon's savings were squandered in the
most reckless fashion.   Their house was crowded
at all hours with Napoleon's supporters, many of
whom, either because they had come long dis-
tances, or had been entertained so generously
they were incapable of finding their way home,
might be seen, when night fell, sleeping on
mattresses spread on the floor or on the stairs.
Letizia began to fear that she would be ruined.
"I am almost at the end of my resources," she
sadly remarked one day to Napoleon, "I must
either sell my property or borrow."   The young
officer made an impatient gesture, upon which
she hastened to add : "Oh! it is not poverty
that I fear ; it is disgrace."   "Mother," replied
Napoleon, "take courage and endeavour to sus-
tain me to the end.   We must go forward ; we
have gone too far to turn back.   In ten days, the
battalion will be organised ; then my men will
cease to be a burden to you ; they will be paid by
the Government.   If I succeed, as I hope, our
fortunes will change.   Once superior officer, my
way is made.   A general conflagration is about to
burst forth in Europe, and a brilliant career
awaits those who know how to make use of their

opportunities. The profession of arms will triumph over all others. . . . I hope that I shall be wanted, and, for the rest, I have courage, since I shall know how to render myself necessary. If I do not meet with a premature death in war, I shall undoubtedly find there glory and fortune. Mother, do what you can; but, above all, do not be cast down ; your health might suffer, and I am in need of your endurance, as well as of your devotion." Saying which, he strode away in a great state of agitation.[1]

Although the election was left to the suffrages of the volunteers themselves, the Government sent three commissioners to preside over it, and these officials were expected to exercise considerable influence on the result. There was therefore much speculation as to which of the many offers of hospitality which they had received would be accepted by them, and the consternation of the Bonaparte faction was intense when it was ascertained that one of them named Morati had gone to lodge with Marius Peraldi. They had boasted that their candidate enjoyed the confidence and support of the Government, and here was one of the commissioners a guest at the house of the chief supporter of his most dangerous rival !

Napoleon, however, speedily decided what action to take. On the night before the election, a party of his friends, armed to the teeth, went to

---

[1] Baron Larrey, *Madame Mère*.

Peraldi's residence, and, with many professions of respect, carried off Morati to the Bonapartes' house in the Rue Saint-Charles. "You were not at liberty at Peraldi's," observed Napoleon, in answer to the astonished commissioner's request for an explanation; "here you are in your own house." Morati, a Corsican himself, took the incident in good part, slept at the Bonapartes' house, and next day (April 1, 1792) went under their protection to the poll, which was held in the church of San Francesco. Napoleon's *coup de main* had ensured his success, and he and Quenza were duly elected. "Napoleon," wrote Lucien to Joseph, "is lieutenant-colonel with Quenza. At this moment, the house is full of people and the band of the regiment."

Napoleon paid dearly, in after years, for this trumpery success, for, from that hour, his defeated rival Pozzo di Borgo, once his friend, became his most deadly enemy, and "made of all Europe the *maquis* in which, during a quarter of a century, he pursued with his implacable vengeance the too fortunate companion of his youth."[1]

Nor were its immediate results particularly

[1] "To triumph over the Ajaccian who was his rival, Pozzo visited London, Vienna, St. Petersburg, Constantinople, Syria, seeking everywhere to stir up enmity against Napoleon. Agent in turn of England, Austria, and Russia, he ended by acquiring in the diplomatic world a considerable importance. It was he who incited Bernadotte to turn against his benefactor; he who pushed the Allies to advance on Paris, he who carried off the King of Rome. Finally it was he who, at the Congress of Vienna, had the audacity to propose the banishment to the Isle of Elba, and who invented St. Helena."—Rocca, *le Nid de l'Aigle.*

gratifying. On Easter Sunday (April 8), a quarrel between the volunteers of the Quenza-Bonaparte battalion and the townspeople led to a serious affray, in which several persons on either side were killed or injured, and the interference of the regular troops at the citadel was necessary to restore order. An inquiry was instituted, and, but for the constitutional objection of the Corsicans to wash their dirty linen in public, and the consequent difficulty of obtaining evidence,[1] Napoleon might have found himself in an exceedingly unpleasant position. As matters stood, the bellicose volunteers were ordered to Corte, and their lieutenant-colonel *en seconde*, who had already greatly exceeded his furlough, judged it advisable to return to France. On his arrival in Paris (May 28), he found that he had already been deprived of his commission. Officers, however, were sorely needed, and the War Office accepted his explanation of the delay ; and, on July 10, he was replaced in his old regiment, with the rank of captain, and received his arrears of pay.[2]

[1] The difficulty of obtaining evidence in Corsica in criminal cases rendered a prosecution a mere farce. In 1791, two commissioners sent by the National Assembly to inquire into the condition of the island, reported that, although there had been 130 homicides in the past three years, only one person had been condemned for them.

[2] And this, notwithstanding the fact that, two days earlier, the Minister for War had written to Maillard, the officer commanding the French garrison at Ajaccio, that, having read his report relative to the disturbances on Easter Sunday, he was of opinion that the conduct of M. Bonaparte had been "infinitely reprehensible," and that he regretted his inability to bring him before a court-martial.

Soon after his arrival in Paris, he visited his sister Marianna at Saint-Cyr, who had now been for eight years an inmate of that institution. The days of Saint-Cyr as a seminary for young ladies were numbered, since the democratic spirit of the time refused to tolerate any longer the existence of institutions reserved for the children of the nobility. But the Bonaparte family do not seem to have anticipated the closing of the school, which actually took place in the following autumn; and they were in doubt as to whether it was advisable to remove Marianna, now that she had reached an age when in Corsica most girls were already married, or to allow her to remain until she was twenty, when she would receive, on leaving, a trousseau and a *dot* of 3,000 livres—a large sum in Corsican eyes.

After his visit to Saint-Cyr, however, Napoleon wrote to Joseph, strongly advising that she should return to Corsica. " Marianna is ingenuous," he writes ; "she will easily accustom herself to household ways. There is no malice in her. In this respect, she is less advanced even than Paoletta (Pauline). We could not marry her before keeping her six or seven months at home. . . . I am of opinion that she will be unhappy in Corsica, if she remained in her convent until she was twenty, whereas now she will come thither without perceiving the difference."

Men far older and more experienced in woman's ways than Napoleon had been sadly at fault in

their estimate of the demure daughters of Madame
de Maintenon, who were trained to write in
stilted phrases, to speak, with their eyes bent on
the ground, in softly-modulated tones, and to
curtsey gravely whenever any one addressed
them ; to dissimulate, in short, their natures, their
characters, and their aspirations as they concealed
their tresses beneath the taffeta caps and black
gauze veils which their foundress had selected for
them.   Marianna, in point of fact, was a very
different person from the ingenuous damsel her
brother fondly imagined her to be.   In appearance,
she resembled Napoleon more closely than either
of her sisters, and in character, they had much
in common.   Proud, independent, resolute, and
ambitious, she will bring with her from Saint-
Cyr, not only aristocratic predilections and a love
of regularity and order in all her surroundings,
but the rooted conviction that woman is man's
equal, if not his superior, and that she only requires suitable opportunities to prove it.   A few
years hence, we shall see her at the head of a
literary and artistic coterie in Paris, eager to be
regarded as the arbitrix of taste and the tutelary
divinity of the Muses ; a little later on, her own
Minister for Foreign Affairs at Lucca, writing
bulky despatches to Napoleon.   Ah ! If only her
talents had been equal to her pretensions, what a
great woman she would have been !

As for the high moral principles which her
teachers at Saint-Cyr were supposed to have

inculcated, these alas! if they ever took root at all
in the young lady's mind, speedily withered away.
The gay courtiers of the old *régime* used to complain that Saint-Cyr produced nothing but prudes;
those of them who survived the guillotine and
made their peace with Napoleon, found very little
that was prudish about his eldest sister.

On August 16 of that eventful year, Saint-Cyr
was suppressed, by a decree of the Legislative
Assembly, and Marianna had no alternative but
to return to Ajaccio. Napoleon, who, although he
had been "advised" by the Minister for War to rejoin his regiment, was still in Paris, endeavouring
to make up his mind whether to remain Corsican
with Paoli or to become French with the Revolution, was glad of the excuse which his sister's
predicament afforded him to return to Corsica,
and forthwith applied for the necessary *congé*, in
order that he might escort her thither. This
he obtained without difficulty, and, early on
September 1, he went to Saint-Cyr to fetch
Marianna. The authorities of that institution,
however, declined to allow the girl to depart without the authorisation of the municipality and
that of the Directory of the district. Napoleon
accordingly went to find the mayor, and that
functionary, having accompanied him to the
school and satisfied himself that his visitor really
was the young lady's brother, and not a lover
masquerading as such, with whom she was contemplating elopement, gave the authorisation de-

manded. This Napoleon at once forwarded to the administrators of the district of Versailles for their ratification, accompanying it with a request that they would defray the cost of the journey to Ajaccio, in accordance with a clause in the decree of August 16, which provided that the dispossessed scholars should be paid travelling expenses at the rate of 20 sols per league, to enable them to return to their homes. The following is a translation of this letter, which is preserved in the archives of the Préfecture of Versailles, and has been published by M. Turquan, in his *Sœurs de Napoléon:*

To the Administrators of Versailles.

MESSIEURS,—Buonaparte, brother and guardian of the demoiselle Marianne Buonaparte, has the honour to lay before you the law of August 7 and particularly the additional act decreed the 16th of the same month, suppressing the schools of Saint-Louis. He claims the execution of the law, and to take back to her family the said demoiselle his sister, very urgent affairs and the public service obliging him to quit Paris without delay. He begs that you will be willing to order that she may enjoy the benefit of the law of the 16th, and that the treasurer of the district be directed to pay the twenty sols per league as far as the municipality of Ajaccio in Corsica, place of domicile of the said demoiselle, and where she must rejoin her mother.

With respect,   Buonaparte

1 September, 1792

i.—6

At the bottom of her brother's letter, and in a style and an orthography so capricious as to suggest that several very elegant letters penned by her at Saint-Cyr were drafted and corrected by her mistresses, Marianna wrote as follows :

I have the honour to inform the Administrators that never having known any other father than my brother, if his affairs obliged him to depart without taking me with him, I should find myself in an absolute impossibility of quitting the school of Saint-Cyr.[1]   With respect,

Marianne Buonaparte

The Directory of Versailles, after considering these requests, passed the following resolution.

The Directory is of opinion that there is reason to deliver for the benefit of the demoiselle Bonaparte an order for the sum of 352 livres, in order that she may proceed to Ajaccio in Corsica, her birthplace and the residence of her family, a distance of three hundred and fifty-two leagues ; that, in consequence, the sieur Bonaparte is authorised to withdraw from the school of Saint-Cyr the demoiselle his sister, with the clothes and linen for her use.

That same evening, the sieur Bonaparte returned to Saint-Cyr, in a shabby fiacre, and carried the demoiselle his sister off to Paris,

---

[1] " Jay l'honneur de faire observer à messieurs les administrateurs que, *nayant* jamais connu *d'autres* père que mon frère, *sy* ses affaires *lobligoiet* à partir sans qu'il ne *m'amene* avec *luy* je me trouverais dans une *imposibilité absolu dévacuer* la maison de Saint-Cyr.   " Avec respect,

" Marianne Buonaparte "

to the Hôtel de Metz, in the Rue du Mail, where they remained during those terrible days and nights when the prisons of Paris ran with blood and Murder stalked red-handed through the city. On September 10, they quitted the bloodstained capital and set out on their journey to Marseilles, where they arrived without adventure. Their stay in the city, however—for, owing to the difficulty of finding a ship, they were obliged to remain at Marseilles until the middle of October—was marked by a somewhat alarming incident. Marianna having exchanged the modest head-dress of Saint-Cyr for a fashionable hat trimmed with feathers, some *sans-culottes* took offence, and an angry mob surrounded the inn at which they had put up, shouting: "Death to the aristocrats!" Nor was it until Napoleon removed the obnoxious hat from his sister's head and threw it among the crowd, crying: "We are no more aristocrats than you are!" that it consented to disperse.

On October 15, they reached Ajaccio, and, for the first time since Joseph and Napoleon had quitted their homes to go to France, nearly fourteen years before, Letizia found all her children assembled round her.

CHAPTER V

MARIANNA received a warm welcome
from her family, upon whom she made
a very favourable impression, although
the younger children rallied her a little upon
her stately manners and called her "la Grande
Demoiselle." She made a very favourable impression upon another person, also, Admiral
Truguet,[1] to wit, who, in the middle of December 1792, arrived at Ajaccio, in command of
the squadron which was to take part in the

---

[1] Laurent Jean François Truguet (1752–1839). After serving
with distinction, under Guichen and d'Estaing, in the war of
1778–1783 against Great Britain, he went to Turkey to reorganise
the Ottoman navy, in which his *Traité de manœuvres et de tactique*
was long in use. He was Minister of Marine from November 1795
to August 1797, and in the following year was sent as Ambassador
to Madrid, but fell into disgrace and retired to Holland. Recalled
after the *coup d'État* of Brumaire 18, he was made a Councillor of
State, and, in 1801, resumed his command at sea. Three years
later, however, he was cashiered for refusing to give his adhesion
to the Empire, and remained out of favour till 1808, when he was
appointed maritime prefect of Brest, and subsequently entrusted
with the naval administration of Holland. In 1819, Louis XVIII
created him a count and a *pair de France*.

proposed expedition against Sardinia, bringing
with him Sémonville, who was proceeding as
Ambassador to Constantinople, but proposed to
accompany the expedition.

Truguet, who owed his high grade to the emi-
gration of his superior officers, was still a young
man, "handsome, bronzed, and vigorous," and,
though of modest origin, possessed very elegant
manners. Both the admiral and Sémonville stayed
with the Bonapartes, and, as Madame Bonaparte
knew little or no French, and Truguet was equally
ignorant of Italian, the latter and Marianna were a
good deal in each other's company. The sailor made
love to the young lady "with all the ardour of his
profession," and his overtures appear to have been
not unfavourably received ; but, at that moment,
there was little time for love-making, and still less
for marriage.   At the beginning of January 1793,
Truguet sailed for Cagliari, and he did not return to
Corsica.   At a later period, the admiral lamented
that the call of duty had caused him to miss the
great opportunity of his life, though most persons
acquainted with the lady's subsequent history will
probably be of opinion that it was a fortunate
escape.   As for Marianna, she confessed that she
would have preferred him as a husband to the
complaisant Baciocchi, though that was at best
but a mediocre compliment.

The expedition to Cagliari was a dismal failure,
nor did any better fortune attend an attack on
the little island of La Maddalena, in which

Napoleon received his baptism of fire.   No blame, however, attached to the young officer, who did everything possible to ensure success.   He returned to Corsica, deeply mortified by his failure, and convinced that treachery had been at work.

His suspicions were probably well founded. In its early stages, the great majority of Corsicans had welcomed the Revolution; but, as it proceeded on its bloodstained course, its more moderate adherents, who had no desire that the savage violence which was rendering Paris and half the cities of France nightmares to all peaceably-disposed persons should be introduced into the island, began to take alarm, and after the fall of the Monarchy, a strong movement against the French Government began to manifest itself.

At the head of this movement was Paoli himself, who had never had much sympathy with the Revolution, though he had succeeded in disguising his feelings so successfully from its leaders in Paris, that both the civil and military power in the island had been placed in his hands.   His chief adviser was Napoleon's bitter enemy Pozzo di Borgo, who exercised great influence over him and boasted that he was his right hand.

After much deliberation, the Bonapartes had determined to remain true to France.   It was the most honourable course to adopt, since France had materially assisted in keeping the wolf from their door for many a long year, had educated half the family free of all expense, and, in short,

had placed them under the greatest possible
obligations.   It was also the course which promised most, since they had little to expect from
Paoli, particularly now that he had Pozzo di
Borgo at his elbow.   The old general entertained
the highest regard for Madame Bonaparte, of
whose courage and devotion he had been a witness during the War of Independence.   But this
feeling did not extend to her children.   At their
first meeting, Napoleon had shown his contempt
for Paoli's military talents, and the general had not
forgiven him.   He perceived that he was devoured by ambition, restless, and impetuous, and
that Joseph and Lucien were the same, though
immeasurably inferior to their brother in ability.
As allies, they would be both troublesome and
dangerous, for they could never be trusted to
subordinate their wishes to his.   He therefore
showed no desire to avail himself of their services, passed Napoleon over for the post of aide-
de-camp, used his influence to exclude Joseph
from the Council-General of Corsica, and declined to make Lucien his secretary.

Madame Bonaparte's enthusiastic biographer,
Baron Larrey, speaks in terms of admiration of
what he regards as the nobly-disinterested conduct of the Bonaparte family, which, "far from
uniting with the enemies of the nation, preferred
ruin, the burning of its property, the loss and
confiscation of its goods, persecution, finally, and
exile, by remaining faithful to the annexation

of Corsica to France."[1]   But this confiscation,
persecution, and exile ought, we think, to be
regarded rather as disasters unexpectedly brought
upon it by the rashness of Lucien Bonaparte than
sacrifices deliberately made upon the altar of
political principle.   Had it not been for this
mischance, it is probable that Napoleon, aware of
the futility of the republican party in the island
attempting to make head against the Paolists
without the assistance of a French army, would
have returned to France, taking Joseph and
Lucien with him, while Letizia and the younger
children, whom Paoli would certainly have pro-
tected, would have remained quietly in Corsica.
Lucien, however, upset everything.

This precocious young gentleman—he was not
yet eighteen—by the aid of a sublime assurance,
an extraordinarily fluent tongue, and a fervid
imagination, had already made for himself a considerable reputation in the revolutionary clubs in
Corsica, which he was apparently anxious should
extend to the Continent.   Finding himself, in the
last days of March, at Toulon, whither he had
accompanied Sémonville, in the quality of temporary secretary, he hied him to the Republican
Club, and there delivered a most violent tirade
against Paoli—whose refusal to employ him
had deeply wounded his self-esteem—accusing
him of various illegal acts and of treasonable
dealings with England.   His oration made so

[1] *Madame Mère.*

great an impression upon his audience that an
address to the Convention was forthwith drawn
up and adopted, and on April 2 it was presented
to that assembly by Escudier, the deputy for the
Var.   Only the previous day, Dumouriez had
been declared guilty of treason, and the Convention, beside itself with fear and indignation, was
ready to suspect everybody.   After a brief discussion, a decree was passed summoning Paoli
and Pozzo di Borgo to the bar—in other words,
to the guillotine—and orders for their arrest were
despatched to Corsica.

Lucien, proud and triumphant, wrote to his
family : " I have dealt a decisive blow to our
enemies ; you did not anticipate it." They certainly did not, nor did Lucien anticipate that his
letter would be intercepted by the friends of Paoli
and carried to the general, who lost no time in
publishing it.   The Corsicans were exasperated
to the last degree ; they flocked in crowds to
protect Paoli, seized Ajaccio and Bonifacio, and
prepared for a general civil war.   Napoleon
and Joseph, in great alarm, did everything possible to counteract the effect of their younger
brother's folly ; and the former wrote to the Convention, imploring it to recall its decree.   But it
was too late ; the mischief was done, and by the
end of April, Paoli was in open rebellion.

After an unsuccessful attempt to get possession
of the citadel of Ajaccio, which had fallen into
the hands of the Paolists, Napoleon endeavoured

to make his way to Bastia, whither Joseph had
already gone to join the commissioners of the
Convention.   At Bocognano, he was arrested by
some peasants in the service of his enemy Marius
Peraldi ; but they kept a careless watch over him,
and, when night fell, he succeeded in effecting his
escape.   He returned to Ajaccio, where his
friends concealed him for two days, though, on
one occasion, he narrowly escaped recapture, at
the end of which time they procured him a ship
to carry him to Bastia.

In the meanwhile, Letizia, who must have been
enduring torments of anxiety on behalf of her
son, remained at Ajaccio, in the hope that her
presence would suffice to protect her property,
and that she and her younger children would be
left unmolested. The news, however, grew every
day more alarming, and Napoleon sent a message
to his mother, bidding her prepare for flight, as
" that country was not for them."   Paoli, on his
side, caused her to be informed that, if she were
prepared to disavow her son's proceedings, her
property should be respected. But the courageous
woman rejected his offer with scorn. "*Madame*,"
says Napoleon, "replied like a heroine, and as
Cornelia would have done, that she did not
understand two laws ; that she herself, her children, and her family knew only that of duty and
honour."

The consequences of this uncompromising
attitude were soon apparent. A night or two

later, Madame Bonaparte awoke to find her room filled with armed mountaineers. She started up in great alarm, in the belief that the house was in the hands of the Paolists, but was reassured, on recognising, by the light of the pine-torches which the invaders carried, that their leader was one Nunzio Costa, of Bastelica, the most devoted of her son's adherents. " Be quick, Signora Letizia!" cried he ; " Paoli's people are hard on our heels. There is not a moment to lose. I have all my men here with me. We will save you or die with you!"

Rising in all haste, Letizia summoned her frightened children, and, barely allowing themselves time to dress, they quitted the house. Annunziata and Jérôme she left to the care of her mother Signora Fesch, and then, accompanied by Marianna, Pauline, and Louis, and her half-brother Joseph Fesch, and guarded by the faithful peasants, she set off for Milelli.

Here, however, it was impossible for them to remain, for the Paolists were burning and pillaging in all directions, and, when day broke, their retreat would certainly be discovered, even if those who had failed to find them at Ajaccio were not already on their track. They accordingly resolved to take to the mountains, and, when they were safe from pursuit, to make for the Tower of Capitello, on the other side of the Bay of Ajaccio, and there await the arrival of a French squadron which they knew was daily expected.

Lucien Bonaparte relates that presently they beheld smoke and flames rising from Ajaccio, and that one of their escort exclaimed : " Look, Signora, your house is on fire!" To which his mother replied : "Ah! what does it matter! We will build it again finer than before. *Vive la France!*"

M. Masson, however, unlike Baron Larrey, whose discrimination leaves a good deal to be desired, is of opinion that this patriotic outburst is a mere invention of the writer, who was anxious to place his own conduct in a favourable light and to create the impression that it had the approval of his family. Trained as Letizia had been in admiration for Paoli, we can hardly suppose that she could have been so speedily converted to revolutionary ideas, still less that she could have brought herself to approve of one of her sons denouncing to the French the "Father of his Country." Nor could she have regarded with complacency the destruction of the house in which the greater part of her life had been spent, and have contemplated without alarm the future which awaited herself and her eight children, only three of whom were old enough to earn their livelihood.

All that night the fugitives journeyed on, for the faithful Costa knew that even the briefest delay would be dangerous. "The young men of Bastelica formed the advance-guard, those of Bocognano the rear-guard; the Bonaparte

family marched in the centre of these two squads
of volunteers, who were armed with carbines and
stilettos. The Signora Letizia held the little
Pauline by the hand, while Marianna and Louis
kept by the side of their uncle, the Abbé Fesch.
This group of relatives was surrounded by devoted guides, who directed their steps through
the dark night and along the most narrow and
difficult paths of the *maquis*. The shrubs
and brambles tore their clothes and hurt the
faces, hands, and feet of the children, whose
complaints and sobs alone troubled the silence
of the night, as they reached the ears and heart
of their mother. She gave to all the example of a
courage which rose in proportion to the danger."[1]

Once their scouts came hurrying back, with
the alarming intelligence that a band of armed
Paolists was approaching on its way to Ajaccio ;
and, as the poor children, scarcely daring to
breathe, crouched amid the brushwood to allow
their enemies to pass, they could hear them
promising themselves a terrible revenge on those
pestilent Bonapartes, should they fall into their
hands.

At length, towards morning, the party reached
the heights of Aspreto, where the weary children
threw themselves on the grass to snatch an hour
or two's sleep, while the peasants kept watch.
Then they resumed their journey, and, after
travelling all that day and most of the succeeding

[1] Nasica, *Mémoires sur l'enfance et la jeunesse de Napoléon.*

night, for all the surrounding country was infested by marauding bands of insurgents, and they were under the necessity of making frequent *détours* in order to avoid them, they reached the Tower of Capitello. Alas! there was no sign of any ship, and the peasants exchanged anxious glances, while the children burst into tears, and even Letizia's courage began to fail her. Presently, however, a sail appeared on the horizon, and, in response to their signals, rapidly approached the shore. It was a small coasting-vessel, which Napoleon had hired at Calvi, and he himself was on board. He had landed, it appeared, the previous evening and despatched messengers in every direction to ascertain tidings of his family, but, having been pursued by a band of Paolists, had been compelled to re-embark.

After bidding farewell, with many expressions of gratitude, to the brave peasants to whom they owed their escape,[1] Letizia and her children went on board, and were conveyed to Girolato, whence they gained Calvi and took refuge with the Giubega family, a member of which, Lorenzo Giubega, had stood godfather to Napoleon. Napoleon himself rejoined the French squadron, which, in co-operation with those of the inhabitants of Ajaccio who had remained faithful to France, was about to make an attempt to recover

---

[1] In his will, Napoleon bequeathed to Nunzio Costa 100,000 francs, and a similar sum to Geronimo Levie, of Ajaccio, who had aided the future Emperor to escape to Bastia.

the town. The attempt, however, failed, and, in the first week of June, Napoleon returned to Calvi, where Joseph and the two youngest children also joined their mother.

The Bonapartes once more reunited, with the exception of the immediate cause of all their misfortunes, who had prudently remained at Toulon, anxiously deliberated as to what course they should pursue. It was impossible to remain in Corsica, for they were entirely without means of support, and Letizia was too proud to allow her family to live at the expense of their friends, who were themselves suffering serious loss through the war. Moreover, although they were, for the moment, in safety at Calvi, which was garrisoned by fifteen hundred French troops, the insurgents were closing in upon the town, while a British squadron was cruising off the coast. In all probability, they would shortly find themselves closely blockaded both by sea and land, and Napoleon and Joseph shrank from exposing their mother and the younger children to the dangers and privations of a siege. In France, on the other hand, Napoleon would have his pay as captain, while Joseph might obtain some employment, and they would be in a position to contribute towards the support of the others. No doubt, too, the Corsican deputies in the Convention would exert themselves to obtain some assistance for the distressed family from the Government.

And so to France they decided to proceed,

and, on June 11th, Letizia, her seven children, and
Joseph Fesch embarked on a merchant vessel,
which, having had the good fortune to elude the
vigilance of the British cruisers, brought them
in safety to Toulon.

CHAPTER VI

Early days of the Bonaparte family in France—Their distressing poverty — Gradual improvement in their circumstances — Napoleon, made general of brigade and appointed inspector of coast fortifications, invites his mother and sisters to join him at Antibes—Madame Bonaparte and her daughters—Indiscretions of Élisa and Pauline at Marseilles—Life at Antibes—Adventure of Pauline—Marriage of Lucien—Marriage of Joseph —Napoleon imprisoned—Junot a suitor for Pauline's hand—Napoleon as matchmaker—Vendémiaire 13.

THE exiled family only remained a few days at Toulon. The town was in a state of anarchy; Royalists and Girondists, secretly encouraged by Great Britain and Spain, disputed supremacy with the adherents of the Convention, and a sanguinary insurrection might break out at any moment. The Bonapartes had not fled from civil war in Corsica with the intention of seeking it again in Provence, and Napoleon and Joseph perceiving that Toulon, in its present disturbed condition, was no place for their mother and their young brothers and sisters, particularly as they would soon be deprived of their protection, resolved to remove them to the neighbouring village of La Vallette, where they lodged at the house of a widow named Cordeil. Then they bade them farewell, and set off, Napoleon to rejoin his regiment, which was now quartered at Nice, and Joseph to seek employment in Paris.

During the next three months, Madame Bonaparte and the younger children seem to have been continually on the move — as the poor creatures had scarcely any luggage, these removals were easy and inexpensive—though their frequent changes of residence are somewhat difficult to trace. About the middle of July, they left La Vallette, owing apparently to the irrepressible Lucien having got himself into trouble with the dominant faction at Toulon, and seem to have gone first to Bausset, and subsequently to Mionnac, a little village on the road to Brignolles. Then, at the beginning of September, after the defeat of the insurrectionary army of the Bouches - du - Rhone had opened Marseilles to loyal Republicans, they removed to that town,[1] where they lodged on the fourth floor of a house in the Rue Pavillon until they were allotted free quarters at the Hôtel de Cipières, in the Rue Lafon, which had once been the *mairie*.

All this time, the unfortunate exiles seem to have been in the greatest distress. In Corsica, they had been no strangers to poverty, but, as they had always had the produce of their garden and orchard to fall back upon, they had never

---

[1] Baron Larrey says that they arrived in Toulon in June, but his book, so admirable in many respects, is full of chronological errors.

known actual want. Now, however, they found themselves in circumstances where money was a necessity, and, but for the small sums which Napoleon was able to send them from time to time, they must certainly have starved. If we are to believe Barras, "they presented the spectacle of the most distressing poverty, living solely on borrowed money, barely sufficient to provide them with a mattress, which they shared in common, and a cauldron, out of which they all ate together."[1]

And if food and lodging were difficult to procure, clothes were altogether out of the question. They had fled from Ajaccio with "nothing but the clothes in which they were dressed,"[2] and these must have suffered severely from their nocturnal wanderings amid the mountains and brushwood. Louis and Jérôme were boys, and Annunziata was happily too young to appreciate the magnitude of such a calamity; but with Marianna and Pauline it was different, and in their battered hats, their patched frocks, and their broken shoes, the poor girls were ready to die with shame and vexation every time they set foot out of doors.

Never had Letizia's courage and endurance, never had her genius for economy, been so severely tested. She toiled day and night to

---

[1] Barras, *Mémoires*. Barras probably exaggerates; but there can be no doubt the family was at times in the direst straits.

[2] Lucien Bonaparte, *Mémoires*.

supply the needs of her children; she made one franc do the work, not of two, but of three or four—the sum which Marianna had been so desirous of contributing to her schoolfellow's farewell fête at Saint-Cyr would probably have kept the family for a week—and she humbled her pride so far as to wait her turn in the long queue of half-starved wretches at the Bureau de Bienfaisance, to whom the municipality of Marseilles doled out each day a meagre ration of garrison bread.

Gradually, however, their circumstances began to improve. Napoleon bombarded both the military and civil authorities at Marseilles with entreaties "to come to the aid of his unfortunate family, of his poverty-stricken mother," with the result that orders were given by the commandant of the garrison that soldiers' rations, consisting of bread, meat, vegetables, fuel, and salt, should be served out to them. Joseph, who had returned from Paris, obtained a post in the commissariat of the Navy at Toulon; Lucien, after vain efforts to get himself attached to the embassy at Constantinople, condescended to accept a clerkship in the military stores at Saint-Maximin, a little town not far from Marseilles; while Fesch also secured a small civil appointment; and all three presumably contributed something to the support of their relatives. Finally, Barras and Fréron, the commissioners of the Convention at Marseilles, interested themselves in the unfortunate family,

ARRIVAL OF THE BONAPARTE FAMILY IN FRANCE IN JUNE, 1793

FROM AN ENGRAVING AFTER THE PAINTING BY MAUZAISSE

and obtained for them a share of the indemnity
which had been voted by the Convention for
necessitous Corsican patriots who had been driven
to take refuge on the Continent. Madame Bonaparte accordingly received 75 francs a month for
herself, and 45 francs a month for each of her
children under the age of fifteen, in addition to
an immediate grant of 150 francs to each bene-
ficiary. Their difficulties were at an end; it was
wealth in comparison with the grinding poverty
to which they had lately been reduced.

In the spring of 1794, Napoleon, who had been
promoted to the rank of general of brigade, " for
the zeal and intelligence of which he had given
proof in contributing to the surrender of the
rebel town [Toulon]," was charged with the inspection of the fortifications of the Mediterranean
coast, and installed his mother and sisters in a
comfortable country-house close to Antibes, and
within easy distance of his headquarters.

Madame Bonaparte was by no means sorry to
quit Marseilles for a while. Apart from the
pleasure she experienced in being so near her son,
and in exchanging her comfortless lodging in a
town where the Terror was now at its height, and
the tumbrils containing the victims of the guillotine passed daily beneath her windows, for more
healthy and peaceful surroundings, the conduct of
her daughters—or rather of the two elder girls,
Marianna and Pauline—at Marseilles had been
such as to cause their mother no little anxiety,

and to render a period of rustication very advisable.

Admirable mother though Letizia Bonaparte was, and greatly as she was respected and beloved by her daughters, her influence over them was, nevertheless, very slight. Nor is this difficult to understand. In Corsica, as we have observed elsewhere, woman occupied a very subordinate position, and while parents exercised very careful supervision over their sons, their daughters were, for the most part, sadly neglected. At the age of fourteen or fifteen, by which time nearly every girl had had her husband found for her, she had learned to read and write, more or less correctly, and knew something of household management ; but, save for the great lesson of submission to her elders, which was very strictly inculcated, she had received but little moral or religious training. Nevertheless, so strong was the force of tradition, that Corsican women were almost invariably irreproachable wives and excellent mothers, and there is no reason to suppose that the Bonaparte girls would have proved exceptions to this rule, had they remained in their native land. But it was their misfortune to be transplanted from their peaceful island home into the restless, feverish life of revolutionary France, at an age when old habits are most easily discarded and new ones formed ; to find themselves among people who scoffed at religion and openly ignored the precepts of morality ; to taste the bitterness of the most poverty, and then to be raised, by rapid stages, to wealth and influence beyond their wildest dreams, and, eventually, to the very pinnacle of Fortune. Who can wonder, then, that, under these circumstances, the lessons of childhood were speedily forgotten, that most of what was evil in the Corsican character flourished exceedingly, while most of what was good withered away, and that they should have resembled their unstable, extravagant, pleasure-loving father far more closely than their modest, virtuous, and thrifty mother?

Even so early as the last months of their residence at Marseilles, the two elder girls began to show unmistakable signs of the influence of their new surroundings. Marianna, who was now sixteen, was the only one of the family who had no pretensions to beauty. Her friend Rœderer describes her as "of middle stature, thin, flat-chested, with slender arms, a fine leg, and pretty feet; regular features, a classic profile, black hair, a rather clear skin, beautiful teeth, and an extremely mobile countenance." He adds that her usual expression was "animated, but a trifle severe"; that, when with people with whom she was not well acquainted, she "sometimes wore an air of ennui and constraint"; but that, in the company of her friends, she was "merry, frank, and witty."[1]

Other chroniclers, however, are much less com-

[1] *Œuvres.*

plimentary to Marianna than Rœderer. The Duchesse d'Abrantès declares that "never had woman renounced as she had done the grace of her sex; one was tempted to believe that she wore a disguise"; and, though this lively writer's tendency towards exaggeration is well known, the general consensus of opinion seems to be that there was very little that was feminine about the appearance or manner of Marianna.

We must, however, no longer speak of the eldest Mlle. Bonaparte as Marianna, but as *Élisa*. At Saint-Cyr, she had been called Élisa to distinguish her from one of her schoolfellows, also a Corsican, Marianna Casabianca, and, soon after her arrival in France, she adopted this name in preference to her own.[1]

Pauline—or Paulette, as she was generally called by her relatives and intimate friends—who was now in her fourteenth year, but, like most Corsican girls, already almost a woman, was a very different person from her somewhat masculine sister. With her little classic head, her pure oval face, her lovely hazel eyes, her clear olive complexion, and "the bust and shoulders of a goddess," she was the most charming creature possible to behold. "Many persons," says the Duchesse d'Abrantès, "have spoken of her

[1] Du Casse, *Supplément à la Correspondance de Napoléon.* M. Masson is of opinion that the name Élisa was invented for her by Lucien, who had a mania for rebaptising people; but Du Casse's explanation, which is accepted by the lady's latest biographer, M. Paul Marmottan, seems the more probable.

beauty.   One knows this beauty by her portraits
and her statues ; but it is impossible to form a
correct idea of what this extraordinary woman
was in the perfection of her loveliness, because
the majority of people knew her only after her
return from St. Domingo, when she was already
faded, and only the shadow of that Paulette of
the ravishing beauty which we admire sometimes, as we admire a beautiful statue of Venus
or Galatea."   Ricard declares her to have been
"a marvellous beauty."   Madame de Rémusat,
speaking of her on her return from St. Domingo,
"weak, suffering, and dressed in mourning,"
nevertheless, expresses the opinion that she was
"the most lovely woman she had ever seen."
And finally—though we might multiply such
testimonies—Madame Ducrest, who, as an intimate friend of the Empress Joséphine, had no
love for the Bonaparte women, and, indeed,
speaks of Pauline's character in anything but
complimentary terms, writes : " She was the
most lovely woman I ever beheld.   There
was not the slightest imperfection in her delicious face, to which she joined an elegant
figure and the most seductive grace.   She was
an incomparable beauty."

And Pauline knew it—had known it, indeed,
almost before she was out of the nursery, since
it had probably saved her many a castigation in
the old days in Corsica ; and, for her, admiration was henceforth as the breath of life.   Of

education she had received even less than most
Corsican girls, for her schooling had been interrupted by the Revolution, and she had not the
smallest desire to make good the deficiency.
Study, she had heard, had a tendency to make
people ugly ; certainly, it had done nothing for
Élisa's appearance. For herself, she preferred
to remain ignorant and beautiful. And she kept
her resolution.

After allowing for all that may be ascribed to
the malice of enemies and to that tendency to
exaggeration from which few chroniclers are
exempt, it seems impossible to deny that Élisa
and Pauline must have conducted themselves at
Marseilles in a manner that was the reverse of
discreet. Ricard, who was then residing in the
town, and was a frequent visitor to the Bonapartes' house, after expressing his disbelief in certain very scandalous stories in connection with their
sojourn there, adds : " But I must say that opinion
at Marseilles was not favourable to them, and
that it attributed to them gallant and even
scandalous adventures. Bonaparte never forgave
the Marseillais."[1] And he is confirmed by
Madame de Rémusat : " If one ought to believe
the recollections of the Marseillais, these young
girls showed that they had not been brought up
in the severity of a very scrupulous morality.
The Emperor never forgave the town of Marseilles, for having witnessed the want of dignity

[1] *Autour des Bonapartes.*

which his relatives displayed there at that time ; and the unpleasant anecdotes, imprudently repeated by certain Provençals, always militated against the interests of all Provence, so far as he was concerned."[1]

Some writers have accused Madame Bonaparte of encouraging the "dissolute conduct" of her daughters. But, if they were ever guilty of "dissolute conduct," which is extremely improbable, it certainly took place without her knowledge. At the same time, she would appear to have exercised very little supervision over them, and must therefore be considered, to a certain extent, responsible for the scandalous stories which caused Napoleon so much annoyance, though absorbed as she was just then in a ceaseless struggle against poverty, it is difficult to blame her.

Élisa and Pauline were enchanted with their new life. They made many friends, for Napoleon had now come to be regarded as a young officer with a distinct future before him, so far as any one could be said to have a future in those troublous times. They held little receptions, in which Élisa sometimes edified the company by reading aloud, while occasionally comedies were performed, wherein Pauline played the saucy *soubrette* as to the manner born.

Notwithstanding that this young lady was now

[1] *Mémoires.*

nearly fifteen, she had not yet abandoned her impish pranks. One day, while taking a walk, she came to a garden which was one blaze of gorgeous blossoms. Pauline was unacquainted with the owner—a certain M. Baliste—but the gate stood invitingly ajar, and, as there happened to be no more amusing occupation in prospect at that particular moment, she decided to enter and spend a few minutes in improving her knowledge of the floriculture of Provence. Unhappily, roses and carnations were not the only attractions of M. Baliste's garden ; there were thick clusters of purple grapes, there were artichokes, and there were some particularly fine figs, a fruit to which Pauline was particularly partial. Having concluded her inspection of the flowers, mademoiselle thought she would taste one of the figs, just to see if they were as good as those of Ajaccio, and found it so very excellent that she continued to taste until the tree was appreciably lightened. Suddenly, a harsh voice fell upon her ear, and, turning round, she perceived, to her dismay, an old gentleman, with a face purple with indignation and a formidable stick in his hand, hastening towards her. The little marauder fled, but, though she ran her best, the indignant owner ran still faster, and his stick was already suspended over her pretty shoulders, when Desgenettes, a military surgeon, who, in later years, attained some celebrity, happened to pass by, on his way to visit Madame Bonaparte. He interposed, and though the angry old gentleman at first refused to listen to reason, he at length permitted himself to be appeased.[1]

Although the circumstances of the Bonapartes had now become comparatively easy, this did not prevent Letizia from continuing to exercise the most rigid economy wherever possible, and many years later old inhabitants of Antibes used to relate how they had often seen the future Emperor's mother washing linen in the Riou, which flowed not far from the house.

In the summer, when Napoleon was obliged to return to Nice, his family accompanied him, and Élisa and Pauline were invited to several balls, where they danced and flirted with the officers of the garrison and enjoyed themselves so much, that they must have found it difficult to believe that only a twelvemonth before they had lacked the wherewithal for a square meal.

During Madame Bonaparte's sojourn at Antibes and Nice, two of her sons took unto themselves wives. The first was Lucien, who, it will be remembered, had recently obtained a post in the military stores at Saint-Maximin. Saint-Maximin, a small country town of some three thousand inhabitants, was not a very promising field for the exercise of Lucien's talents, but he certainly made the most of his opportunities. He temporarily abandoned his Christian name for that of Brutus, reigned over the local republican club, became

[1] Baron Desgenettes, *Souvenirs.*

president of the revolutionary committee of the municipality, and caused a number of inoffensive persons to be arrested and thrown into prison. Finally, he gave a beautiful example of the equality which he was always preaching, by espousing (May 4, 1794) a daughter of the people named Caroline Boyer, sister of a small innkeeper, with whom he lodged, though, according to his own account, Citizen Boyer does not appear to have given him much choice in the matter.

Madame Bonaparte and all the family were extremely indignant on learning of this *més-alliance*, which, inasmuch as the bridegroom was a minor and had neglected to obtain his mother's consent, might have been annulled, if Letizia had chosen to appeal to the courts. However, Caroline, or rather Christine—for that was the name her husband gave her—who was a sweet-tempered and unassuming, as well as a very pretty, girl, made Lucien an excellent wife, while he, on his side, was entirely devoted to her; and, in time, the Bonapartes grew reconciled to the union.

In the meanwhile, Letizia found abundant compensation for the conduct of Lucien in the marriage of Joseph, who, on August 1, 1794, married Julie Clary, the daughter of a wealthy soap-boiler of Marseilles, whose younger sister, the pretty Désirée Clary, afterwards married Bernadotte and became the ancestress of the Royal

Family of Sweden.[1]   Joseph had rescued one of
the lady's brothers, Etienne by name, from the
chill embrace of Dame Guillotine, the fear of which
alone had driven another brother, François, to
take his own life ; and this service, backed by the
young Corsican's handsome face, elegant manners, and good birth, had completely captivated
Mlle. Clary's heart.

It was a prudent match, for, although the soap-
boiler's daughter was singularly unprepossessing
in appearance, with a "villainous figure, a flat
nose, and a shapeless mouth," she was a very
worthy and sensible young woman, and the pos-
sessor of a fortune which must have seemed to
the Bonapartes like the riches of Golconda itself,[2]
to say nothing of expectations from a relative, a
prosperous usurer.

What more could a fond mother desire for her
son ?   And Letizia's cup of joy would have been
full to overflowing, if only Napoleon could have
paired off with the equally well-dowered Désirée.
But, though the young soldier does appear to
have made some tentative advances in that direction, which were not ill received, he probably had
far too much on his mind just then to have any

---

[1] The civil marriage was celebrated at Cuges, six leagues from
Marseilles ; a religious ceremony took place privately, some
days later, at Saint-Jean-le-Désert.   None of the bridegroom's
relatives seems to have been present at either ceremony.

[2] About 150,000 francs, the purchasing power of which, in 1794,
was, according to M. Masson's estimate, equal to ten times that
sum to-day.

leisure for serious wooing. Besides which, the lady's brothers are said to have expressed the opinion that "one Corsican in the family was enough."

The joy of the Bonaparte family at the good fortune of its nominal head was momentarily quenched by a most alarming incident.

When, a few days after Joseph's marriage, the news of Robespierre's fall reached Nice,[1] Napoleon, who passed for a *protégé* of the incorruptible Maximilien—or rather of the incorruptible one's younger brother, Augustin—was placed under arrest by Albitte, Laporte, and Salicetti, the representatives in mission with the Army of the Alps, and imprisoned in a fortress near Antibes. Letizia and her daughters were in a terrible state of distress, for Napoleon was accused of having intrigued with the younger Robespierre to keep the Army of the Alps inactive, and many a man's head had parted company with his shoulders for a far less serious reason. Happily, however, their anxiety was soon at an end, for, after a diligent, but unsuccessful, search for compromising matter among Napoleon's papers, the representatives, "taking into consideration the utility which his military and local knowledge might be to the Republic," provisionally restored him to liberty. It was not, however, until three week later that they

---

[1] The events of Thermidor 9 and 10 (July 27 and 28) do not appear to have been known at Nice until August 5.

announced to the Committee of Public Safety that he had "reconquered their confidence," and reinstated him in his former position.

In March of the following year, Napoleon sailed from Toulon, as chief of the artillery, with the expedition intended "to deliver Corsica from the tyranny of the English." The expedition, however, never reached Corsica, as off Cape Noli it had the misfortune to fall in with a British squadron under Hotham, and was compelled to fall back in confusion to the French coast, with the loss of two vessels. To his intense disgust, Napoleon found that, during his absence, he had been superseded in the inspectorship of the coast fortifications by his countryman Casabianca; and towards the end of May, he set out for Paris, accompanied by his brother Louis, now a sub-lieutenant of artillery, and his friends Marmont and Junot.

Junot had attracted Napoleon's attention by the courage and coolness he had displayed before Toulon, and he had made him his aide-de-camp.[1] This position gave him many opportunities of meeting the general's relatives, and "his youthful warmth of feeling"—it is his future wife, the

---

[1] One day, Napoleon, wishing to dictate an order, called for some one who could write a legible hand, and Junot was brought to him. While he was taking down Napoleon's instructions, a cannon-ball struck the earthwork of the battery on which he was writing, and covered him and his papers with earth. "*Bien!*" remarked Junot, laughing "We shall not now require any sand."

Duchesse d'Abrantès, who speaks—"could not withstand so charming a creature as Pauline then was; he loved her to infatuation." Being an honourable young man, he considered himself bound to disclose his feelings to Napoleon—a rather unnecessary proceeding, since, by all accounts, the latter would not have required any great amount of perspicacity to have divined them already—and begged him to employ his good offices to obtain Madame Bonaparte's consent.

On the young lady's side, he did not expect to encounter any obstacles, "having a belief, amounting almost to certainty, that Paulette would say 'Yes' with pleasure, so soon as he should be able to offer her an establishment sufficient to be a security against bringing children into the world destined to be miserable."[1]

Napoleon, however, prudently declined to commit himself, though he gave Junot to understand that he would gladly welcome him into the family, if he could show that he had any reasonable prospect of being able to support a wife. Upon which, the enamoured youth straightway wrote to his father to ascertain what assistance he might expect from that quarter.

One beautiful summer evening, soon after their arrival in Paris, Napoleon and his aide-de-camp were walking under the shady trees of the Jardin des Plantes—a very favourite resort of the future

---

[1] Duchesse d'Abrantès, *Mémoires*.

Emperor—when the latter returned to the subject which was nearest his heart, and handed his chief a letter which he had received from his father, in which Junot *père* informed his son that he had nothing to give him during his lifetime, except his blessing, but that his share of the family property would one day amount to 20,000 francs. "You see that I shall then be rich," said Junot, "since, apart from my pay and my prospects of promotion, I shall have an income of 1,200 livres a year. I beseech you, my dear General, write to the Citoyenne Bonaparte, your mother; tell her that I love her daughter, that I demand her hand, and that my father, on his side, is about to write to her to make the formal proposal."

Napoleon listened with a sympathetic smile on his lips to the pleading of the eager lover, and seemed on the point of giving a favourable reply; but when they left the quiet garden and found themselves in the crowded streets, the noise and bustle about him recalled him to the stern realities of life, and, turning to his expectant companion, he said : " I cannot write to my mother to make this proposal, for you are to have eventually, as you assure me, an income of 1,200 livres; but you have not got them yet. Your father wears well; and you may have to wait a long time for them. The truth is that you have nothing but your lieutenant's pay. As for Paulette, she has not so much. So that to sum up : you have nothing, she has nothing. What is the total ? Nothing.

You cannot then marry at present. We must
wait; we shall perhaps see better days, my friend.
Yes, we shall have them, even if I should have
to seek them in another part of the world."

This reply was a sad blow to poor Junot; but
its logic was unanswerable, and there was nothing
left to him but to abandon his pretensions.[1]

If we are to believe the Duchesse d'Abrantès,
although Napoleon had declined to countenance
the impecunious Junot's suit, he was none the
less desirous to find a husband for Pauline, since,
one day, he called upon the chronicler's mother,
Madame Permon, and proposed to unite her family
and his by a whole chain of alliances: to wit, a
marriage between Albert Permon and Pauline,
another between Laure Permon (the future Duchesse d'Abrantès) and either Louis or Jérôme,
and the third between Madame Permon, who had
recently became a widow, and himself. The lady,
however, declined his propositions, observing
that her children were too young to marry, while
she herself was old enough to be her suitor's
mother.

When Napoleon spoke to Junot of seeking
better days in another part of the world, he
was seriously thinking of taking service in
Turkey, where the Sultan was anxious to engage

---

[1] Duchesse d'Abrantès, *Mémoires*. The chronicler adds that
she has transcribed this conversation as she had it from her husband's own lips, "because she considered that the whole attitude
of Bonaparte on that evening was remarkable."

French officers to reorganise his army. The Committee of Public Safety had appointed the young officer to the command of a brigade of infantry in the Army of the West, then engaged in stamping out the insurrection in La Vendée; but Napoleon had little taste for such butcher's work, besides which he considered that his transference from the artillery to the infantry was a reflection upon his abilities. He therefore remained in Paris, on the plea of ill-health, and, in August, applied for permission to proceed to Turkey. This request was on the point of being granted when, on September 15, the Central Committee struck his name off the list of general officers, "on account of his refusal to proceed to the post which had been assigned him." Fortune seemed to have abandoned him, but, in reality, she had never been kinder. Three weeks later, thanks to the critical situation in which the Government found itself and the discernment of Barras, he was restored to his rank and appointed to the Army of the Interior; and, on Vendémiaire 13, his "whiff of grapeshot" saved the tottering Republic from destruction, and established his own fortunes and those of his family.

CHAPTER VII

IN the autumn of 1794, Madame Bonaparte
and her daughters had returned to Marseilles. During their stay at Nice, Letizia
had not been unmindful of her girls' future, and
had made a valiant attempt to secure a rich
soap-boiler named Rabassin—the Bonapartes
appear to have been rather partial to soap-
boilers and their offspring at this period—for
Élisa. M. Rabassin, however, evaded her, and,
in after years, is said to have had the bad taste to
boast in public of the discernment he had displayed
on this occasion. Nor did any better fortune
attend her pursuit of a certain M. de Lasalcette,
a gentleman of Dauphiné, at that time residing
at Marseilles, whom she had marked down as a
suitable husband for Pauline. M. de Lasalcette
greatly admired Pauline, but he had the good
sense to perceive that "beauty unaccompanied by
solid moral principles is scarcely a guarantee of

happiness for a husband," and decided to wait until he could find both combined in the same person.

Thanks to Joseph's prudent marriage, the family found their circumstances still further improved, for the new *ménage* seems to have contributed liberally towards the support of its indigent relatives. However, if the Bonapartes had contrived to surmount their most pressing financial difficulties, other causes of anxiety were not wanting. Vendémiaire 13 was still some distance off, and Napoleon's prospects, which in the previous summer had seemed almost assured, were again very uncertain; while, in July 1795, the adventurous Lucien once more succeeded in destroying the peace of mind of his long-suffering family.

In the violent reaction against Terrorism which had followed the fall of Robespierre, the petty tyrants of the provincial municipalities were everywhere ejected from office and sent to take the place of their victims in prison. Many of them perished by the guillotine, and many more were butchered by the Companies of Jehu and of the Sun, organised bodies of young men belonging to the upper and middle classes, most of whom had lost relatives or friends during the Terror, and who, mad with the lust for vengeance, roamed up and down the country, breaking into the prisons and murdering the incarcerated Jacobins without distinction of age or sex.

Lucien Bonaparte, who, after the reaction of
Thermidor, had prudently lost no time in quitting Saint-Maximin and taking service with the
principal contractor to the Army of Italy, at Saint-
Chamant, near Cette, was permitted to remain
at large for some time. But he had made too
many enemies to escape altogether, and eventually he was denounced as an accomplice of the
younger Robespierre, by a man named Ray—
a member of a family which he had persecuted
when he was Brutus—and imprisoned at Aix.

Lucien was in mortal fear ; it was not so much
the guillotine he dreaded as the knives of the
Companions of Jehu, who had already made one
clean sweep of the prisons at Aix, and might
quite conceivably be contemplating a second
holocaust ; and every night he heard in imagination the dreaded avengers of innocent blood
thundering at the gate. Poor Lucien had shed
no blood ; he had only made bombastic speeches,
and locked up those who refused to admire them
for a few days or weeks, to give them an
opportunity for salutary reflection. But the Companions of Jehu were not wont to draw nice dis-
tinctions ; all was fish that came to their net.

Madame Bonaparte, when the news reached
her, was equally alarmed. She forgot all about
that *mésalliance* which had occasioned her so much
indignation at the time. She thought only of the
peril of her son, and wrote to every one who
might be able to bring any influence to bear to

procure his release. Here is a letter which she addressed to her compatriot Chiappe, one of the deputies in mission with the Army of Italy, who was then at Nice.

Marseilles

3 Thermidor, Year III

(*July* 21, 1795)

Citizen Representative,—I have just learned, by this morning's courier, of the arrest of my son Lucien. Since none of his brothers are here, and I know not to whom to have recourse, I address myself to you, in the hope that, in consideration of your friendship for me, you will interest yourself on his behalf. He has been denounced, at Saint-Maximin, to one of your colleagues, of whose name I am ignorant. I cannot conceive what is the charge against him, since there are no *émigrés* in that part of the country, and no one has been punished by the sword of the Law. There have only been a few persons arrested, and those are denounced; I know not why. . . . I beg you, Citizen Representative, to write immediately to Isoard your colleague, who is here. I await this proof of your friendship and I hope you will not disdain my supplications. If your sister-in-law is still at Nice, recall me to her remembrance. I am, Citizen Representative, with respect, Your concitoyenne,

Letizia Bonaparte[1]

Baron Larrey, whose admiration for his heroine not infrequently inclines him to exag-

---

[1] This letter was probably drafted by Élisa, as Madame Bonaparte was, at this time, almost unacquainted with French.

gerate her influence, asserts that Lucien owed
his restoration to liberty to his mother's intercession. But, though Letizia's representations
no doubt counted for something, his release
seems to have been mainly the work of Napoleon, who brought great pressure to bear from
Paris upon the deputies in mission at Marseilles,
with whom the decision rested. Any way, on
August 5, Lucien was released, and, about a
month later, set off for Paris, where Napoleon
intended to find him employment and to keep
him, if possible, out of further mischief.

Three weeks after the insurrection of Vendémiaire 13, Napoleon had climbed to the top of
the ladder, upon whose lower rungs a month
before he had barely succeeded in retaining a
precarious foothold. On Brumaire 4 (October 26),
he was appointed general-in-chief of the Army
of the Interior.

The most devoted of sons, his first thought
was for his mother, and rich indeed was the
compensation she now received for those few
months of poverty and humiliation at Toulon
and Marseilles. "I have sent the family fifty
or sixty thousand francs," he writes to Joseph ;
"it wants for nothing. . . . It is abundantly
provided for in every way."

Nor were his brothers' interests forgotten.
For Joseph, the post of French consul at
Genoa, letters of marque empowering him to

fit out two privateers to prey upon British commerce — a very promising form of investment, provided the said vessels could contrive to show a clean pair of heels to the enemy's cruisers, when occasion required—and the command of a battalion of engineers for his brother-in-law. For Lucien, an appointment as *commissaire des guerres* in the Army of the North, whither that young gentleman did not condescend to repair until more than three months later, preferring to accompany Fréron—of whom more anon —on a mission to the South, to put the drag on the Royalist reaction and persuade the Company of Jehu to moderate its ardour. For Louis, a lieutenant's commission in the 4th Regiment of Artillery and the post of aide-de-camp to himself. For Jérôme, the College of Juilly, "where he learned Latin, mathematics, drawing, music, etc., everything at the expense of the great brother." And all this in two months. Assuredly, Napoleon was justified in writing to Joseph : " I cannot do more than I am doing for all."

As for the girls, he was resolved that they should marry well. No Albert Permons or Rabassins for the sisters of General Bonaparte, the hero of Vendémiaire, the saviour of the Republic, Commander-in-chief of the Army of the Interior ! And he rejected with contempt the application of a Citizen Billon of Marseilles —another of the soap-boiling fraternity—for the hand of Pauline.

And the family rejoiced in its good fortune, present and prospective, as only those can rejoice who have supported life upon a diet of garrison-bread and stale vegetables, and endured all the undignified annoyances of poverty. But its complacency received a rude shock, when, in March 1796, hard upon the intelligence that Napoleon had been appointed to the command of the Army of Italy, came the news of his marriage with the widow Beauharnais.

The astonishment of the Bonapartes was profound. Napoleon had taken this momentous step, had married this "old woman with grown-up children" and a far from spotless reputation, without asking his mother's consent, without consulting Joseph, without so much as a word or a hint to any of them!

But great as was their astonishment, their indignation and alarm were even greater. It was to Napoleon that they all looked to satisfy their several aspirations: his mother for money to hoard against another rainy day, his brothers for easy and lucrative posts, his sisters for marriage-portions. And now he was married —married not to an ugly, timid, and rich little *bourgeoise*, of simple tastes and contented disposition, like Julie Clary; not to the illiterate daughter of an *aubergiste*, overwhelmed by the honour of being received into such a family; but to a *ci-devant* viscountess, needy, frivolous, and extravagant, with two children of her own, and Heaven only knew how many relatives, friends, and ex-lovers ready to contend with them for the crumbs that fell from the great man's table! Napoleon, they felt sure, would form new ties, new associations, new habits. He would lose the sentiment of Corsican exclusiveness; he would employ his credit for others, he would cease to belong only to his own people.

The marriage threatened the interests of all; but it did more: it outraged Madame Bonaparte in her native prejudices; it wounded the girls in their vanity. Letizia was much attached to Joseph's wife, whose simple tastes were thoroughly in accordance with her own; besides, Julie was rich and wanted nothing from Napoleon. As for Christine Boyer, her modesty, her good sense, her deep affection for her erratic boy-husband, her almost pathetic gratitude for Letizia's recognition of their relationship, had reconciled her to a match which she had at first regarded with so much annoyance. But, with Joséphine, an aristocrat, a Parisian, a woman of the world, of easy morals and expensive tastes, who probably had not a thought in her head beyond the shape of a coiffure or the fit of a gown, unless it were how to obtain the wherewithal to satisfy her extravagance, she could have nothing in common; she would feel awkward and ill at ease whenever they met. And, besides being poor, extravagant, and of indifferent character—any one of which objections was sufficient in Letizia's eyes to disqualify her for the position of her son's wife—Joséphine was thirty-four at least, and scarcely likely to bear Napoleon children. To a Corsican, such a marriage was nothing less than a crime.

For the girls, the prospect was still more alarming. Joseph's wife was too plain to cause them any misgivings, Lucien's too shy and awkward; but Napoleon's was not only said to be pretty, but she was one who had been privileged to move amid the society of the old *régime*, who, until misfortune had overtaken her, had lived in a giddy world, of balls and theatres and receptions and flirtations; who was doubtless the perfection of elegance, good taste, and *savoir-faire*. How could these *gauche* Corsican girls appear in the same room with her without being utterly eclipsed, without being made to look almost ridiculous?

In short, the whole family—with the single exception of Jérôme, too young as yet to appreciate the gravity of the situation—even before they had set eyes upon the hapless Joséphine, hated her as only Corsicans can hate, and had declared against her and her children as bitter, as unscrupulous, a vendetta as ever was waged among the *maquis* of their native island—a vendetta which was to ruin Napoleon's domestic peace, divide the Consular and Imperial courts into two factions, and to continue until the interloper had been driven away.

But, after their first burst of indignation had

subsided, the Bonapartes recognised the wisdom
of appearing to accept the situation, at least, until
a favourable opportunity for commencing active
hostilities should present itself, which was not
likely to occur until the glamour of Napoleon's
passion had begun to wane.   The young general,
on his side, knew his relatives too well to entertain
much doubt as to the manner in which they were
likely to regard his matrimonial escapade, as is
shown by the secrecy with which he had acted.
But he hoped to reconcile them to the situation,
by proving that, if he had not consulted them in
the matter, his feelings towards them were unchanged, and he was none the less anxious for
their advancement.

On March 22, Napoleon arrived at Marseilles,
on his way to join the " half-naked, half-starved "
Army of Italy, with which, ere many weeks were
over, he was to accomplish such wonders. Before,
however, attempting the conquest of Italy, he had
resolved to conquer his mother ; and, of the two
tasks, the latter was by far the most difficult, since
Letizia was still in arms against Joséphine long
after her son had assumed the Iron Crown of
Lombardy.   But it was difficult to refuse Napoleon
any request at such a moment, so Letizia yielded,
doubtless with a mental reservation, though it
was not until nine days after the general's departure that she addressed to Joséphine the
following letter, in answer to one which she had
received from her daughter-in-law :—

To the Citoyenne La Pagerie-Buonaparte, Rue Chantereine, 6, Paris.

Marseilles
12 Germinal Year IV
(*April* 1, 1796)

I have received your letter, Madame, which could not strengthen the idea I had formed of you. My son had acquainted me with his happy union, and, from that moment, you possessed my esteem and approval. Nothing is wanting to my happiness, save the pleasure of beholding you. Be assured that I entertain for you all a mother's affection, and that I love you as much as my own children.

My son encourages me in the hope, and your letter confirms me in it, that you will pass through Marseilles on your way to join him. I rejoice, Madame, in the pleasure that your sojourn here will afford me.

My daughters join me in the hope that you will hasten the date of your journey. In the meanwhile, be assured that my children, following my example, have dedicated to you the same devotion and affection which they entertain for their brother.

Believe, Madame, in the attachment and affection of

Letizia Buonaparte, mother.[1]

The elegant phraseology and correct orthography of this letter, written by a woman who never succeeded in acquiring more than a very imperfect knowledge of the French language,

[1] *Bibliothèque Nationale*, published by Baron Larrey.

and who, when, in later years, she had secretaries
and ladies of honour to do her bidding, was in
the habit of dictating the major part of her correspondence in Italian, and its tone of studied
courtesy and affected cordiality, so foreign to the
brusque and outspoken nature of the writer, all go
to show that Letizia must have had at least one
collaborator.   In all probability, as M. Masson
suggests, it was the work of a family council, while
the delay in despatching it to Paris is accounted
for by the fact that it had been first submitted to
Joseph at Genoa.[1]   However that may be, Napoleon had secured, although somewhat late, the
formal consent which he required, and appearances
were saved.

[1] *Napoléon et sa famille.*   The panegyrical Baron Larrey
seems to have no doubt regarding the authorship or the sincerity of
"this letter of maternal sympathy, which responded so well to the
sentiments of filial sympathy expressed by Joséphine."

CHAPTER VIII

IF Napoleon, in marrying Joséphine de Beauharnais, had obeyed the dictates of his
heart, he had not the smallest intention of
permitting the younger members of his family to
regard his conduct as a precedent which they
were at liberty to follow; and this one of them
was very quickly to discover.

When, in the previous autumn, Napoleon had
pronounced his veto on the proposal that had been
made for Pauline's hand by Citizen Billon, the
soap-boiler, that young lady had accepted the
fraternal decision, not only without demur, but
with considerable relief, inasmuch as a cavalier
very much more to her taste had recently appeared—or rather reappeared—upon the scene.

It will be remembered that, soon after the
Bonapartes arrived in Marseilles, in 1793, they
had been rescued from the poverty in which they

found themselves by the commissioners of the Convention Barras and Fréron, who procured them a pension from the Government. By favour of this service, the two deputies had become frequent visitors at the Hôtel Cipierès, and Fréron seems to have paid Pauline considerable attention. However, in March 1794, he returned to Paris, and she saw him no more, until the beginning of November 1795, when he returned to Marseilles as Commissioner of the Directory for the Departments of the South, with Lucien in his train, and lost no time in picking up the threads of their interrupted flirtation. Before, however, we relate the interesting little romance of Pauline and Fréron, it may be as well to give some account of this singular person, so typical of all that was most base and most sanguinary in revolutionary politics.

Louis Marie Stanislas Fréron was the son of that ex-Jesuit and critic Élie Catherine Fréron, who was such a thorn in the side of Voltaire,[1] and was educated at the famous Jesuit college of Louis-le-Grand, where he had Robespierre and Camille Desmoulins as fellow-pupils. Like them, he embraced with ardour the principles of the Revolution—or rather professed them, since his only principle was self-interest—founded, in May

---

[1] "Wasp Fréron begat him: Voltaire's *Frélon*; who fought stinging, while sting and poison-bag were left, were it only as Reviewer and over Printed Waste-Paper."—Carlyle, *French Revolution*.

1790, the journal, *l'Orateur du Peuple*, became a prominent member of the club of the Cordeliers, and took part in the insurrection of August 10, 1792. Elected to the Convention, in the following September, as one of the deputies for Paris, he sat among the Montagnards and voted for the death of the King "*sans appel ni sursis,*" and for the proscription of the Girondists. In the summer of 1793, he was sent, with Barras, as deputy in mission to the Army of Italy, engaged in reducing the rebellious South to submission. He caused many of the principal inhabitants of Marseilles to be brought to trial and guillotined, confiscated their property, demolished some of the finest public buildings in the city, and even pushed his revolutionary ardour so far as to date his letters from "*la ville Sans-Nom,*" and to demand that the town, which he had already half-ruined, should be deprived of its name, and its walls pulled down. The Convention, however, refused to sanction this extravagance, and Marseilles preserved both its name and its walls. On the surrender of Toulon, he advised that that town should be razed to the ground—though happily the Government was of a different opinion—and the measures he adopted towards the conquered were in conformity with the violence of his language. "Firing-parties are the order of the day here," he wrote to Moïse Bayle, deputy for the Bouches-du-Rhône; "there are more than six hundred persons who will never again take up arms against the Republic. Death is busy among the subjects of Louis XVII.   To-day, all the sergeants, adjutants, and soldiers of the Marine have suffered it, in company with the municipal authorities, who bedecked themselves with the white scarf during the reign of the Marmoset.   Three accursed priests concluded the proceedings."

At the end of the year, he returned to Marseilles to continue his interrupted labours, and, during the next three months, is said to have caused no less than four hundred persons to be brought to the guillotine.

Returning to Paris, in March 1794, he resumed his seat in the Convention, conspired against Robespierre, and was one of the principal agents of his fall, though it is only fair to observe that the incorruptible one would certainly have sent Fréron to the Place de la Revolution, had not the latter had the prudence to forestall him.

In the crimes which he had committed, Fréron had not had the excuse of conviction, which others were able to invoke.   He was one of those who slew and destroyed merely to avoid compromising themselves, or to acquire a lucrative favour, with the party in power.   Now that the reaction against the Terrorists had set in, he renounced his former opinions, turned savagely upon his old allies, became the Marat of the "*Jeunesse dorée*," and paraded the streets of the capital, at the head of bands of young men, known as " Fréron's Army," beating and insulting every Jacobin he

met.[1] He supported the Convention in the insurrection of Vendémiaire, but failed to secure a
seat either in the Council of the Ancients or in
that of the Five Hundred, for his recent *volte-
face* had disgusted many, while his honesty was
not above suspicion, and he had recently been pub-
licly charged with converting to his own use the
confiscated property of some of his victims at
Marseilles and Toulon.   However, he obtained,
by way of compensation, from the expiring Committee of Public Safety, the mission to the South
of which we have already spoken,[2] though, as his
tastes lay in the direction of organising massacres,
rather than of putting a stop to them, it does not
appear to have been attended with much success.

At the time of his return to Marseilles, Fréron
was in his forty-third year, and his personal
appearance was no more calculated to prepossess
any one in his favour than was his political record.
He had a retreating forehead, an aggressively
large nose, sunken eyes, a heavy jaw, and thin
cruel lips ; in short, the man's unlovely character
was stamped upon every line of his countenance.
However, he did his best to atone for the scurvy
manner in which Nature had treated him by
the elegance of his dress and manners.   Like
Robespierre, while embracing the most violent
democratic principles, he had declined to adopt

---

[1] He even proposed that the Hôtel de Ville should be demolished, as it had been "the Louvre of the tyrant Robespierre."

[2] See p. 123, *supra.*

STANISLAS FRÉRON
FROM AN ENGRAVING BY BONNEVILLE, AFTER A DRAWING BY THE SAME ARTIST
(BIBLIOTHÈQUE NATIONALE)

republican fashions in dress, and was the aristocrat of the Revolution, the Beau Brummell of
Jacobinism. He wore his hair carefully curled
and powdered in the fashion of the old *régime*,
a *jabot* of costly lace, a coat with a skimpy body,
an enormous collar, and long square tails, and
knee-breeches of rose-coloured satin, fitting so
tight to the skin that it was a perpetual wonder
to every one how he ever succeeded in getting
into them or, when that feat had been accomplished, how he contrived to get out again, and
carried in his walks abroad an enormous gold-
headed cane, like that wielded by a drum-major
on parade. In his conversation, he spoke the
affected language of the time, lingering lovingly
over his vowels and suppressing his "r's" as
ruthlessly as he had the hapless Royalists of
Marseilles and Toulon. For the rest, he was a
very gallant gentleman, with a marked partiality
for the daughters of Thespis, and for more than
four years he had been the lover of a certain
demoiselle Masson, of the Comédie-Italienne.
Rumour even went so far as to declare that he
was married to the lady, and, since she had
already presented him with two pledges of her
affection, and promised him a third, there was
certainly some justification for the report. However, Fréron troubled himself very little about
what people said, as he was not the man to allow
the gossip of the *coulisses* to stand between him
and an advantageous marriage.

And such a marriage, he believed, had now presented itself. Pauline, beautiful, fresh, and in-genuous, produced on this middle-aged *roué*, weary of painted *coryphées* and soulless courtesans, a very agreeable impression. She was profoundly ignorant, it is true; her pretty little head was as empty as those of the wax dolls which, in moments of generosity, he sometimes bestowed upon his luckless offspring in Paris. But he did not want a clever wife; the girl's beauty appealed to his jaded senses, her prospects—or rather those of Napoleon—appealed to his cupidity and ambition, for he foresaw that the young soldier would go far and rise high, while his own fortunes were decidedly on the down-grade. He resolved to marry Pauline.

The young lady, on her side, was quite ready to respond to his advances. She felt that her *métier* was to inspire love, and had not the slightest desire to avoid it; indeed, by all accounts, she lost no opportunity of practising it, and had already become quite dangerously pro-ficient. Many people had professed themselves her slaves, but no one, with the exception of poor Citizen Billon, whose aspirations Napoleon had so promptly quenched, had carried their adoration so far as to speak of matrimony; and Fréron, with his powdered hair, his fine clothes, and his elegant manners, was a very different type of suitor from the worthy soap-boiler. To her, he was a great man. Had he not sat in the Convention? Had he not been sent on important missions? Did not rebels against the Republic one and indivisible tremble at his frown? Surely she ought to consider herself greatly honoured by his asking her to become his wife! And then he paid her such charming compliments; he wrote her such passionate letters; he composed such beautiful verses in celebration of her charms —like old Élie Fréron before him, Stanislas wielded a fluent pen, though, indeed, he was no honour to literature—and he made love so delightfully. Really there were times when he seemed almost handsome; no one could possibly have imagined him to be forty-two—old enough, in fact, to be her father.

So Pauline loved him with her whole heart— or imagined that she did, which at sixteen amounts to much the same thing—and troubled her head not one jot as to whether he were rich or poor, since at sixteen one does not trouble about such trifles, and, besides, to do her justice, she was never, at any time of her life, mercenary.

But, perhaps happily for Pauline, the financial part of the affair bulked very large indeed in the eyes of her mother and Napoleon. Baron Larrey declares that "this alliance did not please under any aspect Madame Bonaparte *mère*, who refused her consent, in spite of the entreaties of her daughter"; and Madame Tschudi, Letizia's most recent biographer, says that she "inexorably refused her consent to the union." But both writers omit to mention that this refusal was, for some months, merely a suspensive veto, in order to allow the Bonapartes time to inform themselves more precisely as to the ex-deputy's position and prospects, and to see whether some more eligible suitor might not present himself. Thus, on January 11, 1796, we find Napoleon writing to Joseph : "I do not see any objection to Paulette's marriage, *if he* [Fréron] *is rich.*"

If he is rich! It is nothing to him that Fréron is more than double his sister's age ; it is nothing to him that his private life is a scandal ; that he had been one of the worst of that unspeakable gang which had turned Paris and half the chief towns of France into shambles ; that he is a cruel, debauched, hypocritical scoundrel! No ; he is quite ready to give him his young sister, "if he is rich "—if, after due inquiry has been made, it is found that he has contrived to lay his blood-stained hands on sufficient of his victims' property to make him worthy to enter the Bonaparte family! Could cynicism possibly go further?

While Fréron was being weighed in the balance by his inamorata's family, the lovers appear to have been permitted to meet pretty frequently and, in the intervals, found consolation in a very active correspondence. Barras declares that ere long they became lovers in the fullest acceptation of the term, but this is probably a calumny. Nevertheless, to judge by Pauline's epistles—none of Fréron's to her have unfortunately been preserved—the termination of the romance, either by marriage or by a complete separation, was certainly advisable. Take the following, for example :

19 Ventose, Year IV

(*March* 9, 1796)

I was yesterday in the greatest anxiety about thy health, my good friend. I sent . . . but, too silly, he returned without ascertaining how you were. I was in that condition when Nouet[1] arrived. I did not count upon one of thy letters. He told me that thou wast suffering much. Why didst thou write! Thou dost not love me, since thou dost disobey me. I do not wish to see thy handwriting until thou art able to go out. Thou knowest well, my friend, that it is a two-fold privation for me ; but I will endure everything, provided that thou art cured. I will write to thee ; Nouet will bring thee my letter. Tell him to come every day. I am not sorry that thou art frank with him ; I believe him to be discreet. It is enough that he is thy friend for me to trust him.

I did not reply to thy letter of the day before yesterday, since I preferred to speak to thee about it. My heart is the surety for my answer. Yes ; I swear to thee, dear Stanislas, never to love any one but thee. My heart cannot be shared ; it is wholly thine. Who could oppose the union of two souls who seek only happiness, and who find it in loving one another? No, my friend, neither mamma nor any one can refuse thee my hand.

[1] A confidant of Fréron.

Nouet told me yesterday that thou oughtest not to go out all the week. Ah well! we must have patience; we will write, and that will make amends for the privation of not seeing one another. I thank thee for thy attention in sending me thy hair. I send thee mine likewise, not that of Laura, for Laura and Petrarch, whom thou dost often cite,[1] were not as happy as we are. Petrarch was faithful, but Laura, . . . Adieu, Stanislas, my kind friend; I embrace thee as I love thee.

P. B.

Although the result of the inquiry into Fréron's financial position had not been such as to inspire the Bonapartes with any very ardent desire to welcome him into the family, his prospects were, at the moment when the above letter was written, distinctly encouraging. His old accomplice Barras had as good as promised him the much-coveted post of commissary to one of the armies, in which an enterprising gentleman without any scruples worth mentioning might amass a comfortable little fortune in a very short space of time, having the privilege of plundering both the French troops and their conquests; and, if he kept his word, Fréron would become a suitor worthy of all encouragement. When, therefore, on March 22, Napoleon arrived at Marseilles, on his way to join the Army of Italy, he greeted the ex-deputy most cordially, gave him to understand

---

[1] Petrarch was a favourite author of Fréron; he had translated several of his sonnets.

that the marriage had his entire approval, and, as Fréron expressed his intention of spending his honeymoon in Paris, he even promised to give him a letter for Joséphine, "in order that she might not be too astonished at the sudden appearance of Paulette, when Fréron should present her to her."

The delighted Fréron thereupon pleaded for an immediate marriage. They had waited so long, he said, and, further, the expected nomination might arrive any day, and he would be compelled to tear himself away from his bride. Had Bonaparte any objection? None whatever; he only regretted that he would be unable to be present at the ceremony, since his military duties necessitated his departure for Toulon on the following morning. Fréron embraced the general and hurried off to the *mairie*, to make arrangements for the marriage to take place so soon as the necessary formalities had been complied with.

But no sooner had Napoleon departed than Madame Bonaparte began to raise objections. It was impossible for her daughter, she declared, to get married at a moment's notice. There was her trousseau to prepare; there were business matters to discuss; there were friends and relatives who would consider themselves slighted if they were not invited to the ceremony. Finally, such haste was scarcely seemly. No; she was desolated to disappoint Citizen Fréron, but she feared that he must curb his impatience for a few days longer.

Now, there can be very little doubt that
Letizia, in insisting on delay, was acting in concert
with Napoleon ; and their reason was as follows :

Napoleon knew that Barras was anxious to
give Fréron the commissaryship from which so
much was expected, and both he and Letizia
were perfectly willing to welcome him as a relative, *if he obtained it.* But he also knew that,
in the course of his chequered career, his prospective brother-in-law had made many bitter enemies,
in whose hands he had lately had the imprudence
to place a very dangerous weapon, by continuing
to exercise his dictatorship in the South after the
powers which had been granted him had expired.
This matter was about to be brought before the
Council of the Five Hundred.   Napoleon believed that the attack would fail ; but there was a
chance that it would not, in which case matters
might go very hard with Fréron, and it would certainly be impossible for the Directory to nominate
him commissary.   Any way, a few days would
see the matter decided.   For which reason,
though he allowed Fréron to believe that he had
no objection to an immediate marriage, he privately instructed his mother to oppose it.

Fréron chafed at the delay.   He was probably
aware of the machinations of his enemies in
Paris, and wished to secure his bride and her
brother's powerful support before they had time
to strike the blow they were meditating.   Accordingly, after vainly endeavouring to induce

Madame Bonaparte to relent, he addressed the following letter to Napoleon at Toulon :

Germinal 4, Year IV

(*March* 24, 1796)

Thou didst promise me, before leaving, my dear Bonaparte, a letter to thy wife ; we had agreed that thou shouldst announce to her my marriage, in order that she should not be surprised at the sudden appearance of Paulette, when I should present her to her. I am sending an orderly to thee at Toulon, to fetch this letter, of which I will be the bearer.

Thy mother opposes a slight obstacle to my eagerness. I hold to the idea of being married at Marseilles within four or five days. Apart from the possession of that hand which I burn to unite to mine, it is probable that the Directory will nominate me at once to some distant post, which will perhaps entail a speedy departure. If I were obliged to return here, I should lose precious time, and the Government which, with reason, troubles itself very little about the affections of the heart, may blame an absence which will retard the object of the mission which will be confided to me. I entreat thee, write on the instant to thy mother to remove all difficulties ; tell her to allow me the greatest latitude for determining the time of this auspicious moment. I have the entire consent, I have the avowal of my young friend. Why postpone these ties that the most tender love has formed? My dear Bonaparte, assist me to overcome this new obstacle. I count on thee.

My friend, I embrace thee, and am thine and hers for life. S. F.

But the "auspicious moment" so eagerly anticipated by Fréron never arrived; the few days gained
by Napoleon and his mother proved fatal to his
hopes.   For ere they had expired, a courier drew
rein at the ex-deputy's door and handed him a
big official-looking letter.   Eagerly he broke the
seals, believing that it contained his expected
nomination as commissary; but his feelings may
be imagined when he found instead an imperative summons to return to Paris to answer for his
"anarchical operations" in the South.   Napoleon's prudence was justified.

Bidding a hasty farewell to the tearful Pauline,
Fréron posted off to Paris, and defended himself
with the courage of despair.   But the day of
reckoning had come; enemies rose up on all
sides to denounce "this man who, whilst still
young, had already achieved immortality in
crime,"[1] and Barras and his other accomplices
did not dare to defend him, from fear of compromising themselves.   He escaped punishment,
but his career as a public man was ended, and,
when some months later, thanks to the influence
of Jeannet-Dervieux, the French commissioner
in Guiana, he was elected deputy to the Council
of the Five Hundred, his election was immediately annulled, without a single voice being
raised in his favour.

When the news of Fréron's disgrace reached
Napoleon in Italy, he at once decided that his

[1] Isnard à Fréron, Brochure of the Year V.

engagement with Pauline must be put an end to, and wrote to his wife : " I beg thee, my friend, to let Fréron understand that my family does not intend him to marry my sister, and that I am resolved to prevent it." And to Joseph he wrote : " I beg thee to arrange Pauline's affairs ; I do not intend her to marry Fréron. Tell her this, and make her tell him."

Fréron, however, was far from disposed to throw away the only card left him, and firmly refused to resign his pretensions ; while Pauline, on her side, was equally disinclined to listen to reason, being encouraged in her resistance by Lucien—who, seven years later, was to come into violent conflict with his imperious brother over a similar affair[1]—and by certain of Fréron's friends at Marseilles, who declared that she was in honour bound to remain true to her lover.

And so the amorous correspondence continued —indeed, the more strenuous the opposition, the more tender did Pauline's letters become. Often, after writing the body of a letter in French, she added a postscript in Italian, of so inflammable a description, that—to borrow the well-known

---

[1] On June 19, Lucien wrote to Fréron : "What turn are public affairs taking, but, above all, in what situation are thine? Here are two questions of which I demand a frank explanation in thy reply. What art thou doing? What are thy hopes? What are thy intentions, thy plans, thy means? I am asking many questions ; they would be indiscreet, if the most lively friendship and a sentiment still more lively did not justify them. A line [no doubt from Pauline] enclosed with this letter explains this enigma, which thy heart already divines."

observation about the epistles of Mlle. de Les-
pinasse—it seems almost a miracle that the
paper did not ignite under her pen.   Fréron was
"her life," "her soul," "her divinity," "her
beautiful idol"; she "breathed only for him," she
"idolised him," and so forth.

(*May* 19)

I have just received thy letter, which has given
me the greatest pleasure, for I was beginning to
complain of thy silence; and, on the other hand,
it has keenly affected me, because of what you
tell me of that woman.[1]   Do not be uneasy; I
am not ill, except from ennui and lassitude.   Write
me as often as possible.   Thy letters will afford
me some comfort in my distress.   I am very
anxious to learn the result of that woman's affair.
I put myself in her place, and I pity her.

Adieu, I cannot write to thee any more, notwithstanding all the desire I have to talk with
thee.   I have not yet had my portrait painted;
when I am better, I will have it done, as I am
not able at present to endure the fatigue of the
sittings.   Thy portrait is a great consolation to
me: I pass the days in company with it and talk
to it, as if thou wert there.   I hope by the next
post to be better and to write to thee at greater
length.   Remember me kindly to Nouet; I have
received his letter, and will reply by the next
post.   Adieu, my good friend; I love thee more
than myself.   Adieu.

Tell Lucien to write to me; I have already
written him twice.   Excuse my scrawl; in bed
one is not at one's ease.

---

[1] Presumably, Mlle. Masson, whose jealousy was causing
Fréron some embarrassment.

Marseilles

14 Messidor, Year IV

(*July 2*)

I received, on my return from the country, thy charming letter, which occasioned me all possible pleasure. My mind is more tranquil since I have re-read it, for I did not sleep even in the country, where they endeavoured to distract me by all kinds of amusements. Thou hast come near to losing thy Paulette; I fell into the water in trying to jump into a boat. Happily, I was rescued in time. Do not let that trouble you; this accident has had no consequences. Lucien starts for Paris in six days. . . . I am pleased that he is going to Paris; thou wilt be able to take counsel with him in regard to our interests. I speak no more of thy mistress; all that you tell me reassures me. I know the uprightness of thy heart and approve the arrangements thou art making.[1] The water that I imbibed in the river has not chilled my heart towards thee; it must surely have been nectar that I swallowed, if it be possible for it to become still warmer . . .

Adieu, my soul; I love thee for ever, my life.

> Non so dir se sono amante;
> Ma so ben che al tuo sembiante
> Tutto ardor pressa il mio cuore,
> E gli è caro il tuo pressar.
> Sol tuo volto, s'io ti miro,
> Fugge l' alma in un sospiro,
> E poi rìede nel mio petto
> Per tornare a sospirar.[2]

[1] Presumably, Fréron had decided to pension off Mlle. Masson.

[2] These verses are Petrarch's.

From the next epistle, we learn that Joséphine
is taking a hand in the game, and is seeking to
confirm Napoleon in his opposition to the marriage; while, on the other hand, Madame Bonaparte, who, since Fréron had fallen into discredit,
had opposed the marriage—probably at Napoleon's
bidding—has become the lovers' accomplice, as
Fréron is directed to send his letters under cover
to her. Pauline also suggests that they shall both
write to Napoleon, in the hope that their combined entreaties may induce him to relent.

(July 6)

My friend,—Every one intends to oppose us.
I see, by thy letter, that thy friends are among
the ingrates; even Napoleon's wife, whom thou
didst believe on thy side. She writes to her husband that I shall be dishonoured if I were to
marry thee, and that she hopes to prevent it.
What have we done to her? Is it possible, everything is against us! How unhappy we are! . . .
But what am I saying? No; so long as one
loves, one is not unhappy. We experience opposition, we have sorrows it is true, but a letter, a
line: "I love thee," consoles us for the tears that
we shed.

All these difficulties, very far from diminishing
my love, only serve to augment it. Courage, my
well-beloved; our constancy will witness the day
when all these obstacles will be removed, I hope.
I counsel thee to write to Napoleon; I should
like to write. What dost thou say to it? It
seems to me that my letter was not sufficiently
strong to persuade him fully of my feelings for

thee. Perhaps he will be softened by the tears of a sister and the sorrows of a lover. Thou knowest that he can do much ; tell me what thou thinkest of it? I will make every effort to send thee my portrait. Thou canst address thy letters under cover to mamma.

Adieu, my friend, for life thy faithful friend,

P. B.

. . . Be of good courage ; in spite of thy misfortunes, thou art still more dear to me. Perhaps things will change. Love me always, my soul, my blessing, my tender friend ; I breathe only for thee, I love thee.[1]

In the next letter, written five days later, Pauline tells her beloved Stanislas that she has again been confined to her bed—the mental anguish she is enduring is evidently beginning to affect her health,—but she is as devoted as ever, and vows eternal fidelity in both French and Italian.

(July 11)

My good friend,—Thou must undoubtedly be anxious at not having received my letters ; but I was suffering as much as thyself from being unable either to talk with my friend or to pour out my heart to him. I was in bed, and I was somewhat indisposed. Thou knowest my sensibility, and thou art not ignorant that I adore thee. And to see ourselves forced to encounter so many obstacles and so unhappy! No ; it is impossible for Paulette to live apart from her affectionate friend Stanislas.

---

[1] This postscript is in Italian.

Formerly, I had the sweet consolation of being able to speak of thee and to pour out my heart to Élisa; but I have it no longer. Lucien has shown me thy letter; I see that thy situation is still unchanged. Ah! how I have kissed that letter, how I have pressed it against my bosom, against my heart! Yes; notwithstanding all this opposition, sustained by thy love, I feel that I have the courage to endure it. I would that I could be with thee; I would console thee for all the injustice that has been done thee. To conclude, we are leaving this house; to-morrow I will send thee the address.

Adieu, my good friend, write to me often and open thy heart to that of thy affectionate and faithful love

P. B.

Ah! my beloved, my divinity! What suffering thus to be separated so long! But I cling to the hope that we shall be soon reunited. Adieu then, my dear hope, my idol; I believe that, in the end, fate will grow weary of persecuting us. . . . I love thee always, and most passionately, for ever I love thee, I love thee, my beautiful idol; thou art my heart, tender friend; I love thee, I love thee, I love thee, I love thee, lover so tenderly loved.[1]

In the meanwhile, Napoleon and his ragged legions had been carrying all before them in Italy, and, with each fresh success, the young victor's ambition, not only for himself but for his rela-

[1] "Ti amo, sempre, e passionnatissimamente, per sempre ti amo, ti amo, ti amo, sbell' idol mio, sei cuore mio, tenero amico, ti amo, amo, amo, amo, si amatissimo amante."

tives also, increased, and he became more and
more incensed at Pauline's obstinacy. What!
decline to abandon this wretched Fréron, when,
as sister of the conqueror of Italy, she was a
match for any one in France! It was prepos-
terous! M. d'Almeras, Pauline's latest biographer, is of opinion that Napoleon had not as
yet "opposed to Fréron's candidature a formal
and definite refusal"; but he does not appear to be
acquainted with his letters to his wife and Joseph
which we have already cited.[1]   But it is possible that, as Napoleon was under some obli-
gation to Fréron, for the services he had rendered
his family in the past, and wished to spare his
feelings, he may have subsequently given him to
understand that, if the latter's circumstances improved, he might reconsider his decision, in the
hope that Pauline would grow weary of such an
unsatisfactory state of affairs and put an end to
the comedy of her own accord.   Of this, however,
there seemed to be no prospect, and he was therefore much relieved when, towards the end of
1796, Fréron became involved in a very unpleasant scandal, which provided Napoleon with
an excellent pretext for ringing down the curtain.

A woman whose favours the ex-Jacobin had
obtained under promise of marriage, exasperated
at being abandoned by her perfidious lover, came
forward and declared that she was his wife, and,
though she failed to establish her claim, succeeded

---

[1] See p. 145, *supra*.

in raising a scandal which, for some days, formed the chief topic of conversation at Marseilles. Napoleon, promptly informed of this, lost not a moment in despatching letters to his mother and sister, insisting, in the most peremptory terms, on the latter renouncing all hope of ever being permitted to marry Fréron.

Against such positive orders there could be no appeal, and Pauline, finding herself abandoned by those members of her family who had hitherto encouraged her to stand firm, was compelled to recognise the futility of further resistance. She accordingly wrote to Napoleon the following letter, in which, while declaring that no one on earth should prevent her from consecrating her heart to her Stanislas and continuing to receive and reply to his letters, she promised to abide by her brother's decision on the question of marriage:

I have received your letter; it has occasioned me the greatest grief. I did not anticipate this change on your part. You had consented to my union with Fréron. After the promises which you had made me of smoothing over all obstacles, my heart had abandoned itself to this sweet hope, and I regarded it as that which was to fill my destiny. I send you his [Fréron's] last letter; you will see that all the calumnies which have been circulated to his discredit are untrue.

As for myself, I prefer a lifetime of unhappiness to marrying without your consent and bringing down your curse upon my head. You, my dear Napoleon, for whom I have always displayed the

most tender affection, if you were witness of the
tears which your letter has caused me to shed,
you would be touched, I am sure of it.   You, to
whom I looked for my happiness, you wish to
make me renounce the only person whom I can
love.   Young as I am, my character is firm : I
feel that it is impossible for me to renounce
Fréron after the promises that I have made him
to love him only.   Yes, I shall keep them; no one
in the world shall prevent me from consecrating
my heart to him, from receiving his letters, from
replying to them, and from repeating that I shall
love him alone.   I am too well aware of my duties
to depart from them ; but I know that I do not
know how to change according to circumstances.

Adieu ; that is all that I have to say to you.
May you be happy, and, in the midst of all these
brilliant victories, of all this happiness, recall
sometimes the life full of bitterness, and the tears
that are shed every day by

                                              P. B.

Opinions differ as to how far the foregoing
epistle, which is certainly rather a remarkable
production for a young girl of sixteen, particularly for one who had received but the scantiest
of educations, and had never shown the slightest
inclination to supplement it, ought to be considered the work of Pauline.   Some writers are
of opinion that it was drafted by either Élisa or
Lucien ; but M. Masson considers that the writer
had had " no other teacher than Passion," and
M. d'Almeras, the lady's latest biographer, seems
to be of the same opinion.   Any way, it deter-

mined Napoleon to adopt the only remedy likely
to prove efficacious in the circumstances, namely,
to send for Pauline to come to Italy. There,
amid the gallant young officers of his victorious
army, she would be hard to please indeed if she
could not find some one to console her for the loss
of her unworthy lover. But, lest she should experience any difficulty in making her choice, he had
already taken the precaution to select a suitable
husband for her, one Victor Emmanuel Leclerc,
a worthy young man, an excellent officer, a personal friend of his own, and possessed of some
fortune. Leclerc was an old friend of Pauline.
He had met her at Marseilles, while stationed
there three years before, and had conceived for
her a passion which, Napoleon ascertained by
discreet inquiries, had resisted, not only time, but
a full acquaintance with the Fréron affair.

Accordingly, at the beginning of November
1796, Napoleon wrote to his mother, directing
that Pauline should be sent to Italy, under the
care of Joseph Fesch, for whom he had found
a lucrative post in the Commissariat. The dis-
consolate damsel, however, appears to have taken
her brother's recent decision so much to heart that
she had fallen somewhat seriously ill, and it was
not until the end of December that she joined
Napoleon and Joséphine at Modena.

CHAPTER IX

Élisa and Félix Baciocchi—They contract a civil marriage, at
Marseilles, in spite of the opposition of Napoleon—Madame
Bonaparte, the Baciocchi, Caroline, and Jérôme set out to join
the general in Italy—Their journey—Betrothal of Pauline and
General Leclerc—Reunion of the Bonaparte family at the
Castle of Montebello—Wedding of Pauline and Leclerc, and
ecclesiastical marriage of Élisa and Baciocchi—The marriage-
contracts—Joséphine and M. Hippolyte Charles—Antipathy
of the women Bonapartes to Joséphine.

SOON after Pauline's departure for Italy, a
suitor for the hand of her elder sister presented himself. His name was Felice
(Félix) Baciocchi,[1] and he came of an old
Genoese family, a branch of which had emigrated
to Corsica and settled at Ajaccio, apparently
about the middle of the sixteenth century. The
Baciocchi were already connected with the Bonapartes by marriage. In the last quarter of the
sixteenth century, a Tomaso Baciocchi had married
a Caterina Bonaparte, while, about 1615, a Giovanni Maria Baciocchi had taken to wife Laura
Bonaparte, daughter of Geronimo, grandson of
the founder of the Corsican branch of the family.
Félix Baciocchi, who was one of nine children,

---

[1] The name is generally written Bacciochi by French writers ;
but in Félix's baptismal certificate (May 18, 1762) it is spelt
Baciocchi, and he always signed his letters thus.

chose a military career, and, in November 1778, at the age of sixteen, received a sub-lieutenancy in the Régiment du Royale Corse.   Joseph Bonaparte describes him, in his *Mémoires*, as "a young officer distinguished in every respect"; but he would appear to have been more distinguished by incapacity than by merit, since it was not until April 16, 1793—that is to say, after more than fourteen years' service—that he reached the rank of captain.   Twelve months later, being suspected of Royalist sympathies, he was cashiered, and, if he had not had the prudence to emigrate, he would probably have lost his head as well as his commission.

After Thermidor, he returned to France, and, in 1795, found himself at Nice, where he met the Bonapartes, with whom he appears to have been already acquainted.   Letizia and her daughters welcomed him as a relative, and subsequently invited him to take up his quarters with them at Marseilles, in their house in the Rue Lafon. Baciocchi accepted the invitation, and profited by his intimacy with the family to pay court to Élisa. That damsel received his attentions very graciously.   She was now nineteen, and as, in spite of the growing fame of her brother, suitors seemed to be in no hurry to come forward, the situation was beginning to cause her some uneasiness. "*Ce bon et rebon* Baciocchi"—as Lucien calls him—was a poor sort of creature, who cared for nothing but eating and drinking, and playing on the violin, which he did so assiduously as to make his friends detest the very sight of that instrument ; but, notwithstanding a singularly vacuous countenance, he passed for a handsome man, and, as he was indolent and good-natured, he promised to make a complaisant as well as an ornamental husband. She therefore resolved to accept him.

As for Madame Bonaparte, the fact that Baciocchi was a Corsican and an Ajaccian made amends for everything, even for the fact that he was but moderately well off.[1] Besides which, she had nothing in common with her eldest daughter, and was beginning to find her somewhat of a handful.

There remained Napoleon to be consulted. Both mother and daughter wrote, urging him to consent ; but the general had other views for his sister and, moreover, he disliked Baciocchi and all his family. Félix was a friend and near relative of his enemy Pozzo di Borgo, and, during the troubles in Corsica four years before, the Baciocchi had been among the most ardent supporters of Paoli. To the representations of his mother and Élisa he replied by a flat refusal.

Both ladies, however, were now exceedingly anxious for the match ; indeed, some writers incline to the belief that matters between Mlle. Bonaparte and her admirer had already gone too

---

[1] He was not, however, poor, as several writers seem to imagine. Indeed, from a Corsican point of view, he was quite well-to-do.

far for them to draw back.   Since they could not obtain Napoleon's consent, they determined to dispense with it, and to pretend that they had not received his letter until too late.

Accordingly, on Floréal 12, Year V (May 1, 1797), a civil marriage took place at Marseilles. With the exception of Madame Bonaparte, none of the family were present at the ceremony. Napoleon and Louis were with the Army of Italy; Joseph at Parma, where he now occupied the post of French Resident; Pauline, with Joséphine, at Mantua; while Annunziata and Jérôme, of whom the latter had temporarily quitted the College of Juilly and rejoined his mother, were too young to act as witnesses.   Lucien was at Marseilles or, at any rate, in the neighbourhood; but, as he had lately absented himself without leave from his post of commissary in Corsica, to which he had been appointed some weeks before, he doubtless judged it advisable to keep out of the way. He, however, sent his secretary Pierre Faure, who, with Letizia, one Pierre Dominique Salvini, a Corsican refugee, Joseph Elzéard Ardisson, "landowner," and Joseph Massoni, described as "aide-de-camp," signed the marriage certificate.

The question of dowry, a matter which was almost invariably settled prior to a marriage, was postponed until Napoleon's pardon could be obtained.   This Madame Bonaparte determined to seek in person, and, so soon as Napoleon had returned to Italy, after the Peace of Leoben, she wrote to him, suggesting that she and her daughters should join him at his headquarters. The general, who was still in ignorance of the marriage, willingly consented, and Letizia determined to start immediately, fearful lest, if she delayed her departure, Napoleon might learn of what had occurred from some other source. Aware of the character of her son, she believed that, if she were to arrive unexpectedly, he would not be able to resist her tears and entreaties, and would accept the accomplished fact.

Accordingly, at the end of May, the whole household in the Rue Lafon embarked for Genoa: that is to say, Madame Bonaparte, Élisa and her husband, Jérôme, and Annunziata, who was now called Caroline, and must be known henceforth by that name.[1]

The travellers landed at Genoa at a very inauspicious moment. A few days before, there had been a desperate and sanguinary conflict in the streets between the partisans of the Doge and the Senate and the democratic party, which favoured a French protectorate ; and the city and the surrounding country were still seething with excitement. Napoleon, not having been warned of his relatives' arrival, had taken no measures for their protection, and, if hostilities were renewed, they might find themselves in

---

[1] The name Caroline, according to M. Frédéric Masson, was bestowed on Annunziata by her brother Lucien, although Lucien himself states that it was given her by Napoleon.

grave danger. Lavalette, one of the general's aides-de-camp, who had been sent on a mission to Genoa, to obtain from the Senate reparation for outrages committed on French residents, was greatly alarmed when news was brought him that his chief's relatives were in the city.

"I was expecting," he writes, "to be able to take my departure on the morrow, when a vessel which entered the harbour gave me new cause for embarrassment. It brought Bonaparte's mother and two of his sisters, known subsequently as the Queen of Naples and the Grand-Duchess of Tuscany, with M. Baciocchi, recently married. These ladies had not seen the general for some years; they came from Marseilles, and were under the impression that Italy was perfectly tranquil. Bonaparte had not received the letter in which they announced their coming. No measures had been taken, no orders given; the popular disturbances might be renewed, and they might be among the victims. My first thought was to remain with them, and to make some provision for their defence, in the event of their being attacked. But Madame Bonaparte was a woman full of intelligence and courage. 'I have nothing to fear here,' said she to me, 'since my son has in his hands as hostages the most important persons of the Republic. Start at once to acquaint him with my arrival; to-morrow, I shall continue my journey.'"[1]

[1] Comte Lavalette, *Mémoires et Souvenirs.*

Lavalette did as she desired, but, to guard against accidents, he stationed cavalry pickets at different points along the road by which the party was to travel. This precaution was, however, quite unnecessary, for, as Letizia had foreseen, the name of Bonaparte was a better protection than a whole regiment. Everywhere the general's relatives were received with the most profound respect, and, on the first day of June, they arrived in safety at the Castle of Montebello, three leagues from Milan, on the road to Como, where Napoleon had been residing since the middle of May.

The meeting between mother and son was a very tender one, and events proved that Madame Bonaparte had accurately gauged the situation. Though Napoleon was not, as we may suppose, over well pleased to find that his wishes had been disregarded in the matter of Élisa's choice of a husband, he did not like, now that the affair was an accomplished fact, to show himself more difficult to please than his mother had been. He therefore accepted the marriage with a good grace, promised to do his best for both his sister and her husband, and, in return, asked Letizia's sanction to the marriage which he had arranged for Pauline.

Napoleon had judged rightly when he decided that the best cure for Pauline's infatuation for Fréron was to transplant her forthwith to Italy.

In Italy, the damsel speedily forgot the vows of
eternal fidelity she had sworn to her Stanislas;
and when, in March 1797, Napoleon set out, at
the head of his all-conquering army, to carry
the war across the Alps into Styria, leaving his
wife and sister to proceed to Mantua, and subsequently to Milan, she was already betrothed
to Leclerc.

The match appeared a very suitable one. The
son of a prosperous merchant at Pontoise, Leclerc, before entering the army, as a volunteer,
in 1791, had received an excellent education, as
had his brother and sister, the former of whom
was a prefect under the Empire, while the latter
became the wife of Maréchal Davoust. Like
Napoleon, he had distinguished himself at the
siege of Toulon, and had, although only twenty-
four, already attained the rank of adjutant-general,
while he also possessed considerable private
means. Highly esteemed by his chief, he seems
to have been generally liked and respected, both
in the army and in society. Marmont, while
holding but a poor opinion of his professional
ability, tells us that he was an excellent comrade;
while Madame Ducrest describes him as "kind-
hearted and good." In person, he was short and
slight—Pauline was accustomed to speak of him
as "her little Leclerc"—with a pleasant face, a
ruddy complexion, and fair hair.

Although, probably, not without a keen appreciation of the influence such a marriage would

have upon his career, Leclerc seems to have been genuinely in love with Pauline, while that young lady, for a time at least, reciprocated his passion and imagined herself in love for the second time.

If we are to believe Marmont, he himself, and not Leclerc, was the original choice of Napoleon for his sister. " During our residence at Montebello," he writes, " Napoleon occupied himself with the marriage of his second sister, Pauline, afterwards Princess Borghese. He offered her to me, through the medium of his brother Joseph. She was charming ; it was beauty of form in a perfection almost ideal. She was only a few months over sixteen, and already promised to be what she was to become. I declined this alliance, notwithstanding all the admiration I entertained for her and the advantages which it promised me. I had, at that time, dreams of domestic felicity, fidelity, and virtue, seldom realised, it is true, but which often influence the imagination of youth. In the hope of one day attaining this chimera, I renounced a marriage whose results would have exercised an immense influence on my career, and to-day, after the *dénoûment* of the great drama, it is probable that, as matters have gone, I have more to congratulate myself upon than to regret." [1]

Now, even if we had no evidence to the contrary, this statement would deserve to be regarded

[1] Marmont, *Mémoires*.

with suspicion, since, where Napoleon and his relatives are concerned, Marmont is one of the most untrustworthy of chroniclers—have not two works been written mainly to refute his assertions? But, as a matter of fact, it is an obvious invention. Pauline and Leclerc were certainly betrothed before the Styrian campaign, on which the latter accompanied Napoleon, since, when, after the Peace of Leoben, Leclerc was sent to Paris to announce that event to the Directory, he informed his friend, the poet Arnault, of his good fortune, and, moreover, the marriage took place a few days after his return to Italy (June 14, 1797). What then becomes of Marmont's assertion that "during their residence at Montebello"—that is to say, some time between May 16, when Napoleon took up his quarters there, and June 14, when Pauline was married to Leclerc, his chief offered him his sister's hand?

Equally devoid of foundation is the assertion of Mounier that Napoleon's only reason for giving his sister to Leclerc was that he had surprised the pair in a compromising situation.

"The marriage with Leclerc," he writes, "came about in the following manner:

"General Bonaparte was working in his cabinet at Milan; Leclerc was an officer of his staff, and took advantage of a screen to express a little too cavalierly his love for Pauline. General Bonaparte heard a noise, rose up, and saw. The

VICTOR EMMANUEL LECLERC

FROM AN ENGRAVING BY L. G. THIBAULT (BRITISH MUSEUM)

marriage took place without the loss of a moment."[1]

Such an anecdote, related by a man who became the implacable enemy of Napoleon after having eaten his bread,[2] would, under ordinary circumstances, be altogether unworthy of serious consideration. But, since it has been repeated, by several historians with a weakness for the picturesque, and, notably, by Pauline's latest biographer, M. d'Almeras, who considers it "by no means improbable," it may be as well to examine it.[3]

Mounier asserts that the supposed compromising incident took place at Milan, that is to say, some time between the beginning of April, when Pauline arrived there, and the middle of May, when she left for Montebello. During the whole of that time, Leclerc was hundreds of miles away from Milan, in fact, he did not return to Italy until the beginning of June. So much for the veracity of Mounier and the critical discrimination of M. d'Almeras!

The Castle of Montebello, which, at the end of the eighteenth century, belonged to the Marchese Crivelli, was an imposing square building, situated on a wooded eminence and com-

---

[1] Published by Comte d'Hérisson, *le Cabinet noir*.

[2] Mounier was, for some time, one of Napoleon's private secretaries.

[3] M. Henri d'Almeras, *Une Amoureuse: Pauline Bonaparte*.

manding a magnificent view over the fertile
plains of Lombardy. On a clear day, the dome of
Milan cathedral could be seen from its windows.
It was approached, from the direction of the city,
by a beautiful avenue, three *kilomètres* in length,
which terminated at a double flight of steps, leading up to a terrace, which encircled the castle.
The gardens were extensive and tastefully laid
out, and now, in the full beauty of early summer,
presented a veritable feast of colour; while shady
alleys, interspersed with fountains and cunningly-
contrived grottoes, afforded a grateful retreat
from the heat of the Italian sun. The interior
of the building was spacious and admirably
adapted for the reception of company, as well as
for the residence of a numerous family and a
considerable staff of servants.[1]

In this castle, the approaches to which were
guarded by three hundred Polish lancers—men
of the legion recently formed in Italy by the
heroic Dombrowski—in their blue and amaranth
uniforms and legendary shapskas, Napoleon held
a sort of court, where he received the generals
and administrators of the army, the nobility of
the republics he had lately founded, the envoys

---

[1] To-day, the Castle of Montebello, which has been converted
into a lunatic asylum, retains but a shadow of its former splendour.
The avenue, the gorgeous flower-beds, the grottoes, and the
fountains have all disappeared; while the building itself has undergone so many alterations, that those who resided there in the
summer of 1797 would scarcely recognise it, were it possible for
them to revisit it.—M. Paul Marmottan, *Élisa Bonaparte.*

and ministers of the different Italian States, and distinguished artists, savants, and men of letters. To the Italian nobles, the artists, and the literati, he was courteous and sometimes even affable, though the cross-examination to which he was wont to subject them was found a somewhat trying ordeal by the more diffident. To his own officers, he was distant and reserved, as though resolved never to permit them to forget the obedience and respect they owed to him. It was seldom that any of them were invited to dine at his table. Frequently, indeed, he dined before his staff—did this general of a regicide republic— in a semi-regal state which recalled the *grand couvert* of the old kings of France, while the band of the Guides performed a selection of military and patriotic airs, and the good citizens of Milan and Verona, who were admitted to the dining-room, craned their necks to watch him eat, just as in days gone by foreigners and provincials had collected to gape at the *Grand Monarque* making one of his Gargantuan meals at Versailles. "However, he betrayed no embarrassment at this extreme honour, and received them as though he had been accustomed to it all his life."[1]

But, in the evening, when the official receptions of the day and the semi-public dinner were over, and he found himself alone with his family and a few privileged friends, the great man

[1] Miot de Mélito, *Mémoires*.

unbent, laid aside the dignity of the commander-in-chief and the cold reserve of the statesman, and became the kindly brother, the genial host. He would sit on the terrace, sipping his coffee, and laughing and talking with one or the other as though he had not a care in the world, charming all by the unaffected frankness and gaiety of his manner. Sometimes, when the conversation languished, he would propose that the company should take it in turns to tell stories, and would call upon General Clarke,[1] who was a noted *raconteur*, to open the ball. If, when the general had finished, no one seemed inclined to take his place, he would offer to tell one himself, and would relate some terrible adventure or some blood-curdling ghost-story, the effect of which he would enhance by using his voice in a way that any actor might have envied. Then, when darkness fell, and his guests returned to the salon, he

---

[1] Henri Jacques Guillaume Clarke, Comte d'Hunebourg and Duc de Feltre (1765–1818). He was of Irish origin and was, at this time, chief of the topographical bureau of the War Office. Sent by the Directory to Italy to act as a spy upon Napoleon's actions, he entered instead into the general's plans, and was subsequently rewarded by being appointed his private secretary. From 1801 to 1804, he was French Ambassador in Tuscany, and, after following Napoleon in the campaigns of 1805 and 1806, in the former of which he acted as governor of Vienna, and in the latter as governor of Berlin, he became, in 1807, Minister for War. He filled this post with success for some years, but in the crisis of 1813 and 1814 proved unequal to the demands made upon him, and on the entry of the Allies into Paris, he declared himself a Royalist, and during the Hundred Days accompanied Louis XVIII to Ghent. From 1815–1817, he was again Minister for War. It was said of Clarke: "He is the man of the sword who owes most to his pen."

would call upon the pretty wife of Léopold Berthier, the younger brother of the future Prince
de Neufchâtel, who had a remarkably fine voice,
to sing, or, if there were any poet present,
would beg him to recite some of his verses.
Later, when Joséphine had formed a party of
ladies for her beloved *vingt-et-un*, he would draw
one of the men into a corner, and propose a game
of " Goose," of which time-honoured pastime he
was exceedingly fond and played with a seriousness
which was highly diverting, "counting his squares
with his marker like a schoolboy, and, like a
schoolboy, also, becoming angry when the dice
were going against him."[1] If hard pressed, he
had no scruples about cheating ; for he could
never endure to be worsted at anything, even at
a children's game.

A few days after the arrival of the Bonapartes at Montebello, Leclerc returned from
his mission to Paris, bringing with him his
friend, the poet Arnault[2] who, in his *Souvenirs*,
has left us the following little sketch of Pauline,

---

[1] Arnault, *Souvenirs d'un Sexagénaire.*

[2] Antoine Vincent Arnault (1766–1834), author of *Marius à
Minturnès, les Vénitiens, Germanicus, les Guelfs et les Gibelins,*
and other plays, of a collection of fables published under the
title of *Fables et Poésies,* the interesting *Souvenirs d'un Sexagénaire,*
and the sumptuously - illustrated *Vie politique et militaire de
Napoléon.* He also wrote the libretti to Méhul's operas, *Horatius
Coclès* and *Phrosine et Méndor,* and collaborated with Jay, Jouy,
and Norvins, in the once celebrated *Biographie nouvelle des Con-
temporains.* Napoleon always held Arnault in high esteem, and
left him a legacy of 100,000 francs.

upon whose irrepressible frivolity the near approach of marriage and its responsibilities does not appear to have produced the smallest effect :

"At dinner, I was placed next to 'Paulette,' who, remembering that she had seen me at Marseilles, and aware, besides, that I was in his [Leclerc's] confidence, treated me as an old acquaintance. Singular compound of what was most complete in physical perfection and what was most fantastic in moral qualities ! If she were the prettiest person possible to behold, she was also the most frivolous possible to imagine. No more gravity than a schoolgirl ; talking inconsequently, laughing at nothing and at everything, contradicting the gravest personages, putting out her tongue at her sister-in-law Joséphine when the latter was not looking at her, nudging my knee when I did not pay enough attention to her pranks, and drawing upon herself, from time to time, one of those terrible glances with which her brother recalled to order the most intractable of men. But, that had little effect upon her ; the next moment, she began again, and the authority of the general-in-chief of the Army of Italy succumbed before the giddiness of a young girl. A good child, otherwise, by force of nature, rather than by force of will ; for she had no principle ; and capable of doing good, even from caprice."[1]

[1] Arnault, *Souvenirs d'un Sexagénaire.*

On June 14,[1] the marriage took place, the civil ceremony being performed before the *Ordon-nateur-en-chef* of the army, while, a few hours later, the blessing of the Church was bestowed upon the happy pair, in the chapel attached to the castle, by Giuseppe Brioschi, rector of Monte-bello, a licence having been granted by Filippo Visconti, Archbishop of Milan, dispensing with the banns and permitting the marriage to be celebrated with closed doors, in a private oratory.

At the same time, the civil marriage, performed six months earlier at Marseilles between Élisa and Baciocchi, received the ecclesiastical sanction; and it seems not a little singular that Napoleon and Joséphine did not avail themselves of this opportunity to consecrate the civil tie which they had contracted. If Joséphine had demanded it, Napoleon would most certainly have consented, as he could still refuse her nothing.

A few days earlier (June 6), the marriage con-tracts had been signed at Milan, in the presence of one Reina, a notary of that city. During the past twelve months, the fortunes of the Bonaparte family had greatly improved, quite irrespective of the advantages which had accrued to it from the triumphant career of Napoleon. In the previous autumn, the English, who had occupied Corsica soon after the flight of the Bonapartes

[1] And not "in the month of September," as stated by M. d'Almeras.

in 1793, growing weary of the continual insurrections with which they were forced to contend, had decided to abandon their unprofitable conquest, and had evacuated the island, accompanied by Paoli, Pozzo di Borgo, Peraldi, and their principal partisans. The Bonapartes therefore recovered their property, which appears to have been considerably increased in the interval, owing to the death of certain relatives, and was now valued at some 320,000 francs. But, since the property consisted almost entirely of real estate, and there had not been time to dispose of sufficient to pay Élisa and Pauline their shares of the paternal inheritance, Napoleon, Joseph, and Louis decided to advance the money required. Élisa—who is described in the marriage contract as Élisa Marianna—received from her three brothers the sum of 35,000 francs in cash, a small estate in Corsica, situated at Campo dell' Oro, near Ajaccio, and known as Torre Vecchia, and two vineyards, the whole valued at 5,000 francs. Pauline received as her dowry the sum of 40,000 francs, and, in return, both ladies and their husbands formally renounced all further claims upon the family property. Both Baciocchi and Leclerc brought into settlement the sum of 13,300 francs, that is to say, a third of the dowry received by their wives.

It is singular that many usually well-informed writers still persist in regarding the dowries received by Élisa and Pauline on their marriages as donations on the part of Napoleon, whereas, as the contracts, which have been preserved, prove, they were merely in the nature of loans, advanced on the best of securities. Napoleon does not appear, on this occasion, to have given his sisters anything out of his own pocket, though in these years of war and rapine his fortune was rapidly increasing. In his letters to the Directory, he complains bitterly of the horde of French commissaries, contractors, and other civilian harpies who were battening on the spoils of Lombardy, but he himself and his principal lieutenants—notably Masséna, foremost in plunder as in battle—were not above drawing large sums from the conquered territory, through the medium of the commissaries to the army. These illicit gains, joined to his share of the family property, formed the nucleus of a considerable fortune, by which, thanks to his generosity, his brothers and sisters were to profit later.

Brilliant fêtes succeeded this double marriage. Almost every day a constant stream of guests, some in carriages, others on horseback, might have been seen wending its way up the stately avenue which led to the castle, to be entertained in princely fashion until far into the night, when they returned to Milan, through country which appeared to the eyes of the French visitors a veritable fairyland, since every field was ablaze with thousands of fireflies, "which seemed to dance on the turf, springing four or five feet into the air."[1]

On June 17, there was an excursion to Lake Como. Napoleon, with his wife, his sisters, his brothers-in-law, Madame Joseph Bonaparte, the Marchese del Gallo, the Neapolitan Ambassador at Vienna,[2] and several French officers, drove thither, escorted by a squadron of dragoons, and were given a magnificent reception by the authorities of the department of the Lario, of which Como was the chief town. Next morning, the party visited Lugano, where they remained two days, and then returned to Montebello.

Napoleon ought to have been a very happy man during his stay at Montebello. He, who, less than two years before, had been pining in obscurity, was now the most prominent figure in Europe. Honour beyond that of any crowned head was his; he was the hero of a long succession of brilliant victories, the idolised chief of an invincible army, the "Liberator of Italy." And his fame was only just beginning; what he had accomplished, he felt, was as nothing to what

[1] Arnault, *Souvenirs d'un Sexagénaire*.

[2] The Marchese del Gallo, although not an Austrian subject, had been sent to Milan by the Court of Vienna, together with its own plenipotentiary, the Graf von Mersfeld, to negotiate the definitive terms of peace. He was afterwards Neapolitan Ambassador in Paris, and, later still, Minister for Foreign Affairs at Naples during the reign of Joseph Bonaparte, as well as in that of Murat, who succeeded him.

he might achieve. "Every day he seemed to see before him a new horizon."[1] Moreover, he was in the flower of youth, with the woman of his choice by his side, and surrounded, for the first time since the exodus from Corsica, four years before, by the whole of his family, with the exception of Lucien; for Joseph, soon to be appointed French Ambassador at Rome, had come with his wife from Parma to join his relatives, and Fesch was also there.

But in the brimming cup of happiness which Fortune held to her favourite's lips, the fickle goddess, as though half-repentant of her beneficence, had mixed two bitter ingredients. The first was the conduct of his wife; the second, the relations between Joséphine and his family.

As a hostess, Joséphine was inimitable. She did the honours of Montebello with that ease, that tact, that urbanity which she never failed to display; her beauty, her grace, her exquisite taste, her amiability, her kindness, were the theme of universal admiration. But she did not love her husband, or, if she did, her love was a negligible quantity, in comparison with Napoleon's fiery passion. After a violent outburst of weeping, she had torn herself away from her beloved Paris in response to his agonising entreaties, only to reveal to him the shallowness and frivolity of her nature. She admired Napoleon; there were times when she may even

[1] Marmont, *Mémoires*.

have fancied that she cared for him; but a very little of that "violent tenderness almost amounting to frenzy" which had disquieted her during his wooing went a long way with this nonchalant Creole. Many a woman would have been proud indeed to find herself the object of such a man's ardent devotion; Joséphine was merely bored. "When I demand of thee a love equal to my own," wrote Napoleon to her, in one of his first moments of disillusionment, " I am wrong." He was indeed!

But this was not all. As time went on, unpleasant rumours began to be circulated; it was said that the fidelity of the general-in-chief's fascinating wife was something more than problematical. General Leclerc had an aide-de-camp, Captain Hippolyte Charles by name. Hippolyte was not exactly an Adonis, being short, slight, and swarthy; but he was very careful of his appearance, and in his gay hussar plumage looked quite a fine bird. In the salons of Paris, he passed for an "amusing boy," excelled in the art of punning—a form of wit more appreciated at the end of the eighteenth century than it is to-day—"*faisait le polichinelle en parlant,*" and was an adept at paying pretty compliments. These rare qualities quite won the heart of Joséphine, and the very lively interest she evinced in the gallant captain was soon a standing jest in the Army of Italy. No one was therefore much surprised when, one fine day, that

young gentleman was detected in some dereliction
of duty and promptly sent back to France. But
alas! although he disappeared from the scene for
a time, others were not wanting to brave the
general's wrath for the sake of his wife's smiles,
and, if we are to believe Sismondi, during the
first Italian campaign, "Bonaparte dismissed from
his headquarters several of Joséphine's lovers."

Captain Hippolyte had been, as we have mentioned, one of Leclerc's aides-de-camp, and there
is some reason to suppose that it was through
Pauline that Napoleon learned of the tender
relations which existed between his wife and
that too enterprising hussar. Amid the fêtes
and distractions of Italy, and the gallant attentions paid her by Leclerc and other admirers,
Pauline had speedily forgotten Fréron, but she
had not forgotten, nor forgiven, the part which
Joséphine had played in the rupture of that little
romance. From the moment of her arrival at
Modena, at the end of the previous year, her
sister-in-law had treated her with the utmost
kindness and consideration. But nothing could
disarm the hostility of Pauline, who allowed no
opportunity to slip of speaking evil of her
brother's wife, of criticising all that she did, all
that she said, all that she wore even, although,
in the matter of dress, Joséphine's taste was above
reproach. There were occasions when she did
not even trouble to preserve the appearance of
cordiality.

With her mother-in-law and Élisa, Joséphine was no more successful. It was in vain that she overwhelmed Letizia with delicate attentions ; that she treated her with the utmost deference ; that she chanted incessantly the praises of her children ; that she made every possible effort to conciliate her. The icy wall behind which the stern matron had chosen to entrench herself remained impenetrable. From the hour when she learned of Napoleon's marriage, she had resolved to wage war against his wife, and what she had seen of Joséphine had only served to confirm her in this decision. From the pedestal of motherly pride to which the birth of her twelve children had raised her, she looked down with scorn upon this indolent, luxurious Creole, who had borne but two, and was never likely to give her husband an heir to his glory. She could not pardon her her frivolity, her extravagance, her sumptuous toilettes, her innumerable admirers—no, not even her lap-dogs ![1]

[1] Arnault relates an amusing story about these pampered creatures. The future Empress had a pug named Fortuné, who was "neither good, nor beautiful, nor amiable," but whom she, nevertheless, adored. She took him with her wherever she went, and at night he slept upon her bed. "You see that gentleman there," said Napoleon, one day, to the chronicler ; "he is my rival. He was in possession of Madame's bedroom when I married her. I wanted to put him out of it, but I was given to understand that I must sleep elsewhere or share it with him. It annoyed me, but it was a case of take or leave, and I yielded. The favourite was not so accommodating ; I carry the proof on my leg." Fortuné's end was tragic. Taking the air one fine day on the terrace of Montebello, he encountered a large mastiff, belonging to Napoleon's cook, at whom,

Élisa, although less cold and reserved than her mother, since she had more ambitions to satisfy, and was well aware that her own and her husband's prospects of advancement depended entirely on the goodwill of Napoleon, observed towards her sister-in-law much the same attitude, and it was not difficult for a shrewd observer to perceive that beneath the studied courtesy of her manner lay a profound aversion.

Caroline was as yet too young for her opinions to carry much weight, but already signs were not wanting that she was disposed to share the sentiments of her mother and sisters. As for the male members of the family, Joseph—the jealous, suspicious Joseph—though bitterly hostile to his brother's wife, had the wisdom to perceive that

since he tolerated no intruders on what he considered his domain, he had the imprudence to snap. The mastiff, less complaisant than the general, resented the injury ; and, a moment later, Fortuné had ceased to live. Joséphine was in despair, but presently found consolation in another pug, who succeeded to all the privileges of the deceased, and was, if possible, even more arrogant. Soon afterwards, Napoleon, while walking in the gardens, happened to meet the cook, who turned to fly. His master called him back and inquired why he wished to run away. " General, after what my dog did ! " " Well ? " " I was afraid that you hated the sight of me." " Your dog ? Have you not got him any longer ? " " Pardon me ; he never sets a paw in the garden, especially since Madame has another." " Let him come in as often as he likes ; perhaps he will rid me of this other fellow as well."

" This incident," remarks Arnault, " conveys an idea of the empire which the most gentle and indolent of Creoles exercised over the most wilful and despotic of men. His will, before which every one bowed, was powerless to resist the tears of a woman, and he, who dictated laws to Europe, could not in his own home even put a dog outside the door."

the time for open hostilities had not yet arrived, and more prudent and diplomatic than Élisa, dissimulated his antipathy beneath the mask of friendship, the while he kept a watchful eye upon Joséphine's every action and laid by a store of useful information for employment at some future time. Louis—Napoleon's favourite brother—was suffering from that malady which was to transform his physical temperament and his moral character, and to change the light-hearted young soldier into a melancholy, discontented hypochondriac. He appeared but little, spending most of his time in reading, or in long conversations with his friend Cuvillier. Jérôme was still only a boy, and his friendship with Eugène de Beauharnais, formerly his fellow-pupil at the College of Juilly, afforded some ground for hope that, when he grew older, Joséphine might find him a useful ally.

But, if the attitude of Napoleon's brothers towards Joséphine appeared still uncertain, there could be no room for doubt as to the feelings of his mother and his two elder sisters; and this, and in particular the entire want of sympathy and understanding between Letizia and his wife, caused him the keenest vexation.

CHAPTER X

AT the beginning of July, the family gathering at Montebello broke up. Napoleon
removed his headquarters to Passeriano,
whither the negotiations with Austria were now
transferred, and was followed by Louis and
Joséphine; Pauline and her husband went to
Milan, where Leclerc's brigade was stationed;
Jérôme was sent back to the College of Juilly;
Madame Bonaparte, who was impatient to revisit
her native land, returned to Marseilles, from
whence she sailed to Corsica, accompanied by
Élisa and Baciocchi, who, thanks to the good
offices of his all-powerful brother, had been promoted to the rank of general of brigade, and—
since Napoleon had no intention of allowing him
to advertise his incapacity in Italy—appointed

Commandant of the citadel of Ajaccio; while Joseph, who had just been nominated French Ambassador at Rome, set out for the Eternal City, taking with him his wife and his youngest sister Caroline.

· Caroline was now fifteen, and "already bore upon her girlish countenance the indications of a beauty which would have few rivals."[1] "Caroline Bonaparte," writes the Duchesse d'Abrantès, "was a very pretty girl, fresh as a rose; not to be compared, so far as regards the regular beauty of her features, with Madame Leclerc, though more pleasing, perhaps, by the expression of her countenance and the brilliancy of her complexion; but she was very far from possessing the perfection of shape which distinguished her elder sister. Her head was too large for her body; her bust was too short; her shoulders were too round, and her hips too thick; but her feet, her hands, and her arms were models, and her skin resembled white satin seen through pink glass. Her teeth were beautiful, as were those of all the Bonapartes; her hair was fair, but in no way remarkable. As a young girl, Caroline was charming."

To these charms the officers of her brother's staff had been by no means insensible, and several of them had paid her marked attention, notably, a certain dashing cavalry leader, Joachim Murat by name, who had already earned for him-

[1] Arnault, *Souvenirs d'un Sexagénaire.*

self a considerable reputation. But Napoleon, although he had judged it advisable to provide the highly impressionable Pauline with a suitable husband as soon as possible, wisely decided that, since circumstances had deprived his youngest sister of even that modicum of schooling which Corsican girls usually received, it would be as well to give her some kind of education before she thought of marriage, and accordingly intimated that, for the present, he was disinclined to entertain any application for her hand. After she had spent a few months in Rome, where, he hoped, she would make some effort to improve her mind, he intended to send her to the fashionable school for young ladies at Saint-Germain-en-Laye kept by Madame Campan, Marie Antoinette's former waiting-woman, who was endeavouring to impart to the daughters of the new society the elegant and polished manners of the old *régime*.

Joseph, with his wife and sister, arrived in Rome on the last day of August, and, pending his selection of an official residence, took up his quarters at an inn in one of the streets off the Piazza di Spagna. He was apparently unable to find any house to his taste in the neighbourhood of the Corso, the quarter where ambassadors usually resided, and, towards the end of September, installed himself on the other side of the Tiber, in the Palazzo Corsini-alla-Lungara, in the Trastevere.

His choice excited some surprise, since the Palazzo Corsini, although a spacious building with fine gardens, was situated in a remote, unhealthy, and poverty-stricken suburb. There can, however, be little doubt as to Joseph's motive in selecting it as the French Legation. Rome, like all the rest of Italy, was, at this time, permeated with republican ideas, and he had come thither with the not very creditable mission of secretly inciting the subjects of the sovereign to whom he was accredited to revolt; and, as the Trastevere was the stronghold of the popular party, the advantage of residing there was obvious.

Of his intentions, however, the Vatican and Society were as yet unaware, and, while Joseph was carrying on his political intrigues, his wife and Caroline—singular coincidence, that two future Queens of Naples should have found themselves under the same roof!—seem to have passed a very pleasant time. All Rome was eager to do honour to the French Ambassador's relatives. They were, of course, presented to Pius VII, who appears to have received them very graciously, since the audience, we are told, was an unusually long one. The wealthy banker Torlonia, who had recently purchased, from the Caëtani, the title of Marchese di Roma Vecchia, entertained them to a grand dinner, in his beautiful villa outside the Porta San-Pancrazio; the Duchessa Lante gave two balls in their honour, and Cardinal Doria, the Secretary of State, sent them presents of game, fruit, and flowers from the Villa Pamphile. Poets and men of letters, too, vied with one another in chanting the ladies' praises and dedicating books to them ; and one gentleman dedicated "*alla cittadina donzella* Carolina Bonaparte," a volume of verses, entitled : *le Aventure di Saffo, poetassa di Mitilene,* in terms which could scarcely have been more sycophantic if they had been addressed to a queen.[1]

Towards the end of December, Joseph's mother-in-law, Madame Clary, arrived from Marseilles, accompanied by her daughter Désirée—formerly the object of Napoleon's affections—and one of her sons. Désirée was betrothed to General Duphot, a gallant young officer temporarily attached to the Ambassador's suite, and it had been arranged that the marriage should take place in Rome ; but, unhappily, on the evening before the wedding, an event occurred which despatched poor Duphot to a world where there is neither marrying nor giving in marriage, and brought the sojourn of Joseph and his relatives in Rome to an abrupt and tragic termination.

While Julie and Caroline were revelling in balls and receptions, Joseph had been intriguing so successfully that he was soon no longer able to restrain the zeal of the republican section of the

[1] M. Frédéric Masson, *Napoléon et sa famille.* M. Masson adds that the engraving of a bust of Sappho, which serves as the frontispiece, bears a most astonishing resemblance to Caroline.

populace.   On December 28, while the household
of the Embassy were at dinner, a mob of
"patriots," with tricolour cockades in their hats
and armed with pistols and stilettos, gathered
before the palace, and a deputation, headed by
Ceracchi—the same individual who was subsequently concerned in a conspiracy against the life
of Napoleon—entered, and demanded the protection of France.

The Ambassador, much alarmed, ordered Ceracchi and his friends to withdraw; but, before
they could do so, a detachment of the Pontifical
troops arrived upon the scene, with orders to
disperse the mob.   The frightened insurgents
took refuge in the courts and gardens of the
palace, the gates of which had been imprudently left open, and were pursued by the
soldiers.   Joseph, accompanied by Duphot and
three other officers, descended to the court,
reminded the commander of the troops that the
Legation was French territory, and ordered him
to withdraw his men immediately.   The officer
obeyed, but no sooner had the soldiers passed the
gates, than the insurgents, gathering courage,
rushed out after them, brandishing their weapons.

Joseph and his friends, anxious to prevent
bloodshed, accompanied them, marching at their
head, with drawn swords, a proceeding which was
scarcely calculated to give them the appearance
of peacemakers.   Thus they passed down the
Via-della-Lungara, and arrived at the Porta

Settimiana, where stood a guard-house. The men belonging to the guard, hearing the noise, turned out and levelled their muskets at the advancing mob. Duphot thereupon rushed forward to stop the impending volley; but the soldiers, seeing the drawn sword in his hand, and, not unnaturally, mistaking his intention, fired upon him, and he fell wounded to the ground, where he was promptly bayoneted.

The soldiers then fired at the Ambassador and the other French officers, who, however, succeeded in effecting their escape and in regaining the Legation, by way of the palace gardens. Julie and Caroline—Madame Clary and Désirée were, fortunately, spending the evening with some friends—were in a terrible state of alarm, and the palace was crowded with people who had fled thither to seek an asylum. A party was sent out to recover the mangled body of poor Duphot, after which the gates were shut and preparations made for defence; while Joseph despatched a messenger to the Secretary of State, to inform him of his determination to leave Rome immediately and to demand his passports. These did not arrive until two o'clock in the morning, and, four hours later, the Ambassador, his relatives, and suite shook the dust of the Eternal City off their feet and set out for Florence, whence Joseph sent an officer to Mantua to inform Berthier, who commanded there, of what had occurred. Then, while Berthier was assembling

an army to march on Rome, where, six weeks
later (February 15), the Roman Republic was
proclaimed, he and his party continued their
journey by easy stages to Paris, which was
reached on January 22, 1798.

On their arrival in Paris, Joseph and his wife
installed themselves in a furnished house in the
Rue Saints-Pères, while Caroline was sent to
Madame Campan's.   Here she found herself in
the company of several young ladies who were to
become prominent figures in French society in
later years : the two Mlles. d'Auguié, nieces of
Madame Campan, one of whom married Maréchal
Ney, while the other became the wife of M. de
Broc, Chamberlain to the King of Holland ;
Mlle. Hervas d'Almenara, who married General
Duroc, Grand Marshal of the Palace under the
Empire, and Hortense de Beauharnais, José-
phine's daughter by her first marriage and the
future wife of Louis Bonaparte.

Hortense was the pride of the house, the model
pupil, who carried off all the prizes, was exhibited
to parents when they called to see their daughters,
and held up to her schoolfellows as a pattern of industry and virtue.   It is therefore not a matter for
surprise that Caroline, who could scarcely read or
write, and already regarded her brother's step-
daughter as a rival claimant to Napoleon's bounty,
speedily conceived for her one of those intense
hatreds which endure throughout life.

Soon after Caroline was established at Saint-

Germain, her brother Louis, who had returned with Napoleon to Paris at the beginning of the previous December, became a frequent visitor at Madame Campan's. He did not, however, come to see his sister or Hortense, though they were, of course, the ostensible object of his visits, but a cousin of the latter, Émilie de Beauharnais, with whom he had fallen deeply in love, and who appears to have reciprocated his passion. Louis was to accompany his brother on his expedition to Egypt, but, in order not to be separated from his inamorata, he pleaded illness, and declared that a season at the waters of Barèges was absolutely essential to the re-establishment of his health. Feeling, however, the need of a confidant, as do most love-sick youths, he had the imprudence to select his countryman Casabianca, who lost no time in enlightening Napoleon as to what was going on. The latter, who had no mind that his brother should wed a penniless girl, whose father was an *émigré*, and whose mother had been divorced and had contracted a second marriage with a man of colour, decided to nip the romance in the bud. He accordingly, without a moment's delay, packed Monsieur Louis off to Toulon, there to await his coming, and then, in order to leave nothing to chance, proceeded to Saint-Germain, taking with him his aide-de-camp Lavalette, of whom we have already spoken.[1]   Him he presented to

[1] " M. de Lavalette was no bad representation of Bacchus ; a lady might have been proud of his pretty little white hands and

Émilie, and declared that they seemed made for one another. Neither dared to contradict him, and, before they quite realised what they were about, they found themselves married. Which matrimonial *coup de main* accomplished, Napoleon, feeling that he had done his duty by all concerned, set out for Toulon and embarked for Egypt, taking both the newly-wedded husband and the luckless lover with him.

Madame Bonaparte did not see Napoleon before his departure for Egypt.[1] She was still at Ajaccio, together with Élisa, Baciocchi, and Fesch, while Lucien and his wife were residing at Bastia. In April 1798, Lucien was elected to the Council of the Five Hundred, as representative for the district of the Liamone, notwithstanding the fact that he was only twenty-three, while the minimum age for admission to that assembly was twenty-five. Napoleon appears to have anticipated that the election would have been invalidated, since he reserved for his brother a commissaryship in the Army of Egypt. How-

---

pink well-shaped nails. His two little eyes and immoderately small nose, placed in the middle of a very fat pair of cheeks, gave to his countenance a truly comical expression. . . . He had sense and wit, and possessed the essential qualities of a good husband, a good father, and a faithful friend."—Duchesse d'Abrantès, *Mémoires*.

[1] Madame Tschudi, in her biography of Letizia, states that Napoleon visited Corsica on his return from Italy, in December 1797. This is incorrect; he did not visit the island until October 1799, on his way from Egypt to France.

ever, no objection was raised, either at the time or subsequently.

Letizia's chief occupation at Ajaccio was the restoration of the family residence, which, as we have mentioned elsewhere, had been sacked and partly destroyed by the Paolists in 1793. It was a long and difficult business, since it was necessary to bring almost everything that was required from France, even to the tiles for the roof, and the steps and the balustrade for the staircase; besides which, Corsicans are not fond of work and require constant supervision. So assiduously did the good lady devote herself to the task of superintending the labours of the builders, that, in August 1798, she was seized with a severe attack of fever, which confined her to her bed for some time, and left her so weak that she was compelled to prolong her stay in Corsica until a much later date than she had originally intended.

Two letters of this period from Letizia to Madame Clary have been preserved, which are so characteristic of the writer that it would be a pity not to reproduce them :

Ajaccio

5 Frimaire, Year VI of the Republic

(*November* 25, 1797)

My very dear friend,

I have received, Citizeness, with great pleasure your letter of 19 Brumaire. I am very sensible of the kindness of which it is full, and of your assurances of affection, both for myself and our general [Napoleon]. They are nothing new to me, who have received substantial proofs of them, on all occasions. Accept, I beg you, my thanks and offer, if it please you, prayers to Heaven for the preservation of a man who has consecrated his entire life, not so much to the happiness of his family as to the tranquillity of the whole of France. May he be permitted to give happiness to all who have so much right to it.

Captain Bastelica has brought me the things that you mention, the roofing and the little tiles for the floors. But, with regard to these last, I ought to tell you that I have not found as many as I expected. You do not mention the number. Consequently, I shall be glad if you will let me know the precise number, to enable me to make my calculations.

In the meanwhile, you will find enclosed the model, or pattern, of the staircase, which I beg you to have made as soon as possible and forwarded to me, if possible, on the first opportunity. Finally, I shall be obliged if you will send me three thousand tiles for the roof. As for lime, I have sufficient; therefore, do not send any more.

The agent will send you a sack of our native chestnuts. I shall be obliged if you will give a small portion of them to Citizen Four, to whom I beg you to present my compliments. Accept them as a token of my sincere attachment, and my appreciation of all the trouble you are taking on my behalf.

Adieu; convey my regards to your mother and sisters, and believe me while life lasts,

Your sincere friend,

Bonaparte

In case you do not understand the pattern of the staircase, you will oblige me by sending the iron necessary to make it.

To Citizeness Clary, Rue Gay, Marseilles.

Ajaccio
28 Germinal, Year VI of the Republic
(*April* 17, 1798)

I write to you, by Lucien,[1] to ask you to send me, on the return of the same vessel, coloured paper sufficient for two rooms, one red and white, and the other yellow. I beg you, also, to be good enough to let me have three rolls of red paper, like the pattern which the agent Barbun will send you, and eight rolls with a poppy-red border and roses (No. 2). I should also like three small clocks for the bedrooms, and a parcel of white cord for window blinds. I am vexed at the trouble I am giving you.

A thousand remembrances to your mother and to all your family. Adieu, my dear friend.

If you can find eight arm-chairs, with a yellow settee of recent make and of damask, please buy them and send them to me. I should like to have all these things on the first opportunity. Adieu, my good friend; may you keep in good health.

Bonaparte mother[2]

The movements of Élisa during the year which followed her return to Corsica, in company with her mother and husband, in July 1797,

---

[1] Lucien was on his way to Paris to take his seat in the Council of the Five Hundred.

[2] Published by Baron Larrey, *Madame Mère.*

I.—13

seem to be rather uncertain. According to Baron
Larrey, she did not quit Corsica ; but M. Charles
Julliot, a fellow-pupil of Jérôme at the College of
Juilly, speaks of a visit paid by Élisa and
Napoleon to that institution in the month of
December 1798, that is to say, soon after the
latter returned to Paris, covered with the laurels
of Campo-Formio ;[1] while Jung asserts that the
lady was residing in Paris about the time Lucien
arrived there in April 1798. In the opinion of
her latest biographer, M. Paul Marmottan, however, up to the winter of 1799, when Élisa
came to reside in the capital, her visits to Paris
were very brief ones, and she passed the greater
part of her time, as a dutiful wife should, with her
Félix, whom, in June 1798, she presented with
a son and heir, baptized Napoleone. At the end
of the following August, Élisa having expressed
a desire to return to France, Baciocchi was appointed commandant of the Fort Saint-Nicolas
at Marseilles, whither he and his wife removed,
and established themselves in a house in the Rue
Libertad.

As for Pauline, she remained at Milan until the
late summer of 1798. On April 20 of that year,
she gave birth to a son, for whom Napoleon, who
stood sponsor by procuration, selected the name
of Dermide, borrowed from the poems of Ossian,
of which mystical bard the general was a great

[1] M. Paul Marmottan, *Élisa Bonaparte.*

admirer. In accordance with the instructions sent by Napoleon, the child was baptised, on May 29, in the Church of the Capuchins, Sémonville being one of the witnesses. The following morning, the whole garrison of Milan was paraded before the palace in which the Leclercs resided, while Brune, the general commanding the French troops, accompanied by his principal officers, waited upon the proud parents, and, "after having exhibited the procurations given him by Citizeness Marie Jeanne Musquinet-Leclerc, grandmother of the child, and the General-in-chief Bonaparte, requested that the child should bear the names of Dermide Louis Napoléon." And then cannon thundered and drums beat and bands played and church-bells rang and people shouted, just as they did in the old days when news came to Milan that an archduke of Austria had been born. Some three months later, as a result of a quarrel with the officials of the Cisalpine Republic, Leclerc demanded and obtained his recall, and brought his wife and child to Paris, where he established himself at No. 1, Rue de la Victoire, at the corner of the Rue du Mont Blanc, close to the little hôtel occupied by Napoleon and Joséphine.[1]

Pauline was delighted with Paris, and Paris—or, at any rate, the masculine portion of it—was

---

[1] Napoleon resided at No. 6. This street had been known as the Rue Chantereine, until the end of 1797, when, in honour of his Italian victories, its name was changed to the Rue de la Victoire.

equally delighted with Pauline. It is true that her mind was as empty and her conversation as vapid as her face was lovely and her figure perfect ; that when the talk did not happen to run on dress or scandal, and such subjects as music or art, literature or politics, came up for discussion, she was forced to sulk in a corner, in order not to display her ignorance. But then she was so pretty, so merry, so *drôle*, and always so ravishingly " gowned "—for not even Joséphine had more exquisite taste in frills and furbelows, and she was quite aware that even the most beautiful of pictures is the better for an elegant frame— that such shortcomings were readily pardoned, and all the *incroyables* who crowded round her whenever she appeared in public vowed that she was divine.

But, unhappily, those very charms which excited such admiration among the sterner sex, failed not to arouse in her own the most ferocious jealousies, which occasionally manifested themselves in a particularly unpleasant manner.

One evening, Madame Permon, at whose charming house in the Rue Sainte-Croix Pauline was a constant and welcome visitor, gave a ball. It was a very grand function indeed, for there was but very little private entertaining at this period, a few bankers and contractors whom the wars had enriched being the only persons with houses suitable for large assemblies ; and all the most select society of the Faubourg Saint-Germain, all the most accomplished dancing men in Paris, were present. Madame Leclerc, warned in advance by her hostess that she would find herself amidst the very flower of Parisian beauty and elegance, had made her preparations with as much care as did her brother, the general, before a battle, and had ordered for the occasion a toilette, which was, she declared, "to immortalise her." No details concerning this wonderful confection, however, were forthcoming. "You will see when the time arrives; I cannot say anything at present," was her invariable answer to all inquiries; and the secret remained securely locked in the bosoms of her dressmaker and *coiffeur*.

When the eventful evening came, Pauline requested permission to dress at Madame Permon's house, in order to guard against the possibility of her coiffure or gown being crushed during the transit from the Rue de la Victoire to the Rue Sainte-Croix. This was readily accorded, and, some hours before the company was expected to assemble, Madame arrived, and delivered herself into the hands of the priestesses of Fashion.

The result was in every way worthy of so much secrecy, of such infinite precautions; it was a veritable creation, a marvel, a dream! "Only those who knew Madame Leclerc at this time," writes the Duchesse d'Abrantès, "can form any idea of the impression she produced on entering my mother's salon. Her head-dress was

composed of fillets of some very costly fur ; I do
not know the name, but it was of a very smooth
nap, very supple, and covered with little spots.
These fillets were surmounted by bunches of
grapes in gold ; but the hair was not dressed so
high as it is now worn. She was a faithful copy
of a statue or of a cameo representing a Bac-
chante ; and, in truth, the shape of Madame
Leclerc's head and the regularity of her features
emboldened her to attempt this difficult imitation.
Her gown, which was of Indian muslin, exquisitely
fine, had a border of gold tissue, four or five
inches deep, representing a garland. A tunic of
the purest Greek shape, with an embroidered
border similar to the gown, draped her charming
figure. The tunic was caught on the shoulders
by cameos of the greatest value. The sleeves,
which were very short and pleated, were also
caught by cameos, while the girdle, placed below
the bosom, as we see it in statues, consisted of a
band of old gold clasped by a superbly-cut
antique stone. As Madame Leclerc had dressed
in the house, she had not put on her gloves, and
permitted us to see her pretty arms, at that time
so gracefully rounded, adorned by bracelets of
gold and cameos. No ; it is impossible to give
a correct idea of this ravishing form ! She absolutely illumined the salon when she entered it.
There was such perfect harmony in every part of
this delicious *ensemble*, that a murmur of admiration greeted her the moment she appeared. . . .

All the gentlemen thronged about Madame Leclerc, and it was surrounded by them, so to speak,
that she reached the seat which my mother had
reserved for her."

The ladies, as may be supposed, did not share
the admiration of the men. They gathered
together in groups, and cast malevolent glances
in the direction of the young beauty. Was it
not perfectly shameful, they asked one another,
that a little upstart, who, only three or four years
before, had not known where to turn for a meal,
should have the effrontery to parade herself
before them decked out in this fashion? The
creature could have no sense of shame whatever;
she was a brazen-faced hussy! Several of them,
carried away by their feelings, spoke so loud that
good Madame Permon, fearing that her favourite
might overhear them, went round the room, imploring them to lower their voices. But she
might have spared herself the trouble; the
envious glances, the spiteful remarks of her own
sex, were as gratifying to Pauline as were the
compliments of the other. Were they not equally
a tribute to her charms?

But the greatest of moralists has warned us
that a haughty spirit goeth before destruction,
and, on the present occasion, there was but a step
from the giddy pinnacle of success to the nether-
most depths of humiliation. Among the *grandes
dames* present was Madame de Contades, daughter
and sister of the MM. de Bouillé who had dis-

tinguished themselves in the affair of Varennes.
As became a lady so intimately connected with
the old *régime*, she detested and despised the
Bonapartes, and would neither acknowledge the
genius of Napoleon nor the loveliness of Pauline.
Although no very striking beauty, Madame de
Contades did not want for attractions, and
"when she turned round her goddess-like head,
crowned with luxuriant black hair, and cast a
glance at any one, that glance was one that commanded obedience."[1]   At the moment when
Madame Leclerc made her sensational entry, she
was surrounded by a circle of admirers, and her
vanity was cruelly wounded when she beheld
them suddenly melt away, and hasten to swell
the crowd of courtiers which gathered about the
new arrival.   She determined to be avenged, and
to be avenged before the evening was much
older.

But let us allow Madame d'Abrantès to relate
in her entertaining style the tragi-comedy which
followed.

"'Give me your arm,' said Madame de Contades, to a gentleman standing near, and the next
moment her Diana-like form moved across the
salon and approached Madame Leclerc, who had
withdrawn to my mother's boudoir, because she
declared that the heat of the room and the
motion of the dancers made her ill ; but, truth to
tell, because she had found there a long divan,

[1] Duchesse d'Abrantès, *Mémoires.*

which afforded her the opportunity of reclining and displaying all her graceful attitudes to the best advantage. It was an unfortunate manœuvre. The room was small and brilliantly lighted; and Madame Leclerc, in order that her ravishing coiffure might be the better appreciated, was reclining in an attitude which permitted the light to descend full upon it. Madame de Contades regarded her attentively, and, instead of indulging in any of the ill-natured observations which others had had the stupidity to allow the lady to hear, she first praised the gown, then the coiffure, then the face; after which she returned to the coiffure, and declared that it was altogether charming. Then, on a sudden, turning to the gentleman on whose arm she leant, she exclaimed: 'Ah! *mon Dieu! Mon Dieu!* What a pity it is! And such a pretty woman, too! But how is it possible that such a deformity has escaped observation? *Mon Dieu!* What a misfortune!'

"Had these remarks been uttered in the ballroom, the sound of the music and the dancing would have drowned Madame de Contades' voice, although she spoke pretty loud; but in so small a room every word was distinctly audible, and the scarlet that suffused Madame Leclerc's face was much too deep to enhance its beauty.

"Madame de Contades fixed her eyes of fire on Paulette, as if she would look her through, and the tone of compassion in which she uttered the words : ' What a pity ! ' was sufficient to show her that her triumph was at an end.

" ' What is the matter ? ' inquired some one.

" ' Matter ! Do you not see those two enormous ears on either side of her |head ? I declare that, if I had such a pair, I would have them cut off. I shall advise Madame Leclerc to do so. There can be no harm in advising a woman to cut off her ears.'

"All eyes were now turned towards Madame Leclerc's head, not, as before, in order to admire it, but to marvel at the deformity which marred its beauty. To tell the truth, Nature must have been in one of her most capricious moods when she placed two such ears on the right and left of a charming face. They were merely pieces of thin white cartilage, almost without any curling. But this cartilage was not enormous, as Madame de Contades declared ; it was merely ugly, and this ugliness was the more conspicuous, on account of the beautiful features with which it was contrasted. A young woman but little accustomed to society is easily embarrassed, and this was the case with Madame Leclerc, when she read in the faces of her surrounding admirers the effect produced by the remarks of Madame de Contades. The result of this little scene was that Pauline burst into tears and, on the plea of indisposition, retired before midnight." [1]

[1] Duchesse d'Abrantès, *Mémoires*.

CHAPTER XI

Madame Bonaparte, accompanied by Louis, arrives in Paris—
Wealth and consideration enjoyed by the Bonaparte family in
1799—Town and country residences of Joseph, Lucien, and
Pauline—Pauline's jealousy at the admiration which her younger
sister Caroline is beginning to arouse—Growing antagonism of
the Bonapartes to the Beauharnais—War *à l'outrance* decided
upon—Imprudent conduct of Joséphine during her husband's
absence in Egypt—Return of Napoleon—Joséphine accused,
but acquitted—Exasperation of Élisa and Pauline at their
enemy's escape—Madame Bonaparte and Pauline on Brumaire
18 and 19—Scene at the Théâtre Feydeau.

MADAME BONAPARTE remained at
Ajaccio until the end of February 1799.
The irregular and conflicting accounts
which reached her of Napoleon's doings in Egypt
must have occasioned her the keenest anxiety,
but she seems to have cherished the most implicit
confidence in the genius and future of her son;
at any rate, she kept a brave face to the world.
One evening, when she learned that a rumour
that he had been killed was being circulated, she
exclaimed : " My son will not perish miserably in
Egypt, as his enemies desire ; I am persuaded
that he is reserved for the highest destinies."

At the beginning of 1799, Louis Bonaparte,
who had been invalided home from Egypt, arrived
at Ajaccio. He had left Rosetta on November 5,

but had been compelled to undergo a month's quarantine at Taranto, after which the vessel in which he sailed had been chased up and down the Mediterranean by the British cruisers, and once so hard pressed that, believing himself on the point of being captured, he threw into the sea the trophies which Napoleon had committed to his care for conveyance to France.

Louis remained several weeks at Ajaccio, and, on his departure for France, his mother resolved to accompany him.   Joseph and Lucien had, for some time past, been pressing her to join them in Paris, and, towards the end of the previous October, her half-brother had come to escort her thither.   But the attack of fever of which we have spoken elsewhere had left her too weak to undergo the fatigues of the journey for some months.[1]   Now, however, her health was quite restored, and accordingly, on February 20, 1799, she and Louis sailed for Leghorn, escorted by two despatch-boats, *l'Encourageant* and *la Dangereuse*, this roundabout route having presumably been chosen in order to avoid the attention of the British cruisers, which were closely blockading every French port.   Letizia, it is said, had a strong presentiment that she would never see her native land again, and, as she embraced the friends who accompanied her to the harbour, she shed many tears.   From Leghorn, the travellers

[1] Letter of Joseph Fesch to Joseph Bonaparte, 27 Vendémiaire, Year VII (October 18, 1798), published by Larrey.

proceeded by road to Paris, and, on March 11, Letizia beheld for the first time that wonderful city which was already so intimately connected with the fortunes of her family.

And how marvellous a change had those fortunes undergone in the six years which had passed since the arrival of the Bonapartes in France! These needy, obscure Corsicans, who had landed at Toulon, in 1793, with practically nothing but the clothes in which they stood, were now persons of wealth, position, and influence. They had spacious hôtels in the capital and charming seats in the country. They addressed those same Ministers to whom they had once been so subservient as equals, if not as inferiors; they patronised artists and men of letters; they dispensed the most lavish hospitality, and conducted themselves as though they owed the luxury and consideration which they now enjoyed to their own merits, instead of to the genius and generosity of that useful brother, at present sweltering under the Syrian sun.

Joseph, with whom Letizia now took up her quarters, had lately removed from the furnished house in the Rue Saints-Pères which he had occupied on his return from Italy, at the beginning of the previous year, to an imposing mansion in the Rue du Rocher, which had been built by the architect Gabriel for Mlle. Grandi of the Opera, a celebrated courtesan. This house had cost him 60,000 francs, and he had expended

a further 28,000 francs on furniture and improvements.   He had also acquired from the heirs of
the banker Durey, who had been guillotined, in
May 1793, for his relations with the *émigrés*, the
château and estate of Mortefontaine, for which
he had paid 258,000 francs, besides spending
almost as much again on the restoration of the
house and the improvement of the property.

Lucien had installed himself in a fine house
in the Grande-Rue Verte, at the corner of the
Rue Miromesnil, and was in treaty with Pauline
and her husband for the purchase of their estate
of le Plessis-Chamant, near Senlis, which he
acquired in the following August, and proceeded
to improve with a sublime disregard for expense.

Pauline and Leclerc, in addition to their house
in the Rue de la Victoire and their property near
Senlis, possessed a small estate in Italy, at Villa-
Riotino, in the commune of Novellara, while a
little later, after disposing of le Plessis-Chamant,
they bought the beautiful château and estate of
Montgobert, near Villers-Cotterets, to which
they subsequently joined the Abbey of Lieu-
Restaure.[1]

Thanks to the liberality of Napoleon, Madame
Bonaparte herself seems to have had abundant
funds at her disposal, since, in the following
August, we find Joseph Fesch writing to Brac-
cini, the family's man of business at Ajaccio, to
inform him that his sister has drawn upon him

[1] M. Frédéric Masson, *Napoléon et sa famille.*

two bills, one for 10,000 francs, and the other for 6,000, to the order of Citizen Ange Chiappe, formerly deputy for Corsica in the Convention, the same person to whom we found Letizia writing in 1795 to implore his good offices on behalf of the imprisoned Lucien.[1]

When Madame Bonaparte drew these two bills, she was not in Paris, but at Vichy, in company with Louis, who had just been appointed major (*chef d'escadron*) in the 5th Dragoons, which regiment formed part of the garrison of Paris. They returned to the capital at the end of August, when Letizia again took up her quarters at her eldest son's house, while the newly-fledged major went to reside with his brother Lucien. On the strength of his promotion, he began to pay court, *pour le mauvais motif*, to his old flame Émilie de Beauharnais, now Madame de Lavalette, who, however, declined to respond to his advances, and wrote him a severe letter, bidding him "forget a proposal, which accorded neither with her disinterested sentiments nor with his own duties." Deeply mortified by this rebuff, Louis sought consolation in the company of the ladies of the Opera, with the result that he suffered both in pocket and in health, and became more melancholy than ever.

After Madame Bonaparte's arrival in Paris, Caroline came frequently from Madame Campan's to visit her mother, who occasionally took her with her to call upon Madame Permon and

[1] Baron Larrey, *Madame Mère*.

other intimate friends. With her fair hair falling in a shower of curls over her white shoulders,
her dazzling complexion, her delightful smile,
and her unaffected girlish ways, Caroline made
a charming picture, and excited admiration wherever she went, so much so, indeed, that Pauline,
who could not regard without jealousy the success
of another woman, even though that woman happened to belong to her own family, began to take
serious umbrage.

One day, Pauline was sitting in Madame
Permon's salon, listening with a smile of gratified vanity to the insipid compliments which a
certain M. de Montagu, a celebrated *incroyable*
of the time, was whispering into her willing
ear, when her mother and Madame Joseph
Bonaparte entered, accompanied by Caroline,
who had obtained a few days' holiday from
Madame Campan. M. de Montagu looked up,
saw the pretty little *pensionnaire*, and directed
towards her a glance of profound admiration,
which did not escape the notice of Pauline, who
bit her lip with vexation. At that moment,
Caroline caught sight of her sister, and, with a
cry of delight, hurried forward to embrace her.
But what was her astonishment to find herself
repulsed so roughly that she almost fell to the
floor, while the jealous beauty exclaimed : " Be
careful what you are doing ! You are ruining
my gown ! " Then, turning towards her mother,
she continued, in a voice which trembled with

anger: "*Mon Dieu!* Mamma, you must certainly break Annunziata" (since the damsel in question had abandoned her baptismal name, which she considered too absurdly Corsican, for that of Caroline, recommended to her by Lucien, she could not endure to be called Annunziata) "of these rough ways. She has the manners of a peasant girl of the Fium' Orbo."[1]

Pauline had certainly profited by the lesson which she had received from Madame de Contades.

Poor Caroline, with tears in her eyes, returned to her mother, who frowned angrily, but said nothing, since it was her invariable rule never to reprove her children before strangers; while Madame Leclerc, happy in the knowledge that she had amply avenged on her sister the momentary defection of M. de Montagu, became all smiles and amiability once more.

The Bonapartes basked in the sun of prosperity; nevertheless, they were far from tranquil, for they perceived upon the horizon a cloud, which, they feared, might ere long assume such dimensions as to temper materially its grateful warmth.

This cloud was the influence of Joséphine, who, notwithstanding her peccadilloes, still reigned over the heart of Napoleon, since in the early stages of matrimony, passion is far stronger than reason, and jealousy often serves but to accentuate it.

---

[1] One of the most remote districts of Corsica, the inhabitants of which were noted for their primitive manners.

The Bonapartes had received much from the great brother; indeed, when we consider that, with the exception of Letizia, they had no claim upon him beyond that of relationship, and that one of them, at least, had been to him a source of continual annoyance and anxiety, his generosity towards them savours of the quixotic. But they regarded what they had received as only an earnest of what was to come, and felt that it was intolerable that any one should presume to dispute with them the good things to which they were so justly entitled. The more they pondered the matter, the more were they consumed with jealousy and hatred of Joséphine and her children. They grudged their sister-in-law the ample provision Napoleon had made for her before his departure for Egypt, and every time that Joseph, in whose hands the pension had been left, was compelled to draw upon it, he felt as though he were paying money out of his own pocket. They grudged Eugène de Beauharnais his appointment as one of the general's aides-de-camp, though Louis had held the same post, while Joseph and Lucien were not soldiers, infinitely preferring to contend with political opponents in France than with infuriated Turks and brawny British sailors in the breach at Acre. They even grudged poor Hortense her schooling at Madame Campan's.

And so they laid their heads together: Joseph and Lucien and Louis and Pauline and Élisa—

JOSÉPHINE AT MALMAISON
FROM THE PAINTING BY PRUD'HON AT VERSAILLES

who, in January 1799, had lost her little son
Napoleon, and, in order to find distraction from her
grief and Baciocchi's violin, came occasionally to
Paris to visit her relatives—while their mother, if
she did not take any active part in their delibera-
tions, certainly approved of the decision at which
they arrived, namely, that hostilities should be
begun forthwith and continued until a definite
separation between Napoleon and his wife had
been effected.

Circumstance and their enemy's amazing indiscretions combined to favour their designs.   Before Napoleon sailed from Toulon, it had been
arranged that Joséphine, after taking the waters
at Plombières, should join her husband in Egypt,
by way of Naples and Malta.   But at Plombières
she met with an accident, caused by the collapse
of a balcony on which she happened to be standing, and by the time she was convalescent, the
French fleet had been destroyed in the Battle of
the Nile, and Nelson's cruisers swept the sea.
Joséphine accordingly returned to Paris, and
divided her time between her house in the Rue
de la Victoire and Malmaison.   Consolations in
her grass widowhood were not wanting, and she
did not disdain them.   M. Hippolyte Charles, who,
thanks to her good offices, was now a partner in a
wealthy firm of army contractors, again made his
appearance upon the scene, and paid such frequent
and prolonged visits to Malmaison, that strangers
might have been pardoned for mistaking him for

the master of the house; and, if gossip spoke truly, he was not the only favoured admirer.

Nor was this all. As the months went by and no news came from Egypt,[1] Joséphine seemed, in common with many others, to have concluded that the French army was destroyed and Napoleon dead, and decided to seek a support against the hostility of his heirs. With this end in view, ignoring the instructions she had received from her husband, she began to frequent the salons of the Directors—"that gang of scoundrels who envied and hated him"—endeavoured to renew her old intimacy with Barras, and contemplated marrying Hortense to Rewbell's son. All of which afforded the watchful Bonapartes the most lively satisfaction. Joséphine was doubly faithless to her absent husband; every day the evidence against her was accumulating.

They would have been still more overjoyed, had a letter written by Napoleon on Thermidor 9, Year VI (July 27, 1798), to his eldest brother reached its destination, in which he declared that "the veil had been entirely rent asunder," informed him that Joséphine must leave the hôtel in the Rue de la Victoire, and that he "reckoned on him to look after his house"; or if they could have known of a conversation which took place, some

[1] So rigorous was the blockade, that from February 16, 1799, when a courier from Egypt arrived in Paris, until October 13 of that year, when tidings came that Napoleon had landed at Fréjus, no news of him reached France, save that brought by Louis, who had, of course, left Egypt some weeks before the courier in question.

months later, between the general and his faithful
lieutenant Junot, at the wells of Messoudiah,
after the arrival of a courier from France, bearing
fresh accusations from his family and others
against his wife. However, the courier and his
letter fell into the hands of the English, to whom
their enemy's domestic troubles afforded so much
diversion that they caused the epistle to be
printed; while Junot did not return to France
until long after Napoleon.[1]

Suddenly, on the evening of October 9, 1799,
came the news that Napoleon was in France.
Élisa and Pauline were at the theatre, when, in
the middle of the play, a message was brought to
their box. " I saw," writes Chancellor Pasquier,
"much excitement and demonstrations of joy.
They disappeared, and I soon learned that they
were Bonaparte's sisters, and that he had landed;
a courier had brought the news."[2]

Napoleon had embarked at Alexandria on the
night of August 22–3, eluded with his usual
good fortune the British ships cruising between
Malta and Cap Bon, skirted the coasts of Sardinia
and Corsica, and, after a brief stay at Ajaccio, had
landed at Fréjus on the morning of October 8.

One knows what followed: the hurried departure of Joseph, Lucien, Louis, and Leclerc to
meet Napoleon and forestall their enemy; the
fruitless journey of Joséphine, who took the

---

[1] M. Frédéric Masson, *Napoléon et sa famille.*
[2] Pasquier, *Mémoires.*

wrong road; the arrival of the general and his wrath at discovering the absence of his wife; the accusations launched by the whole family against this faithless creature, who cared neither for his honour as a husband, his fortune as a politician, nor his glory as a soldier; the return of the erring wife; the locked bedroom door, the re-proaches hissed through the keyhole; the despair of Joséphine; the entreaties of her children, and, finally, the pardon and reconciliation, to which Lucien was summoned at seven o'clock the following morning to bear ocular testimony.

The wrath of the Bonaparte clan was propor-tioned to their disappointment. The men suc-ceeded in dissimulating it, to some extent, as did their prudent mother; but Élisa and Pauline could not disguise their feelings. "Madame Baciocchi gave free vent to her enmity and scorn; the consequence was that her sister-in-law could never endure her." As for Pauline, she was "of all the members of the family, the most irritated at the pardon which Napoleon had granted his wife," and, from that day forward, it was war to the knife between her and Joséphine. "Never," says Madame d'Abrantès, "have I seen such hatred between two sisters-in-law."[1]

But Napoleon and his family had, for the moment, far more important matters to occupy their attention than the conduct of Joséphine.

[1] Duchesse d'Abrantès, *Mémoires.*

The indescribable enthusiasm which had greeted
Napoleon on his arrival at Fréjus and in every
town and village through which he passed on his
way to Paris, had shown him that the country
would only be too ready to hail him as its
deliverer from the corrupt and incapable oligarchy
which could neither preserve order at home nor
carry on war abroad. "The pear was ripe," and
no sooner had he returned to the capital, than he
began actively preparing for the *coup d'État*
which was to overthrow the Directory and make
him the virtual dictator of France.

Brumaire 18 arrived; the excitement in Paris
was intense. Madame Permon and her daughter
went to Joseph's house in the Rue du Rocher to
visit Letizia. They found her apparently con-
fident as to the result, but her deadly pallor and
a convulsive shudder which seized her every time
any unexpected noise reached her ears, showed
that she was suffering the keenest anxiety.
"Madame Bonaparte," says the Duchesse
d'Abrantès, "appeared to me that day truly like
the mother of the Gracchi."

Letizia, indeed, had abundant cause for anxiety.
It was not only the fate of Napoleon that was
at stake, but that of Louis and Lucien as well.
If the *coup d'État* failed, exile, or even the guillotine, must inevitably be their portion.

The Permons remained with her during the
greater part of that trying day, and only left
her when reassuring messages from Lucien had

somewhat restored her peace of mind.   The out-
works of the fortress had been carried; the
struggle for the citadel was reserved for the
morrow.

Leaving the Rue du Rocher, they drove to
Pauline's house.   That lively lady was but little
perturbed, her frivolous mind being incapable
of appreciating the gravity of the situation.
Nevertheless, she made a great to-do, and
every quarter of an hour dictated to one of her
waiting-women a note to Moreau, who was a
particular friend of hers, to ask the news.

Next day—the day which was to inaugurate
so momentous an epoch in French history—the
Permons returned to Pauline's house.   They
found Letizia with her, and Madame Permon
expressed some surprise that her old friend had
not gone to see Joséphine at so critical a time.
"Signora Panoria," cried Letizia, "it is not to
that quarter that I should look for comfort; it is
to Julie, to Christine.   It is with them that I see
my sons happy; but with the other . . . no, no!"
"And, as she finished the sentence," adds the
chronicler, "she compressed her lips and opened
her eyes widely, which was with her a very characteristic indication that she felt very strongly
about what she had just said."

Slowly the hours passed by, the anxious
mother endeavouring to find some relief from
the agony of suspense which she was enduring
by relating to her sympathetic friends the story

of her early struggles in Corsica, her adventures during the War of Independence, the circumstances relating to the birth of Napoleon, her midnight flight from Ajaccio, and many other matters which we have already set down. She spoke in Italian, for her French was still hardly intelligible, and, though the Permons had often heard her speak of these events before, the knowledge that the fate of three of the children for whom this woman had made so many sacrifices was, at this very moment, trembling in the balance, invested them with a new and thrilling interest.

While her mother was indulging in these reminiscences, Pauline had seated herself before a large mirror, in which she was complacently contemplating her charms, and, at the same time, adjusting the folds of a beautiful Cashmere shawl, which she had thrown over her shoulders. Presently, she proposed that, in order to divert their thoughts, they should go to the play, where it was also possible that they might find some one who was in possession of news from Saint-Cloud. The other ladies agreed, and they all accordingly drove to the Théâtre Feydeau, which was, at this period, the most popular house in Paris. Letizia, as may be supposed, paid but small attention to the performance. She said nothing, but she was evidently wrought to the highest pitch of tension, and her eyes were continually turned to the door of their box, as though awaiting the arrival of a messenger with news of her

sons.   During the interval between the two
pieces, there was an uproar in the *parterre*.
The poor mother, imagining that it was occasioned by some important news from Saint-Cloud,
trembled from head to foot ; but it was only a
thief, who had been detected in the act of rifling his
neighbour's fob, and order was quickly restored.

The curtain rose on the after-piece—*l'Auteur
dans son Ménage*—but it had only been in progress a few minutes when the players were seen
to pause and whisper together, after which, the
actor who took the principal part, advanced to
the front of the stage, intimated that he desired
to address the audience, and cried out, in the
midst of a breathless silence :

" Citizens, General Bonaparte has been nearly
assassinated, at Saint-Cloud, by traitors to their
country ! "

At these words, Madame Leclerc uttered a
shriek so loud and piercing, that, notwithstanding
the excitement which the news had aroused
among the company, every glass in the house
was directed at the box in which the four ladies
sat.   Pauline continued to scream lustily, and her
mother, whose only signs of emotion were her
deadly pallor and tightly-compressed lips, in vain
endeavoured to calm her.   It is not every day
that a lady, however beautiful, has the opportunity
of monopolising the sympathetic attention of so
large an assembly, and Madame Leclerc was
determined to make the most of it.

At length, losing all patience, Letizia grasped her daughter firmly by the arm and angrily exclaimed: "Pauline, why are you making this exhibition of yourself? Be silent! Do you not understand that no harm has come to your brothers? Be silent then and get up, we must go and seek further news."

Her mother's words proved a marvellously efficacious restorative, and in a few moments the stricken lady had sufficiently recovered to make a graceful exit, amid many expressions of sympathy and admiration from the crowd which thronged the corridors and vestibule of the theatre.

From the theatre, they drove to the Rue de la Victoire, since from Joséphine alone were they likely to be able to obtain reliable information of what had occurred. The whole street, however, was blocked with the carriages of people bent upon a similar errand, and for some time it was impossible to get near the house. Presently, however, they learned, from an officer who was hurrying by, that their most sanguine hopes had been realised. The three adventurous brothers were safe; the Constitution of the Year III—that Constitution in defence of which, fourteen months before (September 22, 1798), Lucien and Joseph had sworn to shed their blood, had been abrogated, and three Consuls appointed, of whom Napoleon was the First.

CHAPTER XII

TWO days after the *coup d'État* which had given to France the ruler who was to guide her destinies for more than fourteen eventful years, the three Consuls took up their residence at the Luxembourg, where Napoleon remained until February 19, 1800, when he removed to the Tuileries. His elevation to the leadership of the State was, of course, followed by the elevation of his relatives. Lucien, who had shown such courage and presence of mind at that critical moment, at Saint-Cloud, when his brother's fortunes were trembling in the balance, was elected a member of the Tribunate and appointed

Minister of the Interior; Joseph was elected by the Senate a member of the Corps Législatif, and, in March, 1800, nominated, with Fleureu and Rœderer, one of the commissioners charged to treat for the peace with the United States of America; while Louis, who, it will be remembered, had, in the previous July, received a commission as major in the 5th Dragoons, was, in the following January, actually appointed to the command of the same regiment, to the astonishment and disgust of veteran officers who had fought in a dozen battles before this pampered stripling had so much as donned a uniform. Even a Prince of the Blood under the old *régime* would scarcely have expected more rapid and more wholly undeserved promotion.

The relatives by marriage were, naturally, less fortunate. Leclerc, who had rendered valuable service at Saint-Cloud, was merely given the command of a division of the Army of the Rhine, of which Moreau was subsequently appointed general-in-chief. Seeing that Leclerc had been a general of division since the previous August, this could scarcely be regarded as any very signal favour, though possibly a more distinguished officer might have been found for the post. As for Baciocchi, who was good for nothing in the world, except playing the violin, he received nothing, beyond permission to exchange his command at Marseilles for an appointment as adjutant-general in the 16th Division, quartered in the neighbourhood of Paris; and even this concession he owed to the influence of his wife, who was heartily tired of Marseilles and impatient to enjoy the delights of the capital, of which, up to the present, she had had merely occasional glimpses.

However, the first month of the year 1800 provided Napoleon with a third brother-in-law, and one who had a far stronger claim to advancement than either Leclerc or Baciocchi.

We have mentioned in a previous chapter that when Caroline Bonaparte visited Napoleon at Montebello, in the summer of 1797, her girlish beauty had made a deep impression upon a certain dashing cavalry officer named Murat. The career of Joachim Murat is romantic, even in an age of romance. He was born, on March 25th, 1767, at La Bastide-Fortunière (now La Bastide-Murat), near Cahors, where his father combined the calling of innkeeper with that of subintendant on one of the large estates belonging to the Talleyrand family. The inn was well patronised, the sub-intendancy was a very comfortable berth, and Murat *père* made money, and was able to give his sons good educations and provide his daughters with dowries. Joachim, being the youngest of the boys, was intended for the Church, in which the Talleyrands had promised to provide him with a benefice ; and, after spending some time at the College of Cahors, he was sent to the theological seminary at Aix, where a *bourse* had been obtained for him.   But this strapping lad, with his iron constitution, his restless black eyes, and the hot blood of Gascony coursing through his veins, was as little fitted for an ecclesiastical career as his immortal country-man d'Artagnan himself; and it is therefore not altogether surprising that, one fine day, he ex-changed the sombre garb of a theological student for the very becoming uniform of the Chasseurs des Ardennes, who happened to be passing through Toulouse, on their way from Auch to Carcassonne.   According to one story, the vaca-tion at the seminary had just begun, and Mon-sieur Joachim having been so foolish as to lose the money which his father had sent him for his journey home in a gambling-house, or in some other questionable resort, found himself without a sol in his pocket, and decided that "to go for a soldier" presented the easiest way out of the difficulty.

Murat remained with the Chasseurs des Ar-dennes for two years, and had already attained the rank of quartermaster (*maréchal des logis*), when he committed some breach of discipline, which rendered it advisable for him to apply for his discharge or, at any rate, for an indefinite *congé*.   He returned to La Bastide, but the re-ception he met with from his parents was not such as to encourage him to prolong his stay, and he accordingly entered the service of a draper at Saint-Céré, apparently in the dual capacity of shop-assistant and porter.[1] However, in November 1791, thanks to the influence of the deputy Chavaignac, he was chosen by the Directory of the Lot as one of the three subjects which that department was to furnish to the Garde Constitutionnelle of Louis XVI. The future Maréchal Bessières was one of the other two, and between him and Murat a sincere friendship then began, which death alone was to terminate.

At Paris, his handsome presence, his Gascon turbulence—he is said to have engaged in some half-dozen "affairs of honour" in about as many weeks—and his revolutionary ardour earned him considerable notoriety, and having resigned his place in the Garde Constitutionnelle, he returned to his old regiment, which was now known as the 12th Chasseurs-à-cheval. He appears to have taken part in the first campaign of the Army of the North, and to have been present at the Battle of Jemmapes and other engagements, though his movements during the next twelve months are somewhat uncertain. Any way, his promotion was rapid, and by April 1793 he had attained the rank of major.

We next find him attached to a corps of irregular cavalry, which had been raised on the frontier by one Landrieux, formerly in the service of the Comte de Provence. Murat and Landrieux quarrelled, however, and the former denounced

[1] Marbot, *Mémoires*.

his commanding officer as an aristocrat, with the result that Landrieux was arrested and thrown into prison. At this period, Murat was, or pretended to be, so ardent a Jacobin that, after the assassination of "the Friend of the People," he demanded permission to change the second letter of his name into an "a," and actually signed some of his letters "Marat." The consequence was that when Thermidor arrived and Jacobinism ceased to be the mode, he was cashiered and imprisoned, in his turn, and was perhaps fortunate to keep his head on his shoulders. However, thanks to the intercession of the colonel of his regiment, which had now become the 21st Chasseurs, he was eventually released and his commission restored to him.

In the insurrection of Prairial 2, Year III (May 20, 1795), Murat rendered good service to the Convention, and in the night of Vendémiaire 12–13, it was he who, galloping *ventre-à terre* to Grenelle, with three hundred horse, secured the cannon with which, a few hours later, Napoleon scattered the insurgents of the sections. Contrary to his expectations, and, in spite of several eloquent petitions from the young officer, the Directory did not seem inclined to recognise his services, and Murat, in high dudgeon, had already applied for three months' furlough, when, at the beginning of February 1796, he was promoted to the lieutenant-colonelcy of his regiment, while, three weeks later, Napoleon, recently appointed general-in-chief of the Army of Italy, nominated him as his senior aide-de-camp.

In the first battles of the memorable campaign of that year, Murat so greatly distinguished himself, that, after the armistice of Cherasco, he was despatched to Paris, to convey to the Directory the document which had just been signed and the trophies taken from the enemy. Naturally, he called to pay his respects to his commander-in-chief's wife, who received him so very amiably, that, when he returned to Italy, with the rank of brigadier-general, he is said to have been indiscreet enough to boast about it.[1] Whether on account of this, or because he was suspected, and with reason, of endeavouring to ingratiate himself with the Directory, at the expense of his chief, or perhaps because he had shown himself wanting in energy, if not in courage, in an action before Mantua,[2] he fell into disgrace with Napoleon, and, though he covered himself with glory in several subsequent engagements, notably at Rivoli, where his brigade contributed materially to the victory, he failed to rehabilitate himself in the great man's eyes.

The general's hostility, however, did not prevent Murat from being one of the officers chosen for the Army of Egypt, "as the ladies with whom he was a great favourite," remarks Bourrienne, "interested themselves much on his

---

[1] Duchesse d'Abrantès, *Mémoires*.
[2] Bourrienne, *Mémoires*.

behalf, and were not without influence with the Minister for War." But throughout the voyage he remained in the most complete disgrace, and wrote to Barras, from Malta, that he saw "every day General Bonaparte's friendship for him diminish."[1]

Nevertheless, on their arrival in the land of the Pharaohs, Napoleon showed his appreciation of his military talents by entrusting him with several important commands, in which Murat acquitted himself right worthily, besides performing prodigies of reckless valour. Still the general continued to treat him with marked coldness, and it was not until after the Battle of Aboukir, where Murat, by a brilliant charge, completely routed the Turks opposed to him, and wounded and took prisoner, with his own hand, their leader, Mustapha Pasha, that he at length succeeded in regaining his chief's favour. "The victory in the Battle of Aboukir," wrote Napoleon to the Directory, in his despatch of July 28th, "is principally due to General Murat. I request for him the rank of general of division ; his brigade of cavalry accomplished the impossible."

Admitted to the confidence, as well as restored to the favour, of Napoleon, who regarded him as necessary to the execution of his ambitious projects, Murat returned with him to France, and

---

[1] Letter of Prairial 27, Year VI (June 17, 1798), published by Count Alberto Lumbroso, *Correspondance de Joachim Murat.*

seconded him energetically on Brumaire 19.
When Napoleon, his courage and resolution
momentarily failing him, left the hall of the
Council of the Five Hundred, with the terrible
cry of "*Hors la loi!*" ringing in his ears, and
Lucien, powerless to stem the tumult, quitted the
President's seat and took refuge among the troops
outside, it was Murat, accompanied by Leclerc,
who marched the grenadiers into the Orangery,
and compelled the enraged deputies to disperse.
This service was rewarded by the confirmation of
the rank of general of division, which the Directory had bestowed upon him before its demise,
and, three weeks later, by the post of commander
of the new Consular Guard.

Murat passed for one of the handsomest officers
in the army, though his very thick lips and "nose
which, though aquiline, had nothing of nobility
in its shape," combined with his curly black hair,
black eyes, and swarthy complexion, "gave him
somewhat of the appearance of a negro."[1]   On
the other hand, "he possessed an uncommonly
fine and well-proportioned figure," and "his
muscular strength, the elegance of his manners,
his dignified bearing, and his dauntless courage
in battle, resembled less a Republican soldier,
than one of those accomplished cavaliers of whom
we read in Ariosto and Tasso."[2]   To women, he
was invariably courteous and attentive; with men,

[1] Duchesse d'Abrantès, *Mémoires.*
[2] Bourrienne, *Mémoires.*

affable and good-natured; in short, he was generally popular.

After Napoleon's return from Egypt, Caroline
Bonaparte and Hortense de Beauharnais were
sent for from Madame Campan's to spend a fortnight in Paris, during which Caroline and Murat
met pretty frequently; and the latter did not
fail to resume the attentions which he had paid
the young lady at Montebello. Like Leclerc,
Murat was probably far from insensible to the
material advantages which would follow his
marriage with the sister of General Bonaparte;
but, at the same time, his letters to his relatives
in Gascony, and, indeed, the whole of his subsequent career, prove that he was deeply in love
with his "*chère petite* Caroline."

As for Caroline, this *beau sabreur* had captivated her girlish fancy from the first,[1] and now
that she saw him again surrounded, as it were,
by the halo of romance with which his valiant
deeds in Egypt and Syria had invested him,
her admiration speedily ripened into a warmer
feeling.

And so it came about that when, two days
before the *coup d'État,* she and Hortense were

---

[1] But there seems to be no foundation whatever for Bourrienne's
assertion that "already, at Milan, an intimacy had commenced
between Caroline and Murat which rendered their marriage
eminently desirable"; indeed, Madame d'Abrantès, who is not
over tender towards the ladies of the Bonaparte family, declares
that "Caroline Bonaparte married with a reputation as pure and
fresh as her complexion and the roses of her cheeks."

abruptly sent back to their *pension*, an understanding had already been arrived at. "We
were very far from suspecting the events of the
morrow," says Hortense, "but General Murat,
like a true knightly lover, sent to us, in the night
of Brumaire 19, four grenadiers of the guard
which he commanded. They were instructed to
acquaint us with what had happened at Saint-
Cloud and the nomination of Bonaparte to the
Consulate. Imagine four grenadiers knocking at
the gates of a convent! The alarm was general,
and Madame Campan was loud in her condemna-
tion of this military method of announcing the
news. Caroline saw in it only a proof of gallantry
and love."

But Napoleon's consent had yet to be obtained,
and political exigencies threatened to thwart the
hopes of the lovers. The First Consul had cast
his eye on Moreau, the only general who had
the smallest pretension to dispute his military
supremacy, and whose interests it was therefore
obviously to his advantage to identify with his
own; and he had even gone so far as to announce,
in the *Moniteur* of Brumaire 24, his approaching
marriage with "one" of his sisters. As Caroline
was the only sister unprovided with a husband,
such ambiguity was a little superfluous.

Murat and Caroline were in despair; but, though
they were kept in suspense for some weeks, they
eventually had their way. This unexpected result was due, first, to the refusal of Moreau to

JOACHIM MURAT, AFTERWARDS KING OF NAPLES
FROM THE PAINTING BY GÉRARD AT VERSAILLES

sacrifice his independence for the favours of Napoleon, and, secondly, to the good offices of Joséphine.

Moreau, by his refusal, had rendered the position of the First Consul almost ridiculous. After the paragraph which had appeared in the *Moniteur*, Napoleon found himself decidedly embarrassed, and this facilitated Murat's success. Nevertheless, though he appreciated the necessity of marrying Caroline as soon as possible, he was at first by no means favourable to the idea of an alliance with his former aide-de-camp. He had not forgotten the latter's intrigues with the Directory, nor the tender passages which were supposed to have passed between him and his wife; while his humble origin was a further objection. For which reason, he received his proposal for his sister's hand very coldly, and replied that he would take time to consider the matter.

It was now that Joséphine intervened on the lovers' behalf. Madame d'Abrantès attributes her action to the desire to silence the malevolent rumours which were in circulation concerning her relations with Murat, and to persuade Napoleon that, even if this fascinating cavalier had once been her lover, she had now renounced him. This may have influenced her to some extent; but the true explanation is probably that given by Bourrienne, namely, that she wished to secure for herself a useful ally within the family circle. She believed that, if Murat owed his bride to her, he would feel in honour bound to accord her his support and protection against the animosity with which the majority of the Bonapartes pursued her, and to the danger of which she was now fully alive.

Murat's proposal was, as may be supposed, the subject of much discussion at the Luxembourg. Joséphine used all her powers of persuasion to induce her husband to consent, while Hortense, Eugène, and the First Consul's secretary Bourrienne ably seconded her efforts. Napoleon, however, resisted for some time. "I do not like these love-matches," said he; "these heated brains consult only the volcano of the imagination; I had other views, Who knows what alliance I should have arranged for Caroline? She looks at the matter like a madcap, and does not properly consider my position. There will come a time when perhaps sovereigns will contend for her hand. She proposes, you say, to marry a brave man. In my position, that is not enough; destiny must be allowed to accomplish itself"; and so forth.

But Joséphine and her allies refused to abandon the field. They dwelt on the mutual affection of the lovers; they eulogised the services which Murat had rendered Napoleon at Brumaire, and reminded him of the brilliant courage he had displayed at Aboukir. Napoleon began to show signs of relenting. "I must admit," said he,

"that Murat was superb at Aboukir." Perceiving
their advantage, they redoubled their persuasions,
and, at length, he yielded.

Later the same evening, when the First Consul
found himself alone in his cabinet with Bourrienne, he remarked to his secretary : "Well,
Bourrienne, you ought to be satisfied—for my
part, I am. All things considered, Murat suits
my sister, and then they cannot say that I am
proud, that I seek great alliances. Had I given
my sister to a noble, all you Jacobins would have
cried out for a counter-revolution. Besides, I am
pleased that my wife takes an interest in the
marriage ; you are aware of the reasons. Since
it is settled, I must hasten the matter, as we have
no time to lose. If I go to Italy, I wish to take
Murat with us. I must strike a decisive blow
there."

In the morning, he appeared still more pleased
that he had allowed himself to be persuaded.
"But," observes Bourrienne, "I could easily perceive that he was not aware of the real motive
which had induced Joséphine to interest herself
about the marriage of Murat and Caroline. From
the satisfaction of Bonaparte, it appeared to me
that, in his wife's earnestness, he had found a
proof that the reports of her intimacy with Murat
were calumnies."

The marriage-contract was signed on January
18, 1800, at the Luxembourg, in the presence
of Madame Bonaparte *mère*, the five brothers

(Napoleon, Joseph, Lucien, Louis and Jérôme),
Élisa and Baciocchi, Fesch, Joséphine, Hortense
and Bessières, who is described as a cousin of
Murat, and the surgeon Yvan, a close friend
of the bridegroom. The stipulations were the
same as for Élisa and Pauline : that is to say,
Caroline received from her four elder brothers,
a sum of 40,000 francs in cash, in consideration
of which she renounced all further claims to the
family property. Murat brought into settlement
the sum of 13,300 francs. Caroline was also presented by her family with "diamonds, jewellery,
and objects of trousseau," to the value of 12,000
francs.[1]

The following day, the family left Paris for
Joseph's château of Mortefontaine,[2] and, on the

[1] Bourrienne's story about Napoleon "who had not money
enough to purchase a suitable present for his sister"—elsewhere
he states that, when he returned from Italy, he was worth more
than 3,000,000 francs !—presenting Caroline with a diamond necklace, which he had abstracted from his wife's jewel-case, and which
Joséphine subsequently replaced by one costing 250,000 francs,
which Berthier, the Minister for War, paid for and charged to the
account of the hospital service in Italy, though accepted by M.
Turquan and other writers with a weakness for piquant anecdotes,
is obviously apocryphal. Napoleon, however, did give the bride a
diamond necklace, to which Murat joined three splendid ropes of
pearls.

[2] Before leaving, Murat wrote the following letter to his elder
brother, André Murat :

"Paris
"29 Nivose, Year VIII
"(Jan. 19, 1800)

"I hasten to inform thee, my dear brother, that I am starting for
a country-seat of the Consul Bonaparte, and that to-morrow I am
to marry his sister. The contract was passed and signed yesterday

20th, a purely civil marriage was celebrated in the *Temple décadaire* of the canton of Plailly, in which Mortefontaine was situated. The ceremony was performed by Louis Dubosc, the president of the municipal administration of the canton, the witnesses on behalf of Murat being "Jean Bernadotte, ex-Minister for War, and Étienne Jacques Jérôme Calmelet, *homme de loi*"; and on behalf of the bride, Louis Bonaparte and Leclerc. Madame Bonaparte *mère*, General Lannes,[1] and Fesch were among those present, but no mention is made of the First Consul, Joséphine, or the other members of the family.

Immediately after his marriage, Murat quitted his lodging in the Rue des Citoyennes, to-day Rue

---

evening. Let my sisters know of this. I shall arrange to come and pay you a visit at some future time. Be sure, above all things, to tell my mother that I am longing to see her and to embrace her tenderly. Tell her that my wife looks forward to making her acquaintance and to calling her by the sweet name of mother.

"My dear little Caroline intends to write to her; endeavour to reply in an amiable and courteous manner. Adieu. To-morrow, I shall be the happiest of men; to-morrow, I shall possess the most lovable of women. Write to me. I send the most affectionate greetings to my mother, to thy wife and children, and also to my sisters. Remember me kindly to all our friends, to all our dear fellow-citizens. I look forward eagerly to embracing you all."— Count Alberto Lumbroso, *Correspondance de Joachim Murat*.

[1] M. Turquan, in his *Sœurs de Napoléon*, asserts that Lannes had been Murat's rival for the hand of Caroline, and that he never forgave Bessières for having pleaded his competitor's cause with the First Consul. How could Lannes have had any such pretensions when he was not free to wed, for it was not until seven months after Caroline had married Murat, to be precise, on August 26, 1800, that he divorced his wife (Mlle. Méric)?

Madame, and installed himself with his wife in the Hôtel de Brionne, situated in the northern part of the courts of the Tuileries. The Murats only occupied the apartments on the *rez-de-chaussée*, while M. Benezech, who became Prefect of the Palace when the First Consul, a few weeks later, took up his residence at the Tuileries, occupied the first floor. The young couple seemed very much in love with one another, and when they appeared together in society, people declared that they had never seen a handsomer or more devoted couple. Caroline, whom prosperity had not yet spoiled, charmed every one by her amiability and her unaffected manners. Having received but little education, she was entirely free from the pedantry which characterised her eldest sister; and, although she possessed her full share of vanity, unlike Pauline, she also possessed the faculty of concealing it. She took care to visit all who had shown kindness to her husband in his less prosperous days; she attended balls and danced with every one that desired the honour of being her partner, while Murat, who did not dance, looked on "holding respectfully her gloves and fan." And she invited the general's comrades to breakfast or dinner, where, after an appetising repast had been served on the finest porcelain, a clumsy earthenware pot containing a confection of grapes and pears was placed upon the table, of which Murat invited his guests to partake, observing that it was a dish highly appreciated in Gascony, and that it had been made and sent him by his mother.[1]

Caroline was very attentive to Joséphine, who, since the terrible fright which she had experienced in the previous October, had been a model wife, and had, in consequence, regained much of her influence over her husband, to the profound chagrin of the Bonaparte clan. Caroline, of whom Talleyrand was one day to observe that she had "the head of a Cromwell on the shoulders of a pretty woman," was far too prudent to mix herself up in family quarrels, in which, for the moment at any rate, she had nothing to gain and much to lose. Accordingly, both she and her husband lived on the friendliest terms with Joséphine, though, as a matter of fact, Madame Murat disliked her sister-in-law almost as heartily as did Élisa and Pauline, and was fully resolved to join with them against the Beauharnais the moment it was to her advantage to do so. But, for the present, she had decided that her interests and those of her husband would be better served by conciliating the common enemy, and she was therefore all smiles and compliments. Strange that this girl of eighteen should already have been a past-mistress in the art of dissimulation !

The Murats were not long in reaping the reward of their politic conduct, as, in May 1800, Napoleon presented them with the money to purchase, from Madame de Bullion, the first part

[1] General Thiébault, *Mémoires.*

of the property of Villiers, which was eventually to become the beautiful estate of Neuilly.

While Murat accompanied Napoleon on that brilliant campaign which was to avenge the crushing defeats of the Trebbia and Novi and bring Italy again under French control, his wife remained in Paris, where she continued on the friendliest terms with Joséphine and Hortense, who had now quitted Madame Campan's, accompanying them to the play, visiting them at Malmaison, and, in short, spending nearly all her time in their company.

Joséphine was delighted and was convinced that, in promoting the marriage of Caroline and Murat, she had secured for herself two devoted allies. Under date Messidor 1, Year VIII (June 20, 1800), we find her writing to the latter : " I have only time, my dear little brother, to recommend to you the bearer of this letter, to assure you of my tender affection, and to tell you that you have a charming little wife, who behaves admirably. Adieu, my dear little brother ; I embrace you and love you well."

After the victory of Marengo, in which he had "conducted himself with equal bravery and intelligence," Murat returned to Paris, where the Consuls had decreed to him a sabre of honour, " as a very particular proof of the satisfaction of the French people." This distinction, following so closely upon his alliance with Napoleon, seems to have temporarily turned his head, since he began to give himself the most intolerable airs. He administered a severe thrashing to an unfortunate overseer at one of the barriers, who, when he was returning from the execution of some military duty, had dared to demand the usual toll, on the ground that officers when in civilian dress, as Murat happened to be at the time, could not claim exemption. He "flatly declined" the command of the Army of the West, which the First Consul, who wished to give that of the Army of the Reserve, which Murat desired for himself, to Bernadotte, had offered him, and wrote to Joseph, who was at Lunéville, that, if Bernadotte were given the post in question, he would quit the service altogether.[1] Finally, in November 1800, he condescended to accept the post of "lieutenant of the general-in-chief commanding the Army of Italy," and departed for Milan, to the great relief of Napoleon, who had hitherto borne with his vagaries, in recognition of the good understanding which existed between the Murats and his wife.

Caroline, who was enceinte some seven months, did not accompany her husband, but remained in Paris, which was very gay that winter. The salons, which had been so long closed, had begun to reopen, while the theatres had not been so crowded since the beginning of the Revolution. On Nivose 3 (December 24, 1800), a special per-

[1] Letter of Thermidor 14, Year VIII (August 2, 1800). Bernadotte had married Désirée Clary, Joseph's sister-in-law, and Murat suspected Joseph of championing the claims of that officer.

formance of Haydn's "Creation" was to be given
at the Opera; Garat and Madame Barbier-Wal-
bonne were to sing, and the orchestra had been
increased for the occasion to two hundred and
fifty instruments.   It was a treat which no lover
of music cared to miss, and, at the same time,
a unique opportunity for the display of the very
latest triumphs of the *couturière's* art; and,
though Napoleon had been warned by the police
that a conspiracy against his life was on foot, and
that it would be advisable for him not to quit the
Tuileries, the ladies of his family were so in-
sistent, that he decided to attend with his wife,
Hortense, and Caroline.

Accordingly, at eight o'clock in the evening, he
left the Tuileries to drive to the Rue de la Loi
(Rue de Richelieu), accompanied by Bessières
and the aide-de-camp on duty, and escorted by
a picket of the Consular Guard.   The ladies,
attended by General Rapp, followed in another
carriage.   Just as they were on the point of starting, Rapp happened to remark to Joséphine that
her shawl—a magnificent one which she had
lately received from Constantinople and wore that
evening for the first time—was not adjusted with
its customary coquettish elegance, whereupon the
lady begged him to fold it after the fashion of the
Egyptian ladies.   "Be quick, sister," exclaimed
Caroline, who did not wish to lose a note of the
oratorio; "see, Bonaparte is going!" Joséphine,
however, was not to be hurried, and a minute or

two elapsed before the gallant Rapp had succeeded in arranging the shawl to her satisfaction.
Then they set out, but did not succeed in overtak-
ing Napoleon, and were only crossing the Place du
Carrousel as the First Consul's carriage reached
the northern end of the Rue Sainte-Nicaise.

At that moment, Saint-Régent's "infernal
machine," which had been placed in a cart in
the middle of the latter street, exploded with a
deafening roar.   The shock shattered the windows
of both carriages, and Hortense was slightly
wounded in the hand by the falling glass ; but no
further damage was done to the party from the
Tuileries, although more than thirty unhappy
persons in the Rue Sainte-Nicaise were killed
or injured.   But for the slight delay occasioned
by Joséphine's devotion to her toilette, the occu-
pants of the second carriage must inevitably have
shared the fate of these unfortunates.

When the ladies, whose coachman had made a
détour, the Rue Sainte-Nicaise being encumbered
with dead and wounded and the wreckage caused
by the explosion, reached the Opera, they found
Napoleon already seated in his box, lorgnette in
hand, and, to all appearance, as composed as
though nothing had happened.   "Those scoundrels wanted to blow me up," was his only
remark as his relatives entered.   Then, turning
to his aide-de-camp, he said : "Tell them to
bring me a book of the oratorio."[1]

[1] Rapp, *Mémoires*.

I.—16

The future Duchesse d'Abrantès, who was in an adjoining box and in a position to observe all the movements of her distinguished neighbours, has described for us the attitudes of the various members of the party on this memorable evening.

"The First Consul was calm, and, apparently, only warmly affected when the general murmur conveyed to his ear any strong expression of public feeling. Madame Bonaparte was not equally mistress of her feelings. She seemed to tremble, and to be desirous of hiding herself under her shawl—that very shawl which had saved her life. She wept; in spite of all her efforts to restrain her tears, they were seen trickling down her pale cheeks, and, whenever she glanced at the First Consul, she began to tremble again. Her daughter was also much disturbed. As for Madame Murat, she revealed the character of her family; although her condition would have excused a display of distress and emotion, very natural in the sister of the First Consul, she was perfectly self-possessed throughout the whole of that trying evening."

It was a fortunate circumstance for Caroline that her nerves were so well under control, otherwise, in the advanced state of pregnancy in which she then was, a possibly fatal accident must certainly have followed. As matters were, she continued in excellent health, and on the very same day (January 21, 1801) on which her child —a son—was born, we find her writing to inform

CAROLINE BONAPARTE, ABOUT THE TIME OF HER MARRIAGE
FROM A LITHOGRAPH BY DELPECH

her mother-in-law at La Bastide of the happy event.

Paris

1 Pluviose, Year IX

(*January* 21, 1801)

My dear Mamma,

I write to acquaint you with my happy delivery; I am the mother of a fine boy. I do not doubt that this news will give you pleasure, both on my account and on that of my dear Murat, whom he resembles.

I beg you, my dear and kind mamma, to believe that your fond and affectionate daughter entertains for you sentiments of the most tender regard.

Murat, *née* Bonaparte

I have, personally, good news of my husband, who always speaks of you to me in his letters.[1]

Murat, who was tired of garrison life in Milan, and was on very bad terms with the general-in-chief Brune, had been very anxious to return to Paris for his wife's confinement, and begged the First Consul "to recall him to his dear Caroline." Napoleon, however, refused him permission. "A soldier," he wrote, "ought to remain faithful to his wife, but not to want to return to her, whenever he thinks that he has nothing more to do."

Towards the end of January 1801, the Neapolitans having profited by the resumption of hostilities between France and Austria to march on Ancona, Murat was ordered to occupy

---

[1] Count Alberto Lumbroso, *Correspondance de Joachim Murat*.

Tuscany and advance against them ; but, on the conclusion of the new armistice with the Austrians, Napoleon countermanded the latter order. Nevertheless, Murat advanced into the Pontifical States, and demanded a bribe of 100,000 crowns (500,000 francs) to withdraw his troops. "After having vainly represented to him our poverty," wrote Cardinal Consalvi, "we yielded. . . . We also made him a present of a beautiful cameo worth 200 sequins (about 2,300 francs) to wear on the bosom, which appeared to please him much, and which he at once sent to his wife, who has lately been confined."[1]

The success of his raid so pleased Murat that he decided to pay his Holiness a personal visit, and, on February 22, arrived in Rome, with six of his officers, where he was "lodged and nobly entertained at the Palazzo Sciarra, at the expense of the Apostolic Chamber." The unfortunate pontiff "overwhelmed him with civilities and presents," which latter included a portrait of himself, "a red antique casket," another valuable cameo, and a painting by Raphael. After which, it is distinctly amusing to find Murat naïvely assuring the First Consul that Pius VII was "a worthy man, and that, if they must have a Pope, he was the one suited to the circumstances."[2]

[1] Despatch of February 21, 1801, published by M. Frédéric Masson, *Napoléon et sa famille.*
[2] Count Alberto Lumbroso, *Correspondance de Joachim Murat.*

From Rome, Murat returned to Florence where he had fixed his headquarters, and again solicited permission from Napoleon to return to Paris to see his wife and little son, who had received the names of Napoleon Achille Louis Charles, declaring that "only a father could understand how necessary such a reunion was to his happiness." It is also probable that he desired to place the hundred thousand crowns which he had wrung from the Vatican and other "savings" in safe keeping, but he naturally said nothing about this in his despatches. As, however, Naples had not been included in the peace recently signed at Lunéville, and negotiations with that kingdom were still in progress, Napoleon ordered him to remain at Florence; but, by way of consolation, gave Caroline permission to join him.

Caroline and the little Achille reached Florence on May 6, and Murat wrote to his mother that their arrival had made him the "happiest of men." It is doubtful if his wife, who was beginning to show herself a trifle exacting in her requirements, altogether shared his satisfaction, since, after spending two or three weeks at Florence, she betook herself to the baths at Pisa, and, a fortnight after her return from that city, started off on a visit to Venice.

At the end of July, Murat, to the great satisfaction of himself and Caroline, was appointed general-in-chief of the French troops in Italy,

which necessitated the transfer of his headquarters to Milan. Before leaving Florence,
however, it was his duty to install there the new
"ruler" of Tuscany, the Infant of Parma, who,
as some compensation for his humiliating position, as vassal of the French Republic, had been
permitted to take the title of king, and called
himself King of Etruria, in order to give a
flavour of antiquity to his crown.

This event did not pass off without a very
untoward incident. On the evening before the
Murats departed from Milan, they and the principal officers of the general's staff were invited
to dine at the Court. Caroline was, of course,
placed at the King's right hand, while it was
intended that her husband should occupy a
similar position next the Queen. Unfortunately,
when the party took their seats at table, Murat
happened to be engaged in an earnest conversation with one of his officers in the embrasure
of a window, and Mgr. Caleppi, the Papal Nuncio
at the Etrurian Court, seeing the place at the
Queen's right hand vacant, and believing that it
was reserved for him, took it, with the result that
the general-in-chief had to content himself with
a seat lower down the table. His wrath was extreme, for he was under the impression that the
Nuncio had possessed himself of the coveted
place at the Queen's invitation, and "he had
need to summon to his aid all his powers of self-
restraint to avoid committing some ill-advised

action."[1] As for the French officers, "their countenances revealed their indignation," and, to mark their displeasure at the slight which had been put upon their chief, they one and all refused every dish that was handed to them, and, so soon as the company rose from table, took their departure in a body and went to order dinner at a neighbouring inn. Caleppi subsequently apologised most profusely to the general, but "though they parted the best of friends in the world, at least in appearance," the latter's wrath was not to be so easily appeased, and he revenged himself for this quite unintentional slight by levying in the harshest manner possible the contributions he had been ordered to exact from the Etrurian Government.

About the middle of October, Caroline, who was growing tired of Italy—and perhaps a little of her husband as well—made the circumstance that she was again enceinte a pretext for returning to Paris. Murat begged permission to accompany her, promising that he would only remain a week in the capital; but his inexorable brother-in-law would only allow him to see his wife safely over the Alps. However, some weeks later, tranquillity having been re-established in Italy, Napoleon relented and granted him a three months' furlough; and, at the beginning

---

[1] Despatch of Murat to the First Consul, Thermidor 28, Year IX (August 16, 1801) in Lumbroso, *Correspondance de Joachim Murat*.

of December, Murat found himself again in Paris.

Here he proceeded, like a wise man, to invest the profits of his brigandage in Italy in real estate. On December 15, he acquired, for 470,000 francs, the fine estate belonging to the Corvoisin family at La Motte-Sainte-Heraye, in the Deux-Sèvres, with an annual rent-roll of 32,000 francs. A month later (January 12, 1801), he bought the magnificent Hôtel Thélusson, occupying the space between the Rue de la Victoire and the Rue Saint-Honoré, which had been built, in 1780, for Georges Thélusson, the elder of the two banker brothers of that name.   For this hôtel, of which we shall have something to say presently, he paid 500,000 francs, the exact sum which he had extorted the previous year from the Papal Treasury.   Had the wits of Paris been aware of this little episode, they would doubtless have renamed the building the " Hôtel de Rome," just as they had christened the mansion which the Duc de Richelieu erected out of the profits of the Hanoverian campaign of 1757 the " Pavillon de Hanovre."   Finally, on the following March 12, he purchased, for 153,362 francs, the remaining portion of Madame de Bullion's estate at Villiers.

Thus, in three months, on these properties alone, exclusive of the cost of furnishing and improvements, Murat, who, at the time of his marriage, could not, at the most liberal calculation, have been worth more than 100,000 francs, spent no less a sum than 1,200,000 francs. Assuredly, the hardships and dangers of a soldier's life were not without their compensations in those days!

Before returning to Milan, which he did with an annual salary of 40,000 francs as general-in-chief, and 30,000 francs a *month* for extraordinary expenses, Murat took advantage of the ecclesiastical marriage between Louis Bonaparte and Hortense de Beauharnais (January 4, 1802) to obtain the blessing of the Church on his own union with Caroline.

CHAPTER XIII

WHEN, on February 19, 1800, Napoleon
took up his residence at the Tuileries,
he pressed his mother to join him there,
and offered to place a handsome suite of apartments at her disposal. Madame Bonaparte however declined, preferring to remain in her old
quarters in the Rue du Rocher, with Joseph and
his worthy Julie, to whom she was sincerely
attached. At the Tuileries, she felt, it would be

difficult for her to avoid more or less frequent intercourse with Joséphine, while the luxury and splendour of that ancient home of kings accorded but ill with her simple tastes.

Letizia, indeed, viewed the elevation of her son with very mixed feelings, and was far from sharing the illusion of several members of the family as to the prodigious destiny of Napoleon. She was convinced that a brilliant future awaited him; but she also had a strong presentiment that his triumphs would not endure, and that the higher he rose, the greater would be his fall. Her children and the intimate friends to whom she confided her apprehensions made light of them; but time was to prove how abundantly they were justified.

Moreover she thought with regret of the past, of the old home in her beloved Corsica, of the friends and relatives from whom she was separated, of the days when she was at liberty to spend her time as she pleased. But she had money in abundance, and that was an infinite consolation. What allowance Napoleon made her during the first three years of the Consulate is not known, but it is certain that large sums passed through her hands, while in 1803, he fixed her annual allowance at 120,000 francs, double the amount which he gave his sisters. In addition, Lucien, on his return from his embassy in Spain, in the spring of 1802, during which he had contrived to feather his nest very warmly indeed, made a settlement upon her which added another 24,000 francs to her income.[1]

Her savings, which were very considerable, for her simple habits had survived the elevation of her family, and she was perpetually haunted by the idea that the evil days through which she and her children had passed would one day return, were invested in almost every country in Europe, in order, apparently, that she might find a sort of treasury wherever her destiny might lead her. About these investments she preserved an extraordinary reticence, even preferring to lose them rather than to confess to having made them. Thus, it was only by accident that, in the spring of 1803, the French Ambassador at Naples ascertained that, several years before, Madame Bonaparte had been robbed of a sum of 50,000 francs by a banker of that city named Forquet, to whom she had entrusted the money. Although the Neapolitan Government was then engaged in indemnifying French subjects for the losses they had sustained during the recent war, and would certainly not have hesitated a moment about reimbursing the mother of the First Consul, Letizia had made no claim nor even mentioned her loss to Napoleon; and it was the Ambassador himself who brought the matter to his notice.[2]

[1] In May, 1804, Letizia's allowance was raised to 180,000 francs; in the following September, to 300,000; in 1806, to 480,000; and, finally, in 1808, to 1,000,000.

[2] M. Frédéric Masson, *Napoleon et sa famille.*

Parsimonious herself and caring nothing for the pleasures of society, she was shocked at the extravagance in which her daughters indulged and did not hesitate to reprove them sharply, although her remonstrances fell upon unheeding ears. On one occasion, having been invited by the Leclercs to spend a week at their country-house, she arrived there with only a single gown, and that of very common material. Pauline ventured to remark upon the scantiness of the maternal wardrobe, upon which Letizia retorted angrily : " Be silent, extravagant child! I must save money for your brothers, all of whom are not yet provided for. You are young enough to think of nothing but pleasure ; but at my age we think of more serious matters, and I will not allow Bonaparte to complain that we have devoured all his substance. You abuse his goodness."[1]

When, in August 1800, Joseph sold his house in the Rue du Rocher, which he found too modest for his requirements, and removed to the magnificent Hôtel Marbeuf, in the Faubourg Saint-Honoré, which had formerly belonged to the Marquis de Marbeuf, nephew of the military commandant of Corsica, Letizia did not accompany him, but took up her quarters with her brother Joseph Fesch, who had profited so well by the post Napoleon had obtained for him in the Army of Italy, that he had lately purchased a house in the Rue du Mont-Blanc. Of this house

[1] Madame Ducrest, *Mémoires*.

Madame Bonaparte furnished a part at her own expense.

Letizia went but little into society and seldom visited the Tuileries or Malmaison, for she was exceedingly tenacious of her dignity, and considered that her pre-eminence in the family was compromised by the necessity of yielding precedence to Joséphine on official occasions.[1] The latter, who was aware of her mother-in-law's sentiments towards her, took infinite precautions to avoid any unpleasantness arising in the presence of Napoleon, and, by treating her with the utmost deference, generally succeeded in preserving in their relations at least the appearance of harmony. Now and again, however, circumstances were too strong for her, and the hatred which the elder woman had so long cherished against the "interloper" manifested itself in a peculiarly unpleasant manner.

When, at the end of October 1800, Fouché revealed to the First Consul the indiscretions of Lucien at the Ministry of the Interior,[2] with the

---

[1] At family gatherings, both Letizia and Madame Joseph Bonaparte, as the wife of the nominal head of the family, took precedence of Joséphine.

[2] The chief of these was, of course, the publication of that audacious brochure, *Parallèle entre Cesar, Cromwell, et Bonaparte*, written and officially circulated by the Ministry of the Interior, with the object of preparing the public mind for the establishment of a new dynasty. Lucien denied having written the *Parallèle*, asserting that it had been drawn up by his friend Fontanes, and that the latter had exceeded his instructions ; but the flamboyant style betrayed the author.

result that that too enterprising statesman was
promptly removed from his office and sent into a
sort of disguised exile as Ambassador to Madrid,
there was a painful scene at the Tuileries.   Letizia,
ordinarily so calm and self-possessed, never could
control her feelings when any of her children
were attacked, and on learning of the disgrace of
her dear Lucien, whom she loved even more than
Napoleon, probably on account of his close resemblance, in both appearance and character, to
his father, her anger passed all bounds.

Hastening to the palace, where she found the
First Consul with his wife, she accused Fouché of
having invented the charges against Lucien, and
demanded justice on the wretch who had dared
to slander her son.   Then, turning like a tigress
upon Joséphine, she reproached her bitterly with
her protection of the Minister of Police, and
declared that she was in his pay—an accusation
which was, of course, perfectly true.   Joséphine,
as usual, took refuge in tears, which only caused
Letizia to redouble her reproaches, and Napoleon
was obliged to interfere to protect his wife and
impose silence on his mother.

Lucien himself tells us that, as Letizia was
leaving, she bade Joséphine warn "her friend
Fouché" that she believed that her arm was long
enough to make any man rue the day when he
calumniated her sons.   Whereupon, the First
Consul remarked that it was very evident that
his mother did not read the English newspapers,

in which she would find calumnies enough and
to spare, not only about Lucien, but concerning
himself and every member of the family. " That
is possible," rejoined Letizia, " but I am powerless against the English ; with regard to Citizen
Fouché, that is another matter." [1]

During Lucien's absence at Madrid, his sympathetic mother wrote to him every day, to
console him in his exile.   Here is one of her
letters :

Paris

27 Nivose, Year IX

(*January* 17, 1801)

I have received thy two letters, my dear son,
which have given me the pleasure of knowing
that thou art well and contented ; that makes me
happy. But thy absence is painful for me, though
I find consolation in thinking of thy return :
of the moment when I shall have the satisfaction
of clasping thee in my arms, with the little
Christine.[2]

Lolotte [3] is well and happy.   I shall be able
to tell thee that my portrait [by Isabey] is
finished, I hope, in two days' time, and I am
having a full-length one painted for thee to place
in thy house in Paris ; but it is not yet finished.
All the family are well.   Louis has been ill, but
he is now better,[4] and in a few days he will set

---

[1] Th. Jung, *Lucien Bonaparte et ses Mémoires.*

[2] Christine Egypta Bonaparte, Lucien's younger daughter. She
had accompanied her father to Madrid.

[3] Charlotte Bonaparte, Lucien's elder daughter. She was at
this time a pupil at Madame Campan's.

[4] Louis had left Paris in the previous October, with the

out on his return to Paris. Jérôme has already
gone to sea, but he has not yet written.[1] Thou
canst conceive how uneasy I am at seeing all my
children scattered; I am unwilling to say more
to thee about it.

Adieu, dear Lucien; I embrace thee and the
little Christine. Continue to send me the news.
A thousand greetings to Baciocchi,[2] to whom I
will write. I do not tell thee anything about
Élisa; she is going to write to thee. She is the
only one whom I see every day.

Adieu once more. I am,

Thy affectionate mother,

L. Bonaparte [3]

Although Madame Bonaparte took no part in
politics, she was indefatigable in urging upon the
Government the claims of her countrymen. If
her children, in the midst of their new grandeur,
were tempted to forget their native land, she, at
least, remained faithful to the past, and whoever
came from Corsica to France in the hope of
obtaining some lucrative post, was sure to find in

intention of making a tour through Saxony, Prussia, Poland,
Sweden, and Denmark. After visiting Berlin, where he was
received almost as though he were a foreign prince, by the Prussian
Court, and Dresden, he fell ill at Danzig, and was compelled to
remain there several weeks. He returned to Paris at the end
of January 1801.

[1] At the end of November 1800, Jérôme had been sent into the
Navy, with strict injunctions from the First Consul to Admiral
Gantheaume, upon whose flagship he served, "to make him work."

[2] Baciocchi had accompanied Lucien to Madrid as Second
Secretary to the French Embassy.

[3] Published by Baron Larrey, *Madame Mère.*

the mother of the First Consul a zealous patroness—always provided, of course, that he
belonged to her own faction, for, like all Corsicans, she was terribly vindictive, and never
forgave the Paolists their treatment of her in
1793. Could she have had her way, Napoleon
would have summoned the whole needy Bonaparte clan to France, even unto cousins of the
third and fourth degree, and provided for them
handsomely. But, since he very sensibly refused
to do anything of the kind, she devoted her
energies to furthering the interests of as many of
her relatives and friends as possible, and persecuted the Ministers with applications on their
behalf, couched in an almost imperative tone.
" Permit me, Citizen Minister," she writes to
Decrès, the Minister of Marine, " to recommend
to you the complaint which the Comte Vincent
Bastelica is addressing to you. . . . You will
oblige me by doing justice to his complaint, and
by acquainting me with the decision at which you
arrive."[1]

In June 1801, Madame Bonaparte accompanied
Joséphine, with whom, in order to please Napoleon, she had consented to a nominal reconciliation,
to Plombières. She did not, however, remain
longer with her daughter-in-law than she could
help, for she appears to have spent the greater
part of the summer at Vichy. During her stay

---

[1] Letter of 23 Brumaire, Year X (November 14, 1801), published by Larrey.

at Plombières, Joséphine had overwhelmed her
mother-in-law with delicate little attentions and
endeavoured to humour her in every possible
way. The motive of this was revealed to Letizia,
soon after her return to Paris, when she was
asked to give her consent to the marriage of
Louis Bonaparte and Hortense de Beauharnais.
Letizia, "who saw in this union the triumph of a
strange family over her own," was bitterly opposed to it, as were Joseph, Lucien, Élisa, and
Pauline. But Napoleon had been completely
won over by Joséphine, and Louis, who was, or
believed himself to be, in love, was proof against
all the arguments of his relatives;[1] and, on
January 4, 1802, the singularly ill-assorted couple
were made one.

Élisa, as we have mentioned, had, soon after
the establishment of the Consulate, obtained for
Baciocchi an appointment as adjutant-general in
the 16th Division, quartered in the neighbourhood
of Paris, which permitted her husband and herself to take up their residence in the capital.
The exact date of their arrival is uncertain, but
it would appear to have been either in December
1799 or early in January 1800.[2]

---

[1] Even against the shameful calumnies regarding Napoleon's
relations with Hortense, with which Lucien did not hesitate to
acquaint his brother.

[2] Élisa was still at Marseilles on November 25, 1799, as under
that date we find her writing a letter of recommendation on behalf
of a *protégé* of hers to the Minister for War ; while on January 18

The Baciocchi did not take a house of their own, but went to live at Lucien's hôtel, in the Rue Verte, which he had lately quitted for the Hôtel de Brissac, in the Rue de Grenelle, the official residence of the Minister of the Interior. Madame Lucien was then enceinte and also in very bad health, and the Minister begged his sister, to whom he was greatly attached, to relieve his wife of some of the duties which her new position entailed upon her, and which were altogether too much for her strength. Élisa accordingly presided at most of the official receptions at the Hôtel de Brissac, and, amongst other functions, at the dinner which Lucien gave to the First Consul, who had expressed a wish to meet the famous beauty Madame Récamier, and of which that lady's niece, Madame Lenormant, has left us such an entertaining account.[1]

If Élisa had chafed during her sojourn at Ajaccio and Marseilles at her exclusion from the gaieties of Paris, she certainly did her best to make up for lost time. She was a constant visitor at Madame Récamier's receptions at her beautiful hôtel in the Rue du Mont Blanc, and at her country-house at Clichy. She was an enthusiastic patroness of the drama, and never missed a play

of the following year, she and her husband witnessed the marriage contract of Caroline Bonaparte and Murat, at the Luxembourg Therefore, their migration to Paris must have taken place some time between those dates.

[1] See Madame Lenormant, *Souvenirs et Correspondance d'Madame Récamier.*

at the Théâtre Feydeau.   She attended the subscription balls at the Maison de Salm, Rue de
Lille, and the Hôtel d'Uzès, Rue Montmartre,
which were largely patronised by fashionable
society, notwithstanding the very mixed company
which was to be found at entertainments where
a citizen with a citizeness on either arm could
obtain admission for the sum of nine francs, and
where "any costume was admissible, so long as
decency was observed."   She drove to Long-
champs, as fashion dictated, in cabriolet or *wiski*,
drawn by mettlesome steeds which she guided
herself, and she rode in the Bois de Boulogne,
"in a riding habit of red cashmere, the corsage
decorated with three rows of buttons, and lined
with crimson Florence taffeta."[1]

On May 14, 1800, Lucien Bonaparte, to his
intense grief, lost his much-loved wife Christine,
the gentle, sweet-faced peasant girl, who had long
since succeeded in winning the hearts of all her
husband's family.

"I was left with two little girls," writes Lucién,
in his *Mémoires;* "my sister Élisa (Madame
Baciocchi) was filling the place of their mother at
the moment of the catastrophe, and came to
rejoin me at Plessis.

"It is to my two little girls and to this sister,
then tenderly beloved, that I am indebted for my
first consolations in so cruel a loss.   We wept

[1] M. Paul Marmottan, *Élisa Bonaparte;* M. Henri Bouchot,
le Luxe français sous l'Empire.

together over the tomb which I had caused to be raised to Christine in a remote and enclosed part of my park.[1]   Élisa was almost as assiduous as myself in tending the funereal garden of her whom I so much loved, and who so well merited it.

"Christine, who expired in my arms and in those of our sister Élisa, ought to have at least carried away the hope that her two little girls, Charlotte and Egypta, would find another mother. Sacred promise made and kept by Élisa for four years."[2]

Lucien's grief at the loss of his wife was such that, had he been allowed to consult his own inclinations, he would have closed the salons of the Hôtel de Brissac for an indefinite period. But to this Napoleon would not consent, and in consequence, so soon as decency would permit, he began to entertain again, and Élisa passed much of her time in doing the honours of the house to the distinguished company which attended her brother's receptions.   The duties of the Minister of the Interior included the supervision and encouragement of public instruction, the Fine Arts, and the Drama, and Lucien, with his strong literary and artistic tastes, was certainly well qualified for the post.   Élisa, who aspired

---

[1] The tomb was of marble and bronze, and was always kept covered with beautiful flowers, until the re-establishment of the Catholic religion, when the body was removed to the church of Plessis-Chamant.

[2] Th. Jung, *Lucien Bonaparte et ses Mémoires.*

to play the *rôle* which Madame de Rambouillet and Madame de Sablé had played in the seventeenth century, and Madame Geoffrin and Madame du Deffand in the eighteenth, was in her element in the midst of the artists and literati who thronged the Minister's salons. She discussed poetry with Arnault and Esménard, fiction with Chateaubriand, political economy with Duquesnoy, the drama with Legouvé and Picard —the future Molière of the Empire—architecture with Poyet, and painting with David, Gros, and Isabey; and though some of these celebrated personages must have been considerably amused at her pretensions to knowledge, they were careful not to allow her to perceive it, and appear to have flattered her egregiously. The sister of the Minister of the Interior and the First Consul was a lady whose favour meant pensions and places for the writers and lucrative commissions for the painters and architects; and such desirable things are cheaply purchased at the expense of a little straining of one's conscience.

Madame Baciocchi was so enamoured of the *rôle* she had assumed, that, when Lucien was not receiving, she held literary receptions of her own. "Élisa's house," writes Leclerc to Lucien, on February 22, 1801, "is a tribunal to which authors come to be judged"; and these functions soon became so inconveniently crowded, though for reasons, we fear, very remotely connected with the love of literature, that one day, on the advice of Arnault, the hostess resolved to show herself more exclusive, and erased from her visiting list all the less distinguished of her flatterers.

Presently, Élisa thought she would like to found a ladies' literary society, with herself as president. The fashionable world, which always lends itself so readily to the whims of its leaders, embraced the idea with enthusiasm, and applications for admission were so numerous that one would have imagined that the ladies of Paris were hungering and thirsting after knowledge. The first meeting, at which the principal business under consideration was the all-important question of the costume to be worn by the members, was held on the same day on which the marriage of Junot and Laure Permon took place, and, at its conclusion, Élisa drove to the wedding-dinner at Madame Permon's house in the Rue Sainte-Croix. Here her appearance aroused almost as much sensation as had Pauline's on the occasion of the ball of which we have spoken in a previous chapter, although the feelings which predominated were those of bewilderment and amusement rather than of admiration. "Madame Baciocchi," wrote the bride of that day, many years later, "was attired with a degree of eccentricity which is even now fresh in my mind. She had presided that morning over a ladies' literary society ; and, since she proposed to establish a distinguishing costume for the associates, she decided that the best way to carry out her intentions was to have

ÉLISA BONAPARTE

a model made, and appear in it herself; and in this costume she afterwards came to my mother's house. Her head-dress consisted of a muslin veil embroidered with different-coloured silks and gold thread, twisted round her head, while a wreath of laurel in the fashion of Petrarch and Dante was perched on top of it. She wore a very long tunic, and below it a skirt with a half-train; very short, or, I think, no sleeves, and an immense shawl, arranged in the manner of a cloak. Her toilette was a medley of the Jewish, Greek, Roman—of everything, in short, except French good taste. To see Madame Baciocchi thus attired was not surprising, since we were accustomed to her eccentricities; but it was impossible to resist the ludicrous impression she created by announcing her intention of offering such a dress to the adoption of all good Christians."[1]

Élisa was as much discomfited at what Lucien called his "brilliant disgrace," in November 1801, as their common enemies Joséphine and Hortense were overjoyed, and her chagrin was probably the keener, inasmuch as she seems to have encouraged her brother in the indiscretions which had led to his removal from the Interior and his banishment to Madrid. For, though she had not the smallest talent for political intrigue, she had already developed a decided taste for it. Stanislas de Girardin has sketched for us, in his *Mémoires*,

[1] Duchesse d'Abrantès, *Mémoires*.

the scene which took place in Joséphine's salon at the Tuileries on the evening before Lucien's departure for Spain.

In one corner, a game of *réversi* is going on. The wife of the First Consul reclines gracefully in a large arm-chair by the fire, concealing her satisfaction beneath an air of meditation. Hortense, far less experienced in the art of dissimulating her feelings than her mother, sits opposite, quite unable to disguise the joy which the approaching departure of their implacable foe occasions her. Élisa, seated alone, some distance off, heroically struggling with the tears that rise to her eyes. The other ladies almost silent, but exchanging eloquent glances. Generals, prefects, Councillors of State, coming and going with an abstracted air. Élisa beckons Girardin to her side, and, "in a voice which proves that she is an affectionate friend, that she has wept all the evening, all the day, and that she is even then on the point of bursting into tears," pours her troubles into his sympathetic ear : "The day before yesterday, I returned from Plessis with Lucien. On our arrival, he left me to go to the Tuileries, and an hour later he informed me of his approaching departure and of that of my husband. All those whom I love are leaving me. Judge of my grief! . . . I know not how to hide my sorrow, and I feel ready to weep. . . ." Then she rises, hoping to leave the room unperceived ; but Joséphine, who had not lost sight of her, leaves her arm-chair, approaches, and, with an admirable assumption of sympathy, presses her hand and embraces her."[1]

However, the tears of Élisa were less the outcome of regret on Lucien's account than of anger and humiliation on her own. The thought that the detested Beauharnais had triumphed over her, and that she would no longer be able to play the queen in the salons of the Hôtel de Brissac, was indeed bitter. It would have been easy enough for her, as her sympathetic biographer, M. Marmottan, is fain to admit, to put an end to her grief by accompanying her brother and husband, whom Lucien had appointed as his Second Secretary, into exile, but she preferred to remain in Paris. Madrid offered but little inducement for her to expatriate herself, for she could hardly expect to find there the consideration which, as sister of the First Consul, she enjoyed in Paris; besides which, she was ignorant of the language, the customs, and the rigid etiquette of Spain, and feared, also, that the climate might be unsuited to her health, which was far from robust. She believed, too, that it was advisable for her to remain near Napoleon, in order to counteract the influence of the Beauharnais and to further her own and her husband's fortunes, for she was extremely dissatisfied with what had been done for Baciocchi, although it was quite as much as that complaisant nonentity deserved. Again,

[1] Stanislas de Girardin, *Mémoires.*

Lucien's elder daughter, Charlotte, or Lolotte, whom he had decided to leave in Paris, needed supervision, until arrangements could be made for her to go to Madame Campan's.

But, perhaps, the chief motive which detained her in France was the connection which she had formed with the poet Fontanes, the future President of the Corps Législatif, and the future Grand Master of the University of Paris. Élisa took the keenest pleasure in the society of Fontanes. He was ready to discuss with her politics, literature, art, in short, every subject under heaven; and he was so sympathetic a listener, he flattered her vanity so adroitly, that he made her feel that she must really be a most accomplished young woman.

M. Marmottan defends Élisa energetically from "certain authors little scrupulous, who assert that Fontanes was her lover." According to him, there was nothing between them but intellectual sympathy—"he [Fontanes] loved certainly but as a dreamer, a philosopher, nothing more." This, however, does not seem to be the opinion of M. Arthur Lévy, M. Masson, and M. Turquan. True, Fontanes's appearance was scarcely calculated to inspire a *grande passion;* he was a little fat man, with a round head and somewhat brusque manners, though his fine eyes and very white teeth redeemed him from being altogether commonplace. Moreover, as M. Marmottan is careful to point out, he was twenty

years older than the lady,[1] and possessed a wife,
whose friendly relations with Élisa he regards as
a convincing proof of the innocence of the latter's
relations with her husband.

But Providence has endowed women with
treasures of indulgence for plain men, while the
attentions of distinguished middle-age are frequently very soothing to the vanity of youth. As
for the wife, well, Madame Fontanes would not
have been the first woman to sacrifice her sentiments to her husband's and her own interests.

And whatever may have been the nature of
the relations between the poet and "his amiable
and excellent friend," it must be confessed that
the former exploited the protection of the First
Consul's eldest sister to most excellent purpose. It
was to her that he owed all that he became : deputy,
President of the Corps Législatif, with an additional salary of 60,000 francs a year, Grand Master
of the University, Count of the Empire, senator,
and the rest. These things were certainly worth
a little complaisance on the part of his consort.

During Lucien's absence in Spain, Élisa seems
to have maintained an active correspondence with
him :

Paris

4 Pluviose

(*January* 24, 1801)

Caroline was confined on Pluviose 1, in the
morning ; both she and her child are doing very

---

[1] He was born on March 6, 1757.

well. Bonaparte is the godfather, and Mlle.
Hortense, the godmother. The big boy is named
Achille. . . . I have heard from Joseph.[1] There
is no news, except the armistice of the Army of
Italy. . . . I kept Lolotte with me two days, and
made her go and see her little cousin. She is
beginning to play the piano; I am very satisfied
with the care that Madame Campan is taking of
her. My little one [Lolotte], whose portrait I
will send thee by the first courier, embraces thee;
Lili,[2] also, whom she does not forget. Paulette
amuses herself; she is going to the ball. Murat
is marching on Naples; Leclerc is at Dijon.
Mamma is having her portrait painted by Isabey;
I have given him 2,000 francs for the three portraits.

Adieu, my good friend; I spend nearly all my
time with Caroline. I have formed for myself a
very agreeable society and have cultivated the
pleasant acquaintances I made at the Ministry
(of the Interior); I gather them together occasionally. May you be happy at Madrid. Can
you forget us? No, I do not think so. I like to
believe that thou lovest me well. . . .

Embrace Baciocchi, and a thousand times the
little Christinette.

Toute à toi. Élisa

Paris

27 Pluviose

(*February* 11, 1801)

I have received, my dear Lucien, thy severe
letter. Thy courier did not come to me until

---

[1] Joseph had gone to Lunéville, as one of the French pleni-
potentiaries.

[2] Her younger sister, Christine Bonaparte.

twenty-four hours after his arrival. I have sharply reprimanded him. I wish that thou wouldst give him orders to come at once to the house. . . . Lolotte is very well, and is beginning to write. I am sending thee her portrait and my own ;[1] I have had it made oval, in order that it may not inconvenience thee, if thou dost carry it about. Do what pleases thee with Baciocchi, if thou dost think that it will be more advantageous for him to accompany the Prince of the Peace.[2] I am quite willing, provided that it will further his advancement, and, what is of more account, that he does thee credit. . . . If peace is made, thou wilt send him to bring the news ; perhaps, when thou dost return, he will be able to find employment in Diplomacy, in which he is improving under so good a master. If thou wert in Paris, thou wouldst go to Russia. It is said that Berthier will go ; . . . Talleyrand wishes to buy the *Mercure;* I trust that thou wilt keep it. It does thee honour, and every day there are new subscribers. Do not surrender it, I beg thee.[3]

It has been so cold for the last week, that I have not been able to go and embrace Lolotte. I have received news of her from Madame Campan, who writes to me frequently. She is very amiable, for she loves my Lolotte. I desire, my dear Lucien, to occupy the first place in thy heart, after thy beloved children. . . . Speak to

---

[1] According to M. Marmottan, this miniature by Isabey is the first known portrait of Élisa.

[2] Godoi, the Spanish Prime Minister.

[3] This famous review had been revived in the previous summer, when Lucien Bonaparte became its proprietor. It now appeared fortnightly, and the subscription was 36 francs a year.

them sometimes of me. So soon as the fine weather comes, I shall go to Plessis to spend two months, to put everything in order, to tend the flowers . . . and to continue my journal, which I have temporarily abandoned. Life in Paris is very monotonous; every day the same thing. I see few people; the play is my only pleasure, and I sometimes have a gathering of my friends, who are few in number, for I like to choose them carefully. . . . Nisas[1] has written another tragedy, *Pierre-le-Grand*. I made Lafon read it, for Nisas reads very badly. There are some fine things in it. . . . I hope that it will succeed.[2] M. de Boufflers desires to be remembered to you, also Fontanes and Rœderer. Thy sister and best friend,

Élisa

28 Ventôse

(*March* 19, 1801)

Le Blanc [the courier of the French Embassy at Madrid] came to wake me at 5 o'clock in the morning,[3] and, all joyous, I opened thy packet, to find only reproaches. I confess to thee, my dear Lucien, that I could not refrain from shedding tears on reading thy letter. Could you imagine that I prefer anything to the pleasure of writing to thee? I should not have believed that I deserved thy reproaches.

. . . Thou hast no need to recommend me to

---

[1] Marie Henri François Élisabeth de Carrion-Nisas (1771–1841), soldier, playwright, politician, and military writer.

[2] It was a complete failure, and was mercilessly hissed by the *parterre*, though it would appear to have been not without merit.

[3] Evidently, the "severe reprimand" Élisa had administered to the courier, on the occasion of his last journey to Paris, had not been without its effect.

be with my family. I do not spend a day without seeing mamma. . . . I believe that, after
thee, it is myself whom she loves the most. I
often see Joseph, to whom I am much attached,
like all the rest of the family. I do not see any
other company. Once a month, I go to pass
half an hour with Juliette [Madame Récamier],
and my relations with her are confined to this act
of courtesy, which she returns a hundredfold. I
am going into the country, and, on my return,
I will not see her, if it causes thee pain.[1]

My only pleasure is the play. There is no one
who knows less pleasure than myself. I retire to
rest early; I do not dance, and I am acquainted
with very few people.

Adieu, my friend, return soon; then I shall call
myself, with just title, most happy.

Toute à toi.
                                              Élisa

2 Germinal
(*March* 23, 1801)

Le Blanc has not yet left; he is much distressed by the delay, as you allowed him only
fourteen days, and they have done nothing to
hasten his departure.

Berthier gave a superb fête yesterday; there

---

[1] In the previous autumn, the recently-widowed Lucien had
conceived a violent passion for Madame Récamier, and had
addressed to her, under the *nom-de-guerre* of Romeo, presumably
because the lady's name was Juliette, *billets-doux* couched in the
most grandiloquent language. At first, the fair Juliette laughed at
her admirer and advised him "not to waste in imagination the
time which he might more profitably devote to politics"; but
when the epistles became less ambiguous, she took offence and
complained to her husband. Hence, her relations with Lucien
were just now decidedly strained. For a further account of this
affair, see the author's *Madame Récamier and Her Friends*.

were 2,000 people present; it was very well
arranged.   There was a play suitable to the circumstances, which was performed by actors from
different theatres, but which was rather adversely
criticised.   A Russian dance by Mlles. Chevigni
and Goyon.   The minuet of Paris danced by
Vestris and Gardel.   A supper of three hundred
covers, and after supper a grand ball.   You are
doubtless astonished at Berthier being able to
accommodate 2,000 persons.   He has had a
large gallery built, the counterpart of that of the
Ministry (of War) ; it was decorated very simply.
The columns were formed of cannons, and on
each cannon was the name of a battle.   Dancing
was kept up until nine o'clock in the morning.
Half an hour after midnight, I went to bed,
which is very reasonable.   I do not find more
pleasure in these gatherings.   When wilt thou
return?   Then I shall resume all my gaieties.
Napoleon has gone to Malmaison; he is going to
stay there two months, according to what he says;
I doubt if he will keep to this intention. . . .
Joseph is going to Mortefontaine.   Every one is
in the country, and I myself am going to Plessis
to await thee.

    . . . Madame Campan has written me that
Lolotte was very obedient and that she was playing
the piano.   She embraces thee.   A thousand kisses
to my Lili, whom I love tenderly.   How I long
to see her again!   I have been advised to go to
Plombières, to take the waters.   I cannot make
up my mind to do so.   I should die of mortification, if thou wert to arrive in Paris during
my absence.   I shall await thy return before
deciding.

    Embrace Baciocchi.   I doubt not that his

affection for thee remains always the same. I am exceedingly anxious that, if war breaks out,[1] he should distinguish himself and make people talk about him. I know not what demon of glory troubles me, but I assure thee that all my ambition is confined to that which he has learned to understand. Thousands upon thousands of kisses. Thy best friend

Élisa[2]

Although, during the absence of Lucien and her husband, Élisa went but little into society, she appears to have enjoyed a good deal of the company of her friend Fontanes. "I lead a very retired life," writes that gentleman to Lucien, "and do not leave my house, except to go and talk with her whom you love best. Do not go and imagine that she is one of the thousand Arianes whom your absence makes. She is better than that; she has a soul and a mind like yours. My books, the Rue Verte, and Madrid occupy all my thoughts. Madame Baciocchi can tell you if I am tenderly attached to you. She has the kindness to receive me occasionally; she loves to hear me talk about her brother."

And, in another letter, in reference to Madame Fontanes's approaching confinement, he writes: "If I have a son, he will have your genius; if it

---

[1] Between Spain, assisted by French troops under Gouvion Saint-Cyr, and Portugal. See p. 283 *infra*.

[2] These letters are in the possession of the Baciocchi-Bonaparte family, and have been published by M. Paul Marmottan, in his *Élisa Bonaparte*.

is a daughter, she will have the graces of your sister."[1]

Certainly, M. de Fontanes had a very pretty gift for flattery!

At the beginning of the following autumn, Élisa, whose health, for some time past, had been far from satisfactory, became much worse. She suffered from an acute form of indigestion, and, as her symptoms somewhat resembled those which had preceded the death of her father, she was greatly alarmed. She decided to try the waters of Barèges, and, in the last week of September, set out for the Pyrenees. On the road, she met her husband, hastening to Paris, with the treaty that had just been signed at Madrid in his valise, and let us hope was graciously pleased to express her approval of his diplomatic labours, notwithstanding the disappointment she must have felt that the treaty in question debarred him from earning that glory in the tented field for which she yearned.

Élisa soon decided that the Barèges waters did not suit her constitution—it was late in the season, and the place was excessively dull—and she therefore decided to go to Carcassonne, to consult Barthez, the doctor who had attended Carlo Bonaparte in his last illness, and who enjoyed a great reputation in the medical world. The inns of Carcassonne, in those days, left a good deal to

---

[1] It was a daughter, and was baptised Christine, Lucien and Élisa standing sponsors.

be desired in the matter of cleanliness, and the one which Élisa honoured by her patronage was so dirty, that the poor lady found herself compelled to choose between sleeping on a mattress, on the floor, and disputing possession of the bed with the vermin that infested it. She chose the former alternative, and in this situation was found the next morning by Prosper de Barante, whose father was then Prefect of the Aude, and who came to offer her the hospitality of the Préfecture.

"She was suffering very much from an affection of the stomach," writes the historian of the Dukes of Burgundy. "My father, who was rather unwell, was unable to do the honours of the Préfecture; I presented his excuses and offered my services. Madame Baciocchi received me very graciously. The sisters of the First Consul were then very simple persons; they travelled without any suite, and I found her in a wretched inn, lying on a mattress, on the floor, to escape the vermin. She rose, dressed herself while I waited in an adjoining room, and then, after a conversation, which soon became easy and natural, took my arm to walk in the town. She appeared rather pleased to have encountered me on her way. Her journey bored her; she came I know not from what waters, where she had found no one of her acquaintance. For three or four days, she had received neither letters nor journals. I told her the news. I spoke to her of people whom she knew. As she lived in the literary circle of her brother Lucien, and was on intimate terms with M. de Fontanes, her interests and her conversation inclined particularly to that side. We spoke of plays of the moment, of books recently published, and I gave her the last edition of the *Jardins* of Delille, which I had just received. In short, our *tête-à-tête* lasted two days, and, on leaving, she made me promise to visit her when I should happen to be in Paris."[1]

Élisa did not derive much benefit from her visit to the South, which is perhaps not altogether surprising, since she not only consulted Barthez, but "all the Faculty of Montpellier," and the only point on which these learned men seemed able to agree was the advisability of horse-exercise for their distinguished patient. At length, however, her perseverance was rewarded. "I returned to Paris very ill," she writes to her friend Rœderer. "I procured prescriptions from the most famous physicians of the Faculty. I suffered a good deal for the first few days. After much difficulty, they have succeeded in re-establishing my health. Goat's milk alone, without bread, without water; I am only allowed six cups a day. Apart from a little weakness, I feel very well. And I have been so far to seek the remedy which was so near at hand!"[2]

In the middle of November 1801, Lucien returned from Spain, bringing with him diamonds

---

[1] Baron de Barante, *Souvenirs.*
[2] Letter of October 16, 1801, Rœderer, *Œuvres.*

to the value of over a million francs, which he
had received in recognition of the treaties he had
negotiated with Tuscany and Portugal, and a
maîtresse en titre, the Marquesa de Santa-Cruz.
Although this lady was, for the moment, very
near to his heart, and had a suite of apartments
assigned to her, both in his hôtel in the Rue
Saint-Dominique[1] and at Plessis, it was Élisa
who continued to do the honours of both establishments and to take care of his little girls,
Charlotte and Christine.

Élisa, as we have said, was an enthusiastic
patroness of the drama. She cared, however, but
little for comedy ; tragedy was her delight, and,
not content with watching Mlle. Raucourt and
other celebrated actresses interpreting the heroines
of Corneille and Racine, she aspired to interpret
them herself. To Lucien she confided her histrionic ambitions, and found him a sympathetic
listener. He was almost as assiduous a playgoer
as his sister, and had built a little private theatre
at Plessis with accommodation for three hundred
spectators. Moreover, "he declaimed with a skill
which would have suffered comparison with the
best professional actors,"[2] and the idea of exhibiting his prowess on the boards of the theatre
pleased him not a little. And so, one evening in
the summer of 1802, a performance of *Alzire* was

---

[1] The Hôtel de Brienne. Lucien had taken it for three years
from November 21, 1801, at an annual rent of 12,000 francs.

[2] Bourrienne, *Mémoires*.

given, at Plessis, before the First Consul and a select audience, Élisa playing the title-part and Lucien, Zamore.

If we are to believe Bourrienne, however, it was far from meeting with the success which the distinguished amateurs had anticipated. "The warmth of their declamation, the energetic expression of their gestures, the too-faithful nudity of costume," he writes, "shocked most of the spectators, and Bonaparte more than any one. When the play was over, he was quite indignant. 'It is a scandal,' said he to me, angrily; 'I ought not to suffer such indecencies. I will give Lucien to understand that I will have no more of it.' When his brother, having resumed his ordinary clothes, entered the salon, he addressed him before the company and intimated that he must, for the future, desist from such representations. On our return to Malmaison, he again expressed his annoyance of what had taken place. 'What!' said he, 'when my first duty is to restore purity of morals, my brother and sister must needs go and exhibit themselves, upon a platform, almost in a state of nudity. It is an insult!'"[1]

Nevertheless, his anger was not of long duration, for he was exceedingly fond of witnessing amateur performances, and, a little time afterwards, he invited the same players to give a representation of *Alzire* in his own little theatre at Malmaison; but on the distinct understanding

[1] Bourrienne, *Mémoires*.

that, this time, they should consent to sacrifice historical accuracy in the matter of costume to the proprieties.   Lucien, whose affection for his favourite sister probably inclined him to judge her histrionic efforts rather more favourably than they deserved, declares that " Élisa was a very good tragic actress, particularly in the part of Chimène, which was her triumph."   But this opinion does not seem to have been shared by Napoleon, who, on the present occasion, was heard to remark: " *J'espère que voilà une Alzire bien parodiée.*"

CHAPTER XIV

PAULINE'S husband was far less fortunate than Caroline's, or even than Élisa's. After Brumaire, Leclerc, it will be remembered, had been appointed to the command of one of the divisions of the Army of the Rhine; but it did not fall to his lot to take part in the great victory of Hohenlinden, or, indeed, in any engagement of that memorable campaign, as he fell ill and passed the greater part of the time under the surgeon's care. On the signing of the armistice

which preceded the Peace of Lunéville, Leclerc
returned to Paris and, at the beginning of the
following spring, was sent to Bordeaux to reorganise the troops stationed along the Gironde.
Three months later, when these troops were despatched into Spain, to assist that country in her
war with Portugal, Leclerc accompanied them,
serving as second in command to Gouvion Saint-
Cyr; but the Peace of Badajoz deprived him of
any opportunity of distinguishing himself.[1]

However, Leclerc was soon to have his fill of
fighting, though not of the kind to which he had
hitherto been accustomed, as, at the beginning
of October, he was recalled by the First Consul
to Paris, and entrusted with the command of the
expedition which was being fitted out for the re-
establishment of French authority in the Island

[1] M. Turquan (*les Sœurs de Napoleon*), who seems to be
under the impression that Leclerc was general-in-chief of the
French forces in Spain, instead of only second-in-command,
accuses him, on the authority of General Thiébault, of "engaging
in shameful contraband enterprises, which brought him plenty of
money, but very little consideration," and of "incurring the hatred
of the army by the most atrocious cruelty." We should hesitate,
however, to accept Thiébault's uncorroborated testimony in regard
to the former charge, in spite of the high opinion which M.
Turquan seems to entertain of that officer, even if it were not disproved by Leclerc's own letters to Lucien Bonaparte, in one of
which he states that he is "as poor on leaving Spain as when he
entered it," and, in another, that he is in great need of a present
which Lucien had promised him, in the event of the negotiations
which the Ambassador was carrying on being successfully concluded. Leclerc's well-known kindness of heart, and the fact that
he could not have ventured to commit the acts of which he is
accused without the authority of the general-in-chief, is a sufficient
answer to the latter charge.

of Hayti, or St. Domingo as it was then called ; while, at the same time, Pauline received orders from Napoleon to accompany her husband.

The position of affairs in St. Domingo at this time requires a little explanation.

At the dawn of the nineteenth century, the West Indian islands, now depressed and impoverished, were regarded as of immense importance. In those days, when the name of Australia was almost unknown, when hardly any attempt had yet been made to develop the resources of South Africa, when the population of the United States numbered little more than five million souls, when Europe had not yet learned to make sugar from beet and coffee from chicory, and when the slave trade was still a highly lucrative industry, they were the centre of colonial commerce, and the demand for their produce was enormous. To the general prosperity, however, there was one notable exception.

Since 1791, St. Domingo, the greater part of which belonged to France, and whose trade, at that date, represented more than half of her oceanic commerce, had been a prey to anarchy and bloodshed. The incredible folly of the National Assembly in hastily proclaiming equality between whites and blacks (April 15, 1791), and the refusal of the planters to recognise the decree as binding, led to a terrible revolt of the slaves, in which the island was completely devastated and the most unspeakable atrocities committed

on the unfortunate planters and their families.
An address sent by the French colonists of St.
Domingo to the National Assembly, in October
of that year, thus describes the condition of
affairs :

"One hundred thousand blacks are in revolt,
and in the northern part of the island more than
two hundred sugar manufactories have been
burned and the owners massacred ; and if a few
women have been spared, their captivity is a
condition worse than death itself. Already the
negroes have gained the mountains ; fire and
sword go with them. An immense number of
coffee plantations have also been delivered to the
flames, and those which remain are threatened
with destruction. From all sides, women, children,
and old men who have escaped the carnage are
leaving their hiding-places, and seeking on the
ships the only refuge which is left to them."

On November 30, a deputation from the island
presented itself at the Bar of the Assembly and
described in moving terms the pitiable situation
of the colonists. But, though its representations
were supported by vigorous protests from Nantes,
Saint-Malo, and other towns, whose prosperity
was largely dependent on their colonial trade,
the Assembly declined to interfere, and, on
March 28, 1792, confirmed the decree of the
previous year, and left the "citizen negroes" of
St. Domingo to continue their carnival of pillage
and blood.

The citizen negroes did not fail to show their appreciation of the conduct of their Jacobin sympathisers, and in a few months the whole French portion of the island, with the exception of Port de la Paix and a few other settlements, was in their hands.   Then, thanks to the efforts of Toussaint l'Ouverture, something approaching to tranquillity was restored.   Toussaint, though a much less engaging personage than romantically-inclined writers have depicted him, was undoubtedly a man of remarkable sagacity and strength of will, and the authority he wielded over the horde of blacks which acknowledged his leadership was absolute.   Having made peace with the French governor at Port de la Paix, he rendered him material assistance in repulsing an attempt of the English to get possession of the island.   In return for this service, in 1796, he received from the Directory, who hoped to gain him over altogether, the rank of general of division, which enabled him to strut about in a fine uniform, with a broad sash round his waist, and a gold-laced hat decorated with an enormous plume on his curly locks, to the great admiration of his dusky followers.

However, Toussaint's success had mounted to his head, and, though willing to acknowledge a sort of French protectorate over St. Domingo, he aimed at nothing short of independence.   In 1799, he expelled the French governor, occupied the Spanish portion of the island with an army of 20,000 men, drew up a constitution (May 1801), and declared himself governor of St. Domingo for life, with power to nominate his successor.

These pretensions, and particularly Toussaint's boast that he was "the Bonaparte of the Antilles," greatly incensed Napoleon, and so soon as the truce with Great Britain which preceded the Peace of Amiens opened the seas to the French fleet, he determined to crush him and restore French authority in St. Domingo. At the same time, with characteristic dissimulation, he deemed it expedient to cover his designs by flattering the black chieftain with assurances of his personal esteem and the appreciation of "the great services which he had rendered the French people."

Leclerc seems to have accepted the task entrusted to him by his brother-in-law with considerable reluctance, and certainly it was one in which the perils to be encountered, not only at the hands of a treacherous and savage foe, but from a climate notoriously fatal to Europeans, far outweighed the glory to be won. As for Pauline, if we are to believe Madame d'Abrantès, she was in the depths of despair when first she received Napoleon's orders to accompany the expedition, though she was too proud to allow any but her most intimate friends to suspect her state of mind.

" She appeared delighted to go with 'her little Leclerc,' as she called him, but she was desolated about it, and one day I found her in a paroxysm of despair and tears, very alarming to any one who did not understand her as well as I did.

"'Ah! Laurette,' said she to me, as she threw herself into my arms, 'how happy are you! You are remaining in Paris, you. . . . *Mon Dieu*, how bored I shall be! And then how can my brother have so hard a heart, so spiteful a disposition, as to send me into exile into the midst of snakes and savages? . . . And, then, I am ill. Oh! I shall be dead before I arrive there!'

"And her sobs choked her, so that I feared, for a moment, she was ill.

"I approached her settee, and, taking her hands in mine, I spoke to her, as one would to a child of playthings and toys. I told her that she would be queen over there; that she would ride in a palanquin; that a slave would be attentive to her least movement in order to execute her will; that she would walk about under flowering orange-trees; that the snakes would do her no harm, if there were any in the Antilles; that the savages were equally innocuous; that it was not there that people were roasted on spits, and I concluded my speech by telling her that she would look very pretty, dressed *à la créole*.

"As I spoke, Madame Leclerc's sobs became less violent. 'And thou dost believe then, Laurette (she had a mania for thee and thouing indiscriminately persons who happened to be

with her in her moments of abandon); thou dost
believe that I shall be pretty, *more pretty than
I am*, with a bandana worn *à la créole*, a little
corset, a petticoat of striped muslin? . . .'

"She rang for her maid. 'Bring me all the
bandanas you have,' said she."

And the *coiffure à la créole* was so ravishing,
that Pauline became quite resigned to her fate,
and talked gaily of the picnics she intended to
give among the mountains of St. Domingo.
She had apparently forgotten all about the
snakes and the savages.

Thenceforth, until the time of her departure
arrived, she amused herself in preparations for
her journey, and accumulated such pyramids of
gowns, hats, shoes, *lingerie*, toilette articles,
and impedimenta of every description, that her
friends laughingly remarked that an additional
vessel would be required to transport them. Her
husband ventured to suggest that a few of the
trunks and packing-cases which encumbered the
corridors of his house, might with advantage be
left behind. "Then I remain also," said Pauline
firmly, and, like a wise man, the general said no
more.

Madame de Rémusat asserts that the First
Consul had decided that his sister's disappearance
from France for a season was necessary to put
an end to certain indiscretions in which she was
indulging, and which were occasioning a good
deal of gossip. She does not mention any names,

but other chroniclers, less discreet, declare that Pauline had conceived a violent passion for the actor Lafon,[1] of the Comédie-Française, and that, owing to her reluctance to tear herself away from this fascinating tragedian, the departure of the expedition was greatly delayed and its success seriously compromised. "People were astonished," remarks Salgues, "at this severity on the part of the First Consul towards a sister to whom he appeared to be tenderly attached; but they were assured, to justify it, that the princess was enamoured of a young and talented actor, and that Bonaparte perceived no more certain remedy than to place a distance of fifteen hundred leagues between this beauty and her lover."[2] And Georgette Ducrest writes : "When she [Pauline] started for St. Domingo, she had for Lafon, actor of the Théâtre-Français, an affection about which there was so little secrecy, that Mlle. Duchesnois, on learning that General Leclerc was taking his wife with him, foolishly exclaimed, before a number of people : 'Oh! *Mon Dieu*, how grieved I am! It

[1] The celebrated actor Pierre Lafon was the son of a doctor at La Linde, in Périgord, and was born in 1775. He was originally intended for the Church, and studied theology at the College of Bergerac, but the Revolution compelled him to abandon all idea of an ecclesiastical career. After performing for three or four years in the provinces, he came to Paris towards the end of the year 1799; and, in the following May, appeared at the Comédie-Française, as Achilles in *Iphigénie in Aulis*, and scored an unqualified success.

[2] *Mémoires pour servir de l'histoire de France sur le gouvernement de Napoléon Bonaparte.*

is enough to kill Lafon ; he is so much in love with her.' Many signs were made to her to stop, but she continued for some minutes to bewail the sad lot of her colleague."[1]

Now, what truth is there in the assertions of Salgues and Madame Ducrest, which have been accepted by many historians, including Pauline's latest biographer, M. d'Almeras ? Let us look at the facts.

When, in the early spring of 1801, Leclerc was sent to Bordeaux, Pauline accompanied him, and she remained there until the latter part of June, when the general set out for Spain. She passed the greater part of the time of her husband's absence with Joseph Bonaparte and his wife at Mortefontaine, with occasional visits to her own country-seat of Montgobert, and appears to have been very little in Paris. There would therefore seem to have been but small opportunity for carrying on a *liaison* with an actor of the Comédie-Française of so notorious a nature that her brother believed it advisable to banish her to the West Indies, in order to put an end to the scandal which it was occasioning.

But, it may be objected, there is a reliable witness for the prosecution in the person of Mlle. Duchesnois, a colleague of Lafon at the Comédie-Française, who could not fail to be well acquainted with the gossip of the *coulisses*, who may even have been in the too-fascinating actor's con-

[1] *Mémoires sur l'Impératrice Joséphine.*

fidence, and who, Madame Ducrest tells us, exclaimed, on hearing of the approaching departure of Madame Leclerc : " It is enough to kill Lafon ! "

The answer is that Mlle. Duchesnois, as M. Masson points out, could never have uttered the words imputed to her, inasmuch as she was not at this time a member of the Comédie-Française, or, for that matter, of any other troupe. " Mlle. Duchesnois made her *début* at the Française on August 15, 1803, twenty-one months after the departure of Pauline for St. Domingo, seven months after her return to France."[1]

It was not therefore on account of Lafon that Pauline was temporarily expatriated. Nevertheless, although M. d'Almeras—was there ever a biographer so severe upon his subject ?—is guilty of picturesque exaggeration when he declares that "the list of her lovers rivalled in length those of the mistresses of Don Juan," it is not improbable that her conduct had been sufficiently wanting in circumspection to render her departure eminently desirable from Napoleon's point of view. The First Consul may very well have felt that the sisters of a man with a throne as the goal of his ambition ought to be as much above suspicion as Cæsar's wife.

Next, as to Pauline's alleged responsibility for delaying the departure of the expedition—a delay which, as we shall presently see, was to be

[1] *Napoléon et sa famille.*

THE FIRST CONSUL AT MALMAISON
FROM THE PAINTING BY J. B. ISABEY AT VERSAILLES

the cause of a terrible disaster—by prolonging
her stay in Paris many days after the fleet was
due to sail from Brest. "The squadron had
been ready to put to sea for a fortnight ; sailing-
orders had been received ; the wind was favourable ; nevertheless, it remained in the harbour.
What then prevented its departure ? It was a
woman ! Madame Leclerc ! She was coming,
it was said, travelling in a litter, borne by
men. . . . If the King of Prussia, the great
Frederick, had been then alive, he would have
inveighed, as he did in his time, against the petticoat. In fact, the petticoat has sometimes a
baneful influence on affairs, and, on the present
occasion, also, one could ascribe to it the series
of misfortunes which subsequently overtook our
army. If the First Consul had been aware that
the delay in the sailing of the expedition was
occasioned by his sister, no doubt he would have
given orders for it to start without her ; but, if he
were informed of it, it was not until later."[1]

The aforegoing, written by an officer of the
Army of St. Domingo, would merit consideration, were it not disproved by the facts which
M. Masson has been at pains to collect. So far
from Pauline unduly prolonging her stay in Paris,
she actually left the capital four days before her

---

[1] Lemonnier de la Fosse (*ancien officier de l'armée de Saint-
Domingue*), *Seconde campagne de Saint-Domingue, précédée de
Souvenirs historiques et succincts de la première campagne*,
Le Havre, 1846.

husband, on November 13, in order to allow of her sleeping *en route*, and, though Leclerc, who travelled day and night, overtook her at Rennes, where they both accepted the hospitality of Bernadotte, then in command of the Army of the West, and preceded her to Brest, she rejoined him on November 20, the day after his arrival.

There was certainly a tedious delay before the squadron weighed anchor—one, in fact, of twenty-three days—but this occurred *after* Pauline reached Brest, and was the result of a combination of circumstances, and in no sense attributable to her caprices. In the first place, when the Leclercs arrived, the fitting-out of the squadron had not been completed. Then, a violent north-easterly gale sprang up and blew without intermission for some days, causing an enormous amount of damage to the shipping on the coasts of France, Holland, and Spain. Next, there seems to have been a good deal of rivalry between Leclerc and Villaret-Joyeuse, who was in command of the fleet, and the more the general pressed the admiral to hasten, the more excuses the latter, jealous of his independence and authority, found for delay. Finally, when the wind had abated, and all the preparations had been completed, Villaret insisted on giving a splendid fête on board his flagship, *l'Océan*, on which the Leclercs were to make the voyage, in honour of the sister of the First Consul, and this consumed two further days.

At length, on December 13, the Brest squadron set sail for the Canaries, where it was joined by other squadrons from Lorient, Rochefort, and Toulon, the united armaments mustering thirty-two ships of the line and thirty-one frigates, having more than 20,000 troops on board. Among the civilians who accompanied the expedition, was Pauline's ex-Romeo Stanislas Fréron. Since his matrimonial fiasco, six years before, the once all-powerful deputy in mission had fallen on somewhat evil days, for the odious part he had played during the Terror made it difficult for Napoleon, though always grateful to those who had assisted him or his family in their early struggles with Fortune, to protect him. For the past three years, he had occupied a poorly-paid post as an inspector of hospitals, which scarcely sufficed to provide him with the necessaries of life, and when the First Consul offered him the appointment of prefect of the southern portion of St. Domingo, he was glad to accept it. As Fréron made the voyage on the same vessel as Pauline, it is singular that some of the libellous pamphleteers and imaginative chroniclers of the time have not made her renew with her once " dear idol " the romance so cruelly interrupted in 1796. But, since they are silent, we may presume that she had come to regard him with complete indifference. Probably, time and adversity had dealt hardly with Fréron, and to the spoiled beauty who had all the handsomest *incroyables* in Paris ready to fall at her pretty feet, he appeared merely an uninteresting elderly man.

After a voyage of a little over six weeks, the ill-fated expedition arrived in sight of the French colony at Cap-Français; but Villaret, who, with criminal negligence, had omitted to engage the services of a pilot acquainted with that dangerous coast, refused to attempt an immediate landing, notwithstanding the entreaties of Leclerc. The result was that Toussaint, who, warned by his friends in Europe of the coming of the French armada, had already taken up arms and was ravaging the maritime settlements, stormed and set fire to the town and butchered the inhabitants before their countrymen could come to their aid.

On the disembarkation of the French troops, the cunning Toussaint retreated into the interior, whither Leclerc followed him, at the head of 15,000 men. The difficulties which the French encountered were immense, for they were in a land where Nature fought on the side of the inhabitants and opposed to an invader inexhaustible resources : pathless forests, dense thickets, where every bush was covered with needle-like thorns, treacherous swamps, steep ravines, and rivers, which the rains had changed into torrents. But, roused to fury by the sight of the mutilated bodies of murdered whites, which were to be found at every place where the negroes had halted, the troops pressed on with the utmost courage and determination, and in less than three months practically the whole island had been reconquered, and Toussaint and his chief lieutenants had made their submission.

The First Consul, greatly pleased with his brother-in-law's zeal and energy, wrote to him in terms of the warmest praise: "The nation is about to award to you, as well as to your chief generals and the officers and soldiers who have distinguished themselves, handsome recompense. You are on the way to achieve a great reputation. The Republic will enable you to enjoy a suitable fortune, and the affection I entertain for you is unalterable."

But before this letter reached St. Domingo, the situation of affairs in the island had undergone a disastrous change.

The submission of Toussaint had been merely a feint, intended to secure a truce until the advent of the unhealthy season, when he calculated that disease would quickly thin the ranks of the invaders, and enable the blacks to resume hostilities with every prospect of success.

His anticipations were ultimately realised, though he himself was not destined to witness their fulfilment. In May, yellow fever—that terrible scourge of the West Indies—broke out among the French, and, as the summer advanced, its ravages steadily increased, until, by the beginning of July, generals and administrators, officers and soldiers were dying like flies.[1]

Among the victims of the epidemic, was the sometime lover of the general-in-chief's wife. "Fréron is dead," writes Leclerc to Decrès, the Minister of Marine, on August 2, 1802. "I recommend to you his wife and children; he has been useful and kind, and he endeavoured to be of service to me in the days when he possessed influence as representative of the people with the Army of Italy."[2]

Leclerc, who with Pauline and her little son had retired to the Île de la Tortue, to recruit his health, already shattered by the fatigues of the recent campaign, hastened to Cap-Français immediately the news of the outbreak reached him. Suspecting Toussaint's designs, he caused that personage and some of the other negro leaders to be arrested and transported to France, where the black chieftain died, the following spring, from the hardships to which he was exposed in his prison among the Jura snows. If his treatment by the First Consul were indefensible, the same cannot be said of his arrest. Although denounced by insufficiently-informed writers as an act of shameful treachery, it would appear to have

---

[1] "Out of two companies of carabiniers of the 11th Legion," wrote General Duplanque, "only forty-five men are fit to march; many houses are transformed into hospitals." From August 8 to September 7, 30 officers and 398 soldiers died in the hospital at Port-Margo alone.

[2] Published by M. d'Almeras.

been justified by all the laws of war, for of
Toussaint's intention to resume hostilities, so
soon as he judged the invading army to be
sufficiently weakened by disease, there can be no
possible doubt.[1]

Leclerc and the medical staff struggled heroically against the fell disease, but it was to no
purpose. The medical stores sent from France
were so damaged during the voyage that they had
to be thrown into the sea; those for which they
applied to the Spanish colonists only arrived after
endless delays, and, when they came, there was
no money to pay for them. Further, many of the
surgeons themselves succumbed, and the sur-
vivors were so ignorant of the proper treatment of
a malady unknown in European hospitals that
they frequently became its unconscious allies.[2]
By the middle of August, the number of deaths
had risen to 18,000.[3]

But what of Pauline while her husband was
campaigning in the interior and wrestling with
the disease that was devastating his army?

Pauline, on her arrival, had established herself
with her little son at the half-ruined town of
Cap-Français, where one of the few commodious

[1] And here is a proof: Towards the end of May 1802, Toussaint wrote to one of his spies at Cap-Français : " La Providence
[the hospital at the Cap] is coming to my assistance. . . . How
many journeys are made by night to la Fosette [a cemetery near
the Cap]? . . . Notify me when Leclerc falls ill."

[2] M. Frédéric Masson, *Napoléon et sa famille.*

[3] Report of Decrès, November 1802, published by M.
d'Almeras.

houses which the insurgents had spared was
made ready for their reception, and dignified
by the title of palace. Then, in the late spring,
when the island had apparently been pacified,
and Leclerc was at liberty to rejoin her, she
removed with him, as we have mentioned, to
the Île de la Tortue, the healthiest part of the
colony, where a cool sea-breeze tempered the
heat of the sun, and where life was altogether
more pleasant. When, however, the increasing
ravages of the epidemic necessitated Leclerc's
presence among his troops, she returned to the
main island, and she was at Cap-Français when
the second insurrection broke out.

Pauline's biographers, M. Turquan and M.
d'Almeras, while admitting that they have "no
precise information" on the subject, both incline
to the belief that during these months the lady
conducted herself in an exceedingly dissolute
manner; and the latter goes so far as to
insinuate that even certain gentlemen of colour
were not permitted to sigh in vain.

But on what evidence do they base this
charge? On the testimony of the mendacious
compiler of the so-called *Mémoires* of Fouché,
on Chancellor Pasquier's malicious insinuations,
and on the *Histoire secrète de la cour et du
cabinet de Bonaparté* (*sic*) of the unspeakable
Lewis Goldsmith! Reliable evidence, in good
truth!

What is certain, is that this frivolous pleasure-loving woman showed, in the midst of perils which might have daunted even the boldest, a courage and a *sang-froid* worthy of the highest admiration. She refused to fly before the pestilence, and, though her husband repeatedly urged her to leave him and return to France, she answered that it was but just that she should share his ill fortune, as well as his good, adding, with a gratified smile: " Here I reign like Joséphine; I am the first."

And right gaily did she queen it over the society of that fever-stricken colony. Although she was in very indifferent health herself, and therefore peculiarly susceptible to contagion, she confronted the terrible scourge which was striking down all around her with that charming smile which had played havoc with so many hearts, and firmly declined to discontinue the round of amusements in which she delighted to spend her time. Every evening she kept open house; she gave receptions, concerts, and balls, at which the surviving musicians of the general's band, garbed in the gay uniform which she herself had selected for them, played as merrily as if they had been in a Paris ball-room, though each was aware that after that night he might never handle his cherished instrument again.

Some there were, who, as they left those gaily-lighted rooms and caught sight of the long procession of carts wending its way to the cemetery of La Fosette, shook their heads and remarked that these festivities were sadly out of place at such a time, stigmatised them as " *les rendez-vous du cercueil,*" and expressed their opinion that Madame Leclerc must be either a trifle mad, or absolutely without heart, to dance, so to speak, on the graves of her countrymen.

But Pauline was very far from mad, and, without perhaps her being fully aware of it, the balls and receptions which she gave, and the indifference which she displayed in the face of such imminent danger, had a most beneficial influence on the spirits of the community, by diverting the thoughts of the more timid from the perils which surrounded them and calming their fears. Nor was she without heart, since, whenever in her drives she came across soldiers lying on the ground overcome by thirst or suffering from sunstroke, she would at once order the unfortunate men to be placed in her carriage and conveyed to the hospital. These acts of mercy are vouched for by one of those whose lives she had saved.

But, in the early autumn, a new and even more terrible danger than pestilence confronted the inhabitants of Cap-Français. On September 13, the negro regiments which Toussaint had organised, and which, after the nominal submission of their leader, had been taken into French pay, deserted *en masse*, and, three days later, swooped down upon the Cap.

For this fresh insurrection Leclerc has been

often, and most unjustly, blamed. But, happily,
the results of recent research have cleared the
memory of this excellent officer from the asper-
sions cast upon it. Let us listen to Dr. Rose,
always so well informed and so impartial :

" In the Notes dictated at St. Helena, Napoleon submitted Leclerc's memory to some stric-
tures for his indiscretion in regard to the proposed
restitution of slavery. The official letters of that
officer expose the injustice of the charge. The
facts are these. After the seeming submission of
St. Domingo, the First Consul caused a decree
to be secretly passed at Paris (May 20, 1802),
which prepared to re-establish slavery ; but
Decrès warned Leclerc that it was not for the
present to be applied to St. Domingo, unless it
seemed to be opportune. Knowing how fatal
any such proclamation would be, Leclerc suppressed the decree ; but General Richepanse,
who was now governor of the island of Guade-
loupe, not only issued the decree, but proceeded to
enforce it with rigour. It was this which caused
the last and most desperate revolts of the
blacks, fatal alike to French domination and to
Leclerc's life." [1]

The French forces at Cap-Français were, by
this time, so reduced by disease, that out of the
2,000 men, which were all that Leclerc could
muster to oppose between 10,000 and 12,000
insurgents, only 500 were soldiers ; the remain-

[1] *Life of Napoleon I.*

der were civilians, who had taken up arms in
defence of their families. Well aware that, if
victorious, the blacks would spare neither age
nor sex, and that a fate worse than death would
befall the younger women, the general made
arrangements for the non-combatants to be transferred to the ships in the harbour, in the but
too probable event of the French troops being
unable to hold the enemy at bay. After which,
he bade farewell to his wife, whose beautiful face
betrayed not the slightest sign of fear, and
marched out to meet the insurgents, at the head
of his little army.

Soon the sound of firing, growing every moment more distinct, told the terrified inhabitants
of the Cap that the defenders were being gradually driven back upon the town. One of Leclerc's aides-de-camp came galloping up, with
orders to the general's wife and child to retire at
once to the ships; but Pauline, who was reclining
gracefully in an arm-chair, to all appearance, perfectly composed, answered that her house was
more to her taste, and that she preferred to remain
there. All the ladies who had taken refuge at
the "palace" implored her to embark and to take
them with her, whereupon she exclaimed, with a
gesture of disdain : "You are afraid! But, as for
myself, I am Bonaparte's sister, and I am afraid
of nothing! I will embark in company with my
husband, or I will die."

Presently, the aide-de-camp, who, perceiving

the futility of expostulation, had returned to his chief for further instructions, appeared once more, and gave orders to the soldiers who had been left to guard the house to remove the lady and her little son, by force if necessary. As Pauline still refused to leave her arm-chair, four grenadiers lifted it from the ground and carried it and its fair occupant off, while another bore the little Dermide in his arms, and all the servants of the house and a crowd of weeping women followed. "It is all the same," observed Pauline; "I will not go on board." And she laughed heartily, declaring that it was as amusing as a masquerade.

They had reached the harbour, and Pauline in her arm-chair was on the point of being lowered into the boat which was to convey her to the fleet, when another aide-de-camp arrived, with the news that the courage and discipline of the French had prevailed over the numbers opposed to them, that the blacks were in full retreat, and that the fugitives might return to their homes. "I was certain that I should not go on board," remarked Pauline, complacently. "Was I not right in being unwilling to put myself to inconvenience?"

When the First Consul received the report of this affair, he wrote to Leclerc: "I am very satisfied with the manner in which Pauline has behaved; she ought not to fear death, since she would die gloriously in dying with the army and in being of service to her husband. Everything passes away quickly on earth, except the opinion which we leave inscribed in history."

Leclerc did not live to receive his brother-in-law's letter. The unfortunate officer had done everything that was humanly possible to ensure the success of the task entrusted to him, but, through no fault of his own, he had failed. With the feeble remnant of what had once been a powerful army, it was all that he could do to hold Cap-Français and a few other coast settlements; the rest of the colony was in the hands of the insurgent blacks. Neither the reinforcements nor the money he had confidently expected from France arrived, for Napoleon, with the prospect of an early renewal of the war with England before him, had no mind to spare fresh troops or incur further expenditure for an enterprise which was already becoming unpopular. Louisiana, his base for supplies, failed him, and he had the utmost difficulty in provisioning his troops. Finally, he learned that some of his principal officers were actually negotiating with the enemy.

On October 22, he was attacked by yellow fever, and, though he courageously continued to transact business and issue orders for some days, worn out as he was by the incessant labours, anxieties, and mortifications of the past few months, his case was hopeless from the first. On October 31, aware that his end was near, he bade a tender farewell to Pauline, who had braved the danger of contagion and nursed him with unremitting care, and gave orders that she and her little son should be escorted to the Île de la Tortue.   In the night of November 1–2, he died, regretting in his last moments of consciousness that he had not been permitted to be of more service to his country.

France lost in Leclerc a brave, capable, and honourable soldier, who, at a time when so many officers in high command did not hesitate to enrich themselves by all kinds of dubious practices, had always observed the most scrupulous integrity ; and Pauline, a kind and devoted husband, whose worth she probably appreciated far more than her detractors would have us believe. So far as her shallow nature was capable of a sincere affection, she undoubtedly loved "her little Leclerc," and, if her manner of expressing her regard for the dead was somewhat theatrical, it was genuine enough.

Having resolved to transport the general's body to France, she caused it to be embalmed in the Egyptian fashion, and wrapped in bandages as far as the head, "where the bandage terminated in a cap enclosing the tresses of Madame Leclerc, which she desired should be placed on the body, as a token of conjugal love, in exchange for those of her husband, which she had asked for."[1]   It was then placed in a leaden coffin

---

[1] Leclerc, as his portraits show, had continued to wear his hair long, though many French officers had already had theirs cut short, in imitation of the First Consul.

enclosed within another of cedar-wood, an arrangement which, on its arrival in France, gave rise, as we shall see, to a ridiculous rumour as to the contents of the casket. His heart she enclosed in a leaden vase, and this within a gold urn, which bore the following inscription :

"PAULINE BONAPARTE, married to General Leclerc, 20 Prairial, Year V, has enclosed within this urn her love, with the heart of her husband, whose perils and dangers she shared. Her son will not receive this sad and precious heritage of his father without receiving that of his virtues."

Pauline's preparations for leaving St. Domingo were soon completed, and, a week after Leclerc's death, she and her son Dermide sailed for France, in the *Swiftsure*.[1]

The careful researches of M. Frédéric Masson have enabled him to dispose of the odious story, accepted by M. Turquan, M. d'Almeras, and so many other historians, that, during the voyage from St. Domingo, Pauline consoled herself for the loss of her husband—that husband whose remains she was transporting to France—by indulging in a *liaison* with General Humbert—the leader of the

[1] The *Swiftsure* was an English ship of the line, of 74 guns, which, having become separated from Lord Keith's squadron, had been attacked and captured by Gantheaume's fleet on June 24, 1801. Jérôme Bonaparte had taken part in this engagement, and had been sent on board the *Swiftsure* to receive the captain's sword and to bring the prize to Toulon.

abortive French invasion of Ireland in 1798—who was a fellow-passenger on board the *Swiftsure*. M. Masson shows that Humbert, suspected of being in communication with the negroes, convicted of converting stores intended for the army to his own profit, and accused of cowardice, had received orders from Leclerc to leave the colony, and had sailed for France on October 17, 1802, a fortnight before the general's death and three weeks prior to Pauline's departure! Thus another edifice of calumny crumbles into dust before the unanswerable evidence of fact.[1]

The *Swiftsure* reached Toulon on New Year's Day 1803, but the passengers and crew had to submit to a fortnight's quarantine at the Nozarettes before they were allowed to land. "I have arrived at Toulon after a frightful passage and terrible sufferings," wrote Pauline to the First Consul, "and this is, however, the least of my misfortunes. I have brought back with me the

---

[1] Unhappily, however, in the present case, the process of demolition would appear to be a very gradual one ; for, in a study of Humbert, which appeared in *la Revolution française*, July 1906— nine years after M. Masson had published the facts related above—we find M. Marcellin Pellet repeating the old slander : "She [Pauline] returned to France between the brilliant officer [Humbert] and her husband's coffin. This 'return of the ashes' considerably scandalised public opinion, at an epoch when it was not easily scandalised."

M. Pellet is of opinion that the charges brought by Leclerc against Humbert, which, after investigation by the military authorities in Paris, led to that officer being cashiered (January 13, 1803), were merely a pretext "to dishonour a Republican general of whom one desired to get rid, and to avenge the conjugal honour of General Leclerc."

remains of my poor Leclerc. Pity the poor Paulette, who is very unhappy."

The writer did not exaggerate her condition, which was certainly such as to deserve compassion. Not only did she find herself, at the age of twenty-two, bereft of an excellent husband, whom she had loved as much as it was in her nature to love any one; but her health had suffered severely from the climate of the tropics and the trials through which she had passed. Never having completely recovered from her first confinement, she had been attacked while in St. Domingo by "a serious complaint which always pursued her,"[1] and which rendered walking and travelling extremely trying; and, at the moment of her arrival in France, it was causing her acute suffering. Moreover, she had had, for some time, a painful ulcer on one of her hands, which taxed all the skill of the Paris physicians before it disappeared, and which returned at intervals.[2] Finally, she had suffered so much from sea-sickness that she does not seem to have quitted her cabin during the entire voyage.

Napoleon, who had already been informed of the death of Leclerc, by a vessel bearing despatches which had preceded the *Swiftsure*, sent one of his aides-de-camp to Toulon to meet Pauline and to escort her to Paris, so soon as she had complied with the quarantine regula-

---

[1] Madame de Rémusat, *Mémoires.*
[2] Duchesse d'Abrantès, *Mémoires.*

tions. At the same time, he gave orders that honours which had never before been rendered to a general who had lost his life on active service were to be paid to his brother-in-law's remains. The *Moniteur* of Nivose 19 (January 9, 1803) contained an announcement that "the First Consul would go into mourning and wear it for ten days"; and his example was followed by all the Ministers and the chief State officials; while the bishops were invited to celebrate Requiem Masses in their cathedrals and to vie with one another in the eloquence of their funeral orations. On January 27, the coffin of Leclerc was removed from the *Swiftsure* to another vessel, which conveyed it to Marseilles, the citadel of which the deceased general had formerly commanded. It was received by the garrison under arms and by all the civic functionaries in their robes of office, while cannon fired salutes and the bells of the churches were tolled. Then, guarded by a mounted escort, under the command of a brigadier-general, it was conveyed to Montgobert, where Leclerc had expressed a wish to be interred, receiving in every town through which it passed similar honours to those it had received at Marseilles.

The passage of the funeral *cortège*, however, excited little interest or sympathy among the general public, who showed not the slightest desire to imitate the example of the Consular Court and go into mourning; and, if Napoleon

had hoped, by this means, to arouse the nation
and the army from the apathy with which they
regarded colonial enterprises, he must have been
sadly disappointed. The only remarks made were
not of a nature to afford the First Consul much
satisfaction, and it was just as well that they did
not reach his ears. Unaware that the cedar-wood
coffin enclosed another of lead, and observing the
difficulty of transporting it, people declared their
belief that it did not contain a corpse at all, but
was the repository for the treasures which Pauline
had brought from St. Domingo and desired to
conceal from curious eyes; and it was in the
midst of absurd rumours such as these that the
remains of poor Leclerc were borne to their last
resting-place.

As for Pauline, the quarantine regulations and
the delicate state of her health necessitated her
remaining at Toulon for nearly a month, and it
was not until the end of January that she set
out for Paris. At Lyons, she remained for three
days, as the guest of Joseph Fesch, who, on the
re-establishment of the Catholic religion, had
returned to his sacred duties, and had lately been
consecrated Archbishop of Lyons; after which,
she resumed her journey to the capital, where she
arrived on February 11.

CHAPTER XV

IN the autumn of 1802, Napoleon granted Élisa an annual allowance of 60,000 francs. This made her altogether independent of the hospitality of Lucien. Nevertheless, she continued to reside at the Hôtel de Brienne until early in the following spring, when she purchased, from the family of Moreton-Chabrillan, the Hôtel Maurepas, in the Rue de la Chaise, Faubourg Saint-Germain, an imposing mansion —almost a palace—with spacious apartments, a large courtyard, and an extensive garden.

Élisa was now a very important personage indeed, and Prosper de Barante, who came about this time to pay his respects, in fulfilment of the promise he had made her some time before, "found her very much more the great lady than when they had walked together in the streets of

Carcassonne." However, she received him very graciously, and would no doubt have interested herself in his future, had not the youth been of too independent a nature to enroll himself among her courtiers.[1]

But these she had in abundance, and "she took more pleasure than ever in seeing the cele- brated *littérateurs* of the time crowd into her salon," where our friend Fontanes held sway, by the authority of his brilliant poetic aureole. M. de Chateaubriand, Esménard, Arnault, Andrieux, and many other poets were very assiduous visitors at my sister's."[2]

Next to Fontanes, Chateaubriand stood highest in the lady's favour; a position which it is prob- able that he owed quite as much to Élisa's appreciation of his high-flown compliments as to her admiration of his genius. She was "always adorable," "the beautiful and excellent protec- tress," "the best of women," "the most noble of protectresses," and so forth. At a fête given by Caroline, at Neuilly, she presented the author of *le Génie du Christianisme* to the First Consul, and subsequently informed him that the great man had "found pleasure in his conversation," though Chateaubriand assures us that Napoleon had done all the talking, and that he himself had not had an opportunity of opening his lips. However, for the moment, he had undoubtedly created a

---

[1] Baron de Barante, *Souvenirs*.
[2] Th. Jung, *Lucien Bonaparte et ses Mémoires*.

favourable impression, and when, in April 1803, Joseph Fesch, who had now blossomed into a cardinal, was sent to Rome as French Ambassador, Élisa obtained for him the post of First Secretary of Legation.

But the Ambassador and his secretary did not agree—in fact, they were soon at daggers drawn—and the latter succeeded in making his Eminence the laughing-stock of Rome. Not content with this, he drew up and despatched to the First Consul a most imprudent memoir, in which he accused his chief of incapacity, parsimony, and almost of treason. Napoleon was highly indignant that a returned *émigré*, and a man whose appointment had only been conferred upon him as a special favour, should dare to bring such charges against his uncle. But Élisa defended her *protégé* energetically and maintained him at Rome, even after his adventure with the fair Madame de Beaumont, with whom his relations were perhaps less platonic than the *Mémoires d'Outre-Tombe* have represented them. Finally, when M. de Chateaubriand began to weary of Rome, she persuaded the First Consul to send him as French representative to the little republic of the Valais, with the title of Ambassador, which must have aroused no small amusement in diplomatic circles, though, doubtless, very gratifying to the distinguished author's vanity.

However, almost on the eve of Chateaubriand's departure for Switzerland, all Paris was horrified by the news that the young Duc d'Enghien had been shot at Vincennes. Élisa was particularly indignant. If we are to believe Mlle. Lenormand, she had the courage to say to Napoleon, some hours before the execution of the duke : " Take care, brother, lest one of the balls which will pierce the prince does not rebound and break the sceptre in your hands ".;[1] while Lavalette declares that she addressed to the First Consul a letter of remonstrance, which Fontanes had drawn up, and which brought upon her a reprimand, though not a very severe one.[2] As for Chateaubriand, he immediately resigned the post to which he was about to proceed, on the pretext of his wife's delicate health—a transparent fiction which deceived no one. " Madame Baciocchi," he writes, "exclaimed loudly against what she called my 'disloyalty' ; she sent for me and addressed to me the most lively reproaches." Finding, however, that he was not to be persuaded, "she interposed her kindness between her brother's anger and my resolution," in consequence of which the First Consul received the author's defiance with equanimity and, some days later, smilingly inquired of his sister if she had been " very much alarmed for her friend."[3]

Élisa was more successful in her efforts on behalf of several of those implicated in the con-

---

[1] *Mémoires historiques et secrets de l'impératrice Joséphine.*
[2] *Mémoires.*
[3] Chateaubriand, *Mémoires d'Outre-Tombe.*

spiracy of Georges Cadoudal and Pichegru, of all
connection with which it is now generally acknowledged that the unfortunate Duc d'Enghien was
entirely innocent.   Jealous perhaps of the popu-
larity which Joséphine had acquired, owing to
her successful intervention in the case of Armand
de Polignac, both she and Caroline were most
active in the work of mercy.   " The sisters of
the First Consul," writes Madame de Rémusat,
"anxious to obtain some share of the public
favour for themselves, gave the wives of the
condemned men to understand that they might
apply to them also.   They then conveyed the
petitioners in their own carriages to Saint-Cloud,
in a sort of semi-state, to solicit the pardon of
their husbands.   These proceedings, as to which
the Emperor I believe had been consulted before-
hand, were less spontaneous than those of the
Empress, because they savoured too much of
prearrangement ; but, at any rate, they served
to save the lives of several persons." [1]

When, at the beginning of February 1802,
Murat returned to Milan to install the authorities
of the new Italian Republic, Caroline, who, it
will be remembered, was again enceinte, remained
in Paris.   On March 23, Murat reappeared unexpectedly in the capital, having made the
journey from Milan in only five days.   He gave
out that anxiety as to his wife's health was the

[1] *Mémoires.*

cause of his hurried journey, but his true motive seems to have been the necessity of justifying himself from the attacks of his enemies in Italy, who had accused him of accepting bribes from candidates for office under the new constitution, and of having planned visits to Rome and Naples "merely to reap a harvest of presents." These charges would appear to have been but too well founded, since Napoleon, we are assured, "fell into a violent passion with his brother-in-law." However, thanks in a great measure to the efforts of Caroline, who, at the beginning of April, gave a superb fête to the First Consul at Neuilly, he eventually forgave him, and accorded him permission to pay the proposed visits to Rome and Naples, where the harvest of presents was duly reaped, and included "a beautiful cameo of the value of 3,000 piastres" and "a sabre with its hilt set with diamonds."

On April 25, Caroline gave birth to her second child—a daughter, who received the names of Marie Letizia Joséphine Annunciade. Joséphine was to have stood godmother, but, for some unknown reason, the ecclesiastical ceremony never took place. At the beginning of October, she accompanied her husband, who had passed all the summer in Paris, to Milan, where she was received with every honour by the authorities of the Italian Republic.

Caroline's second sojourn in Italy, which lasted some ten months, was marked by little which is

of interest; it would appear to have been chiefly
employed in endeavouring to keep the peace
between Murat and the Vice-President, Melzi,
who quarrelled perpetually and wrote the most
violent denunciations of each other to the First
Consul. Murat's object seems to have been to
discredit Melzi and the other Ministers of the
new Republic, in order to procure its annexation
to France and his own appointment as its ruler,
for his post of general-in-chief with a princely
salary was far from satisfying his desires. But
Caroline, whose ambition was tempered by a
shrewdness in which her husband was wholly
wanting, perceived that there was little chance
of these intrigues proving successful, and that
their only result would be to bring upon Murat
the displeasure of the First Consul, whose
patience he had already tried rather severely.
She therefore employed all her influence in the
cause of peace and concord, and "conducted herself on all occasions with the utmost prudence,
justice, and sagacity." In the spring of 1803,
when she was expecting her third child, she intimated to Melzi that she would be very willing to
accept him as godfather. The Vice-President
hastened to act upon the suggestion, and wrote
to Napoleon that "he had visited the general-in-
chief and demanded of him permission to hold
his child at the baptismal font." Murat could
not but express his sense of the honour which
Melzi desired to pay him, and for the remainder

of his stay in Milan harmony reigned between them, at least in appearance. The child—a son —was born on May 16, and baptised by the names of Lucien Napoleon Charles François, the last out of compliment to Melzi, whose Christian name was Francesco. "I have learned with pleasure of the delivery of Madame Murat," writes the First Consul to the proud father; "she has done well to make a fine boy. I hope that you will soon inform me that her health is re-established."

Early in August, Caroline returned to Paris, where, at the end of the month, her husband joined her. Murat was now anxious to leave Italy, which, though it had proved an exceed- ingly profitable field for the exercise of his rapacious qualities, did not at present afford sufficient scope for his ambition. He had set his heart upon securing some high military appointment in France, and for this he and Caroline intrigued very busily during the ensuing months. Their efforts were crowned with suc- cess, and, in January 1804, Murat was nominated Governor of Paris and commandant of the troops of the 1st Division and of the National Guard, with a salary of 60,000 francs and permission to retain the rank and pay of general-in-chief. At the same time, Caroline received an annual allow- ance of 60,000 francs on the Grande Cassette, the same which Élisa and Pauline had already received.

It might have been supposed that Caroline
and her husband would have been satisfied with
the splendid position to which they had now
attained. Their fortunes were established on a
solid basis ; they took precedence of every one
after the Consuls and their wives ; they possessed,
in Neuilly, one of the most beautiful estates in
France, and, in the Hôtel Thélusson, one of the
finest, and certainly the most sumptuously furnished house in Paris ; they were courted and
flattered by all. But the Murats placed no limit
to their ambition ; they regarded all this as but
a step to far higher things. They knew that
Napoleon's goal was a throne, and when he rose,
they were determined to rise with him.

Murat had not made a fortune in Italy in order
to hoard it, and not since the Revolution began
had such luxury, such lavish hospitality, been
displayed as that in which this Gascon adventurer
and his wife delighted to indulge. The spacious
apartments of the Hôtel Thélusson, with their
alabaster columns, their costly Aubusson carpets,
their gilded consoles, their glass doors, their exquisitely carved chimney-pieces, their velvet and
lace curtains, their massive candelabra, their
bronzes, their statues, their paintings, were the
wonder and admiration of all who were privileged
to view them. And to what exquisite dinners
did the Governor entertain his friends in that
splendid dining-room, where all the chairs were of
mahogany and the table of cedar ! What mag-

nificent receptions did Caroline hold in the grand
salon, with its six windows, furnished throughout
in blue velvet bordered with gold, and lighted in
the centre by a lustre of thirty-six branches, and
in each corner by a candelabrum supported by a
marble statue! And what a perfect hostess she
was, how gracious, how amiable, how kind! She
seemed never so happy as when using her
influence on behalf of her friends and acquaintances. Was any one working to get a relative
erased from the list of *émigrés*, it was Madame
Murat to whom he went, certain to find in her
a powerful and sympathetic ally. Did a young
man want a commission in the army, Madame
Murat would speak at once to her husband,
"who loved young men and interested himself
in their future." If a stern father opposed the
union of two loving hearts from financial con-
siderations, Madame Murat would intercede with
him and smooth away all obstacles.[1]

The majority of people believed that all this
amiability and kindness sprang from real goodness of heart. Never was there a greater mistake. There was no more spontaneity about it
than there was about the splendid entertainments
at the Hôtel Thélusson and Neuilly. Both were
the result of the most careful calculations, both
were but a means to an end. Although still
hardly more than a girl, Caroline's intuition told

[1] Ricard, *Autour des Bonaparte;* Stanislas de Girardin, *Journal
et Souvenirs.*

her that the road to power and influence is smoothed by the goodwill of one's fellows ; and both she and her husband, over whom her ascendency was daily increasing, made it their invariable rule to conciliate every one, holding with the celebrated Madame de Tencin, the mother of d'Alembert, that while nine persons out of ten will give you not a sou for your trouble, the tenth may become a useful friend.

Caroline was a much less frequent visitor than Élisa at the Tuileries and Malmaison, though her gaiety and good-humour made her presence always welcome. She, however, generally took part in the representations of the "dramatic troupe" of Malmaison, which included Duroc, Bourrienne, Hortense and Eugène de Beauharnais, the painter Isabey, Lauriston, and Junot and his wife, who declares that Madame Murat was an excellent actress.

M. Turquan is inclined to attribute Caroline's comparatively infrequent appearances at Malmaison to her dread of giving colour to the scandalous rumours which had been for some time in circulation as to the relations between her and the First Consul—rumours for which, let us at once observe, there does not appear to have been a shadow of foundation, and which, with one or two exceptions, the best-informed chroniclers of the period have repudiated with indignation.[1]

---

[1] This abominable scandal would appear to have owed its origin, or, at any rate, its propagation, to the malicious Madame

But, though this may have influenced her to some extent, the principal reason would appear to have been the hatred with which she regarded the Beauharnais, and which now that she had nothing more to gain by simulating cordiality, she could with difficulty contrive to conceal. The future of her children and those of Hortense was the chief bone of contention, and the First Consul's preference for the latter exasperated her to such a degree that Napoleon could not fail to be aware of her sentiments.

At the time when the First Consul, to the profound indignation of Joseph and Caroline, was contemplating the adoption of Louis's and Hortense's little son, Napoleon Charles, and, indeed, appeared to have resolved upon it, he was sitting one day, surrounded by his family, with the boy upon his knee. "Dost thou know, baby," said he, "that thou dost run the risk of being a king some day?" "And Achille?" immediately asked Murat, who was present. "Oh, Achille!" replied the First Consul; "Achille will be a good soldier."

"This reply," adds Madame de Rémusat, who relates the anecdote, "deeply wounded Madame

Hulot, Moreau's mother-in-law, who, "being one day at Malmaison, permitted herself to indulge in biting jests in regard to the intimacy which was suspected between Bonaparte and his youngest sister, Caroline, who had lately married." (Madame de Rémusat, *Mémoires*.) If we are to believe General Ségur, Moreau did not scruple to repeat the detestable calumnies of the "Prussian corporal," as Napoleon had dubbed Madame Hulot, and jested freely on the subject at a dinner which he gave to a number of his officers at Augsburg, during the campaign of Hohenlinden.

Murat, but Bonaparte appeared not to notice her, and, stung by his brother's opposition, which he believed, with reason, to have been prompted by her, went on to say to the boy : 'At any rate, I advise thee, my poor child, if thou dost wish to live, not to accept any invitations to dine with thy cousins.'"

Napoleon delighted in unpleasant jests, but, on the present occasion, he was not jesting. He desired to show his sister that he perfectly understood her ambitious and egotistical nature, and that, under certain circumstances, he believed her capable of going to almost any lengths to ensure her pre-eminence and that of her children. "Did he already in the clouds of the future catch a glimpse of the treason of 1814?"[1]

From that moment, in concert with Joseph and her husband, Caroline used every possible persuasion to induce the jealous and suspicious Louis to refuse the honour which Napoleon intended for his son, and did not scruple to point to the First Consul's affection for the child as a proof of his incestuous passion for Hortense, of which it is notorious that his younger brother suspected him. She succeeded, and Louis repulsed with indignation Napoleon's offer, even going so far as to threaten to leave France and take his son with him, and the First Consul, all-powerful as he was, found it impossible to overcome his opposition. Not content with this, he forbade his wife to hold

M. I. Turquan, *les Sœurs de Napoléon.*

any familiar intercourse with her mother or to
sleep a night at Malmaison, surrounded her by
spies, caused her letters to be intercepted and
opened, threatened to separate her from her son
and to shut her up in some remote place, from
which no power on earth should deliver her, and,
in short, "made her experience the full weight of
conjugal despotism."[1]

Caroline, however, gained nothing by her
machinations, beyond the gratification of her
animosity against the Beauharnais. The First
Consul never showed the least inclination to
place the little Achille Murat in the line of
succession to the prospective throne ; indeed, he
appears to have rather disliked the boy than
otherwise, as the following anecdote will show :

Napoleon, as is well known, had a singular
fondness for pulling the ears, not only of children,
but of grown-up people, and this he occasionally
did so vigorously as to cause his hapless victims
considerable pain. One day, when Achille happened to be the recipient of this unpleasant form
of caress, he began to cry, upon which his uncle,
with the intention of "teaching him to be a man,"
pulled all the harder. At length, the pain became
so unbearable that the child wrenched himself
from his tormentor's grasp, and rushed at him,
with clenched fists, crying : "You are a wretch,
a wicked wretch!" Napoleon, who could not
endure the least sign of insubordination, instead

[1] Madame de Rémusat, *Mémoires*.

of endeavouring to soothe his nephew and cause him to forget the injury which he had so needlessly inflicted, replied with a sound slap on the cheek, which sent the poor boy sobbing pitiably to the sympathetic arms of his uncle Lucien, who relates the incident. Madame Murat was so overcome by her brother's brutality that she seemed on the point of swooning—"a faintness," says Lucien, "occasioned by the efforts she made to control the indignation she felt at the violence which her child had suffered." On his side, the First Consul left the room, with a shrug of his shoulders, banging the door behind him, and remarking that Caroline had always been "*une mijaurée*," and it was thus that fathers and mothers spoiled their children.[1]

[1] Th. Jung, *Lucien Bonaparte et ses Mémoires.*

CHAPTER XVI

Pauline after her return from St. Domingo—She purchases the
Hôtel Charost, in the Rue Faubourg Saint-Honoré—Her
despair at the retired life which the First Consul insists upon
her leading—Her flirtation with Admiral Decrès—Napoleon
offers his sister's hand to Francesco di Melzi, Vice-President of
the Italian Republic, who, however, declines the proposal—
Prince Camillo Borghese in Paris—Diplomatists as match-
makers—A marriage between him and Pauline negotiated—
Refusal of the First Consul to permit the ceremony to take
place until his sister has completed a year of widowhood—
Mariage de conscience celebrated, at Mortefontaine, without his
knowledge—Indignation of Napoleon at the deception practised
upon him—The legal marriage—Visit of the Princess Borghese
to Joséphine—Her departure for Rome—Lucien Bonaparte
and Madame Jouberthou—Fury of the First Consul on learning
that his brother has married the lady—Madame Bonaparte
espouses Lucien's cause, but without success, and resolves
to withdraw for a time to Italy, as a protest against Napoleon's
severity—Letizia and Joséphine—Singular scene at a family
dinner-party at Mortefontaine—Lucien's imaginative powers—
Madame Bonaparte sets out for Rome—Extraordinary consideration shown her by Pius VII and the Papal Court—
Napoleon disapproves of his mother being received *en
souveraine*—His letter to the Pope.

ON her arrival in Paris, on February 11,
1803, Pauline went to live with Joseph
and his wife, at the Hôtel Marbeuf, in the
Rue Faubourg Saint-Honoré. Although she was
commonly reported to have brought back such
treasures from the Antilles as to render her by
far the wealthiest of the whole Bonaparte family,

she found herself, in reality, in possession of a very moderate fortune, compared with those which her brothers and sisters enjoyed,[1] and she had contracted so many debts that her estate of Montgobert had to be sold to satisfy the claims of her creditors. Indeed, if the First Consul had not given her a pension of 60,000 francs on the Grande Cassette, similar to those which he had already granted Élisa and Caroline, she would have found herself quite unable to maintain the position to which she had been accustomed since her marriage.

However Napoleon's generosity relieved her of all financial anxieties, and, speedily wearying of the Hôtel Marbeuf, and the supervision which Joseph considered it his duty to exercise over her, she began to look about for a house of her own. Her search was a brief one, as, in the following April, she purchased, from the *ci-devant* Duchesse de Charost, the palatial hôtel of that name, in the Rue Faubourg Saint-Honoré, close to the Hôtel Marbeuf, with a spacious garden, which extended as far as the Champs Élysées.[2] The purchase money of the Hôtel Charost was

---

[1] Leclerc's property, real and personal, was valued at about 1,100,000 francs, which was divided between his wife and child, Pauline having also a life interest in half of her son's share. But this valuation included large sums owing to the deceased officer, who seems to have been of an extravagantly-generous disposition, some of which were irrecoverable; while the title-deeds of his Italian property had been lost.

[2] It had been built, in 1720, by Mazin, for the Duc de Charost, *gouverneur* of Louis XV.

400,000 francs, and its new owner spent a further 50,000 francs on furniture and improvements.

Pauline was, for a week or two, as pleased with the Hôtel Charost as a child with a new toy, but she soon became profoundly bored. It was no doubt delightful to possess a house of her very own, which she could furnish from cellar to attic exactly as her taste dictated, in which she was her own mistress, able to enjoy for the first time in her life the most absolute liberty. But what, she asked herself, was the advantage of possessing a beautiful and sumptuously-furnished house, if no one came to admire it—no one, that is to say, but her relatives and a few old friends of the family? What was the use of a splendid ball-room, if it were impossible to give a ball, or of one of the finest gardens in Paris, if one might not give a fête? What, in short, was the use of her having a house at all, if she were compelled to live the life of a nun?

For, be it remembered, Leclerc—that husband whose image was already becoming so faint—had been dead but some five months, and until nearly seven more had passed, etiquette and the First Consul exacted that Pauline should remain in the most complete retirement and wear mourning, which she detested. Her relatives, to console her, declared that black became her *à merveille*, but this, so far from producing the result they desired, only made her the more miserable; she shed tears of mortification at the thought that so few were able to admire her in her weeds.

At length, she decided that death itself would be preferable to a continuance of such an intolerable existence, and gradually the doors of the Hôtel Charost began to open to a select few of her innumerable admirers. "Bonaparte," writes Madame de Rémusat, "strongly exhorted her to conduct herself better than she had done before she went to St. Domingo; she promised everything, but soon broke her word."[1] On the other hand, M. Turquan's assertion that "her conduct was marked by a levity which surpassed all imagination," and that she "carried on several *liaisons* quite openly," is based on very untrustworthy evidence.[2] The most prominent of her adorers at this time, indeed, was Admiral Decrès, the Minister of Marine, whose intentions appear to have been strictly honourable. The Minister was an abnormally stout man, but he became so infatuated with the beautiful widow, who, in default of admirers more to her taste, flirted with him outrageously, that people declared that he was growing quite thin. However, Pauline had not the smallest intention of bestowing her hand upon a bluff sailor, almost old enough to be her father, and possessed of but a very moderate fortune; the widow of a general-in-chief and a sister of the First Consul might look very much higher than

[1] *Mémoires.*   [2] *Les Sœurs de Napoléon.*

that, and the only result of this affair was to convince Napoleon that, unless the lady were speedily provided with a second husband, she would, out of sheer ennui, end by seriously compromising herself.

He, therefore, began to look about him for a suitable *parti*, and cast a favourable eye upon Francesco di Melzi, the Vice-President of the new Italian Republic, the gentleman with whom Murat had quarrelled so vehemently during his residence at Milan. Melzi was a very great personage indeed, and, in respect both of birth and position, he was everything that Napoleon could desire as a brother-in-law : count at Milan, marquis at Turin, prince at Naples, and grandee of the first class at Madrid. Moreover, he was a man of real ability and high character, and was held in much esteem throughout Italy ; and to attach him more closely to his interests by marrying him to his sister would be to greatly strengthen Napoleon's influence throughout the peninsula. There was but one drawback : he was nearly thirty years older than Pauline, but that, in the First Consul's eyes, was a mere detail and unworthy of serious consideration.

Accordingly, he despatched one of his aides-de-camp to Milan, to inform the Vice-President of the signal honour which he proposed to confer upon him, but, to his chagrin, the honour was declined. Having got along excellently well for more than fifty years without a wife, Melzi was not unnaturally disinclined to have his ways of life revolutionised by a young and pretty woman, particularly by one who, if rumour did not lie, required an unusually firm hand over her.

However, compensation for Napoleon's disappointment was not long in forthcoming, and from the same country in which he had experienced this rebuff. What Milan had refused, Rome hastened to accept.

At the beginning of April 1803, there arrived in Paris a visitor whose advent occasioned quite a little flutter of excitement in society, particularly among families who had daughters *à marier*. Prince Camillo Borghese—for that was the visitor's name—was the head of one of the most illustrious, and indisputably the most wealthy, of the great Roman families—a family which, though it had only been enrolled among the Roman aristocracy for two centuries, had some of the oldest blood in Italy running in its veins—that of the Orsini, the Aldobrandini, the Colonna, the Salviati—which owned a principality of eighty estates in the Roman campagna, a splendid residence in Florence, a palace in Rome "as big as a town," a villa outside the Porta del Popolo—the incomparable Villa Borghese—and the finest private art collection in all Europe.

The heir of this great fortune was, at this time, a young man in his twenty-eighth year, with regular features, brilliant dark eyes, curly black hair, and a figure which, if rather deficient in the matter of inches, was supple and well-proportioned; amiable and good-natured, and "not without a certain natural intelligence," though deplorably ignorant, since his father, Marco Antonio Borghese, had never troubled himself about his children's education, declaring that "they would always know enough to be the subjects of a Pope." For the rest, a brave soldier, a great dandy, a fine horseman, and "one of the most skilful coachmen in all Christendom, counting no rivals in the art of driving a phaëton drawn by four spirited horses."[1]

Like so many of the younger members of the Italian aristocracy, Camillo Borghese had embraced with enthusiasm republican ideas, and when the French entered Rome in 1798, and the short-lived Roman Republic was proclaimed, he and his younger brother, Prince Aldobrandini, had hastened to enlist in the National Guard. A little later, he saw some fighting, under Championnet, against the Neapolitan troops, in which he exhibited considerable courage and appears to have been slightly wounded. The restoration of the Papal authority naturally placed him in a very embarrassing situation, but, thanks to the influence of his powerful relatives, no steps were taken against him, and he remained in possession of his property, though, as he found himself far from a popular figure either in official circles or

---

[1] Maxime de Villemarest, *le Piémont sur l'Empire et la Cour du Prince Borghèse, Souvenirs d'un Inconnu*, 1808-9.

PRINCE CAMILLO BORGHESE

in society, he judged it advisable to withdraw to Florence, where he had been residing for the last three years.

The day following his arrival in Paris, Prince Borghese was presented to Napoleon, by Cardinal Caprara, the Papal Nuncio, on which occasion he appeared "in a dove-coloured suit, and carrying under his arm a hat of black taffeta decorated with feathers." Greatly to its disappointment, however, society saw nothing more of the distinguished foreigner for several weeks, the reason apparently being that the latter was, at this time, profoundly ignorant both of the French language and of French ways, and wished to acquire some knowledge of both before running the gauntlet of the salons. With this object in view, he cultivated the acquaintance of the concierge of the Hôtel Pinon, in the Rue de la Grange-Batelière, in which he had taken a suite of apartments, and spent a good deal of his time in conversation with him in his lodge. In after days, it is said, the prince was heard to declare that nothing in Paris had astonished him so much as the intelligence and refinement of this worthy man and his family.

Although, at first, these humble people and the art-dealers and bric-à-brac merchants, about whose shops Borghese was fond of pottering, were almost the only Parisians who could boast of the honour of the prince's acquaintance, he mixed freely in the foreign society of the capital, and was a frequent visitor at the Legations of the different Italian States. In diplomatic circles, his particular friend was Angiolini di Serravera, the official representative of the ex-Grand-Duke of Tuscany, whom the Treaty of Lunéville had removed to Wartzburg. Angiolini was on intimate terms with the Bonapartes and a great friend of Joseph, at whose house he had frequently met Pauline. He was also in the confidence of Cardinal Caprara, the Papal Nuncio, who was seeking by every means in his power to promote a better understanding between the French Government and the Papacy.[1] The Nuncio and Angiolini laid their heads together, and decided that it would be "productive of great good" if a marriage could be arranged between the wealthy Borghese and the beautiful Madame Leclerc. The alliance of a Roman prince with the favourite sister of the First Consul could not fail to dispose the latter more favourably towards the Holy See, and it might even be regarded as a sort of guarantee of peace; while Angiolini's share in bringing about such a match would increase his own influence at the Consular

---

[1] "Cardinal Caprara was one of the most crafty emissaries that ever obtained, even from the See of St. Peter, a temporary share in the commerce of diplomacy. Notwithstanding the decrepitude of his appearance, the weak and subdued tones of his musical voice, the humility of his bearing, and the stealthy inquisitiveness of his glance, that head concealed under its grey hairs and the scarlet cap of his Order, more subtlety, more cunning, more petty perfidy, than can well be imagined."—Duchess d'Abrantès, *Mémoires*.

Court, and possibly enable him to secure more suitable "compensation" in Germany or elsewhere for the dispossessed Grand-Duke, his master. Caprara, who, it is highly probable, was acting on instructions received from the Vatican, was undoubtedly the moving spirit in the affair; but he very prudently remained in the background and left the negotiations in the hands of Angiolini.

At the beginning of June, without, however, saying anything to Borghese, Angiolini approached Madame Bonaparte and Joseph on the subject. His proposition was received very favourably indeed, and it was agreed that the young people should be brought together without loss of time. Joseph accordingly invited the prince, together with Angiolini, Caprara, and some other Italian diplomatists, to spend a day at Mortefontaine; and Borghese, who, thanks to his frequent conversations with the concierge at the Hôtel Pinon, had by this time succeeded in acquiring some familiarity with the French language, accepted the invitation and was duly presented to Pauline. The latter, warned in advance of the object of the party, had made as elaborate a toilette as her recent loss permitted, and brought every weapon in the arsenal of her charms to bear upon the distinguished foreigner.

The match-makers had every reason to be satisfied with the first move in the game. The

prince did not attempt to disguise the profound
admiration with which the lady inspired him;
while the lady was graciously pleased to approve
of the prince, and still more of the prince's position and fortune. Her grief for her husband's
death, sincere enough at the time, had not long
survived her return to France, and her separation
from everything that might have served to recall
it. Indeed, its very violence had militated against
its continuance. A nature like hers is incapable of
harbouring any sentiment for long, and the more
lively the first impressions, the more speedily are
they effaced. Love, hatred, joy, grief—all pass
away; vanity alone remains.

And then she was so tired of the habiliments
of woe—those detestable black silk gowns, those
odious crape bonnets with their white trimmings!
—so weary of the semi-monastic seclusion on
which the First Consul continued to insist! A
second marriage would enable her to escape from
these restrictions earlier than would otherwise
be possible, and, in the meanwhile, the preparations which it would necessitate would serve as
a welcome distraction from her ennui.

And what a marriage it was that offered itself!
She would be a princess—a real princess—a princess by the grace of the Pope, if not by the grace
of God! How jealous Élisa and Caroline would
be! How furious Joséphine and Hortense! As
for Madame de Contades and all the spiteful
crew of the Faubourg Saint-Germain, who

affected to despise her as an upstart, they would be ready to die of mortification!

And she would not only be a princess, but a very wealthy woman, in a position to indulge all her extravagant fancies, to gratify all her caprices. She would reside in palaces as big as the Tuileries, and in villas in comparison with which Malmaison, Mortefontaine, Neuilly, and Plessis were but modest farm-houses. She would wear the famous Borghese diamonds—finer than any which Paris could boast—and toilettes which even a queen might envy. Finally, she would have a husband, young, handsome, amiable and, she did not doubt, devoted. It was indeed a glorious prospect!

A few days after the meeting at Mortefontaine, Angiolini was authorised by Joseph Bonaparte to ascertain Borghese's views upon the matter. The First Consul had already been approached, and had signified his full approval, although he judged it best not to appear in the affair personally, and to leave Joseph, in his quality of nominal head of the family, to conduct the negotiations. On June 20, Angiolini wrote to Joseph that he had had a long conference with the prince, "who seemed more alarmed than astonished at the prospect." He had been unable to obtain from him a definite acceptance of his proposals, but he had no doubt what his answer would be, "since he had discovered that the essential object had been achieved : the lady pleased him."

A night's reflection, in fact, sufficed to determine Borghese, who was not only in love—or, at any rate, within measurable distance of that condition of mind—but was conscious that he would derive considerable advantages from his connection with the First Consul's family, notably, his immediate restoration to the position he had formerly enjoyed in Rome ; for who would dare to cold-shoulder the brother-in-law of the man who held the future of the Papacy in the hollow of his hand ?   Accordingly, he sent for Angiolini, and authorised him to inform Joseph that "the Prince Borghese would be only too happy if the First Consul were willing to accord him the honour to espouse his amiable sister, Madame Paulette," stipulating only that the betrothal should remain a secret until he had obtained the consent of the princess-dowager, with whom, since his adhesion to republican principles, some years before, his relations had been far from cordial.   This matter would seem to have occasioned the prince and his diplomatic advisers considerable anxiety, and to have necessitated more than one conference to decide upon the terms of the letter, since it was not until a week later that Borghese's secretary set out for Rome, bearing the epistle in question, and another from Caprara to the Secretary of State, to announce the marriage and to solicit the consent of the Holy Father.

The news appears to have been received at Rome with positive enthusiasm.   " His Holiness," writes Fesch to the First Consul, "was enchanted; the Roman nobility has testified its satisfaction, and the Princess Borghese is extremely pleased, and sighs only for the moment when she will be able to embrace your sister. She has sent to Paris Prince Aldobrandini, her second son, in token of her approbation. She is a good woman, who will make Paulette's life happy. It is a family which has a revenue of 100,000 piastres. . . . Behold me related to the first family in Rome!" And, in view of the extra expense which the relationship cannot fail to entail, he demands an increase of salary.[1]

If we are to believe the *Mémorial de Sainte-Hélène*, the enthusiasm was not confined to Rome. "My origin," Napoleon is made to say, "caused me to be regarded by all Italians as a fellow-countryman. . . . When the marriage of my sister Pauline with the Prince Borghese was announced, there was only one voice at Rome and in Tuscany, in the family in question, and in all those connected with it : "It is good! It is a marriage between ourselves; she is one of our family!"

In France, too, the effect of the announcement was all that the First Consul could have desired. "There will then, at any rate, be one princess in the Bonaparte family," observed those who foresaw that Napoleon's assumption of the vacant

---

[1] Letter of Messidor 24, Year XI (July 3, 1803), published by M. Masson, *Napoléon et sa famille.*

throne was only a question of a year or two ; and the Royalists of the Faubourg Saint-Germain, who had obstinately persisted in regarding him and his relatives as low-born adventurers, felt that in future it would be impossible to refuse them a certain measure of consideration. " In the eyes of many people," writes Villemarest, "an alliance with a Roman prince was a very great honour for the head of the Government. Neither the laurels of Italy, nor those of Egypt, nor the still fresher laurels of Marengo, were, in the opinion of a certain world, titles to esteem comparable with the right of displaying two crossed keys in one's armorial bearings."[1]

The one discordant note in the general chorus of congratulation was struck by the libeller Peltier, who, from his safe retreat in London, ironically felicitated the First Consul, in an "open letter," in *l'Ambigu* :

I offer you my sincere congratulations on the approaching marriage of the widow Leclerc and the Prince Camillo Borghese. I feared, at first, in perusing the details of her grief, that she would be unwilling to play the widow of Malabar ; but I see that La Fontaine was perfectly right when he said that there was a great difference between the widow of a year and the widow of a day. I do not despair of seeing her one day a female pope, in whose train you will lead the world.[2]

[1] *Souvenirs d'un Inconnu.*
[2] Published by M. d'Almeras, *Une Amoureuse: Pauline Bonaparte.*

At the beginning of August, Angiolini, acting on behalf of Borghese, and Joseph Bonaparte, representing Pauline, drew up the articles of the marriage-contract. The First Consul agreed to provide his sister with a dowry of 500,000 francs, to which Pauline added a sum of 300,000 francs. These 800,000 francs were to be paid to the husband, who, however, was only to enjoy a life interest in the sum, and, out of the income it produced, to pay his wife 20,000 francs a year for the expenses of her toilette. In the event of the prince predeceasing her, the dowry was to revert to Pauline, who was also to receive an income of 50,000 francs, to retain, so long as she lived, certain apartments in the Palazzo Borghese, and to have the use of two carriages. The articles were duly signed by Pauline and Borghese, at the Hôtel Charost, on August 23. Nothing remained but to fix the date of the marriage ceremony.

Here, however, a difficulty presented itself. By Article 228 of the recently promulgated Civil Code, a widow was at liberty to contract a second marriage ten months after the death of her husband, and, as Leclerc had died on November 2, 1802, Pauline might legally wed Borghese almost immediately. But Napoleon, in accordance with his determination to put a stop to the licence which had so long prevailed, and restore that decorum which he held to be inseparable from the form of government which he was seeking to establish, had, at the beginning of the Year XI of the Republic, that is to say, at the end of September, 1802, formally re-established at the Consular Court the custom of the *ancien régime*, which prescribed a year and six weeks of mourning for the loss of a husband, and had announced his intention of strictly enforcing it. To allow this usage, to which every one was aware he attached so much importance, to be violated by a member of his own family would be to stultify himself, and was not to be contemplated for a moment; and he therefore intimated to his sister and Borghese, who pressed for an immediate marriage, that the happy event could not take place before November 3. The only concession he would make was to shorten the period of his sister's mourning by the odd six weeks.

What followed is certainly very singular. A few days after the signing of the marriage-contract, probably, M. Masson thinks, on August 31, Pauline and Borghese were privately married, at Mortefontaine, by an Italian priest, very possibly Caprara himself, in the presence of Lucien, Joseph, and Angiolini, quite unknown to Napoleon, but with the full knowledge and consent of Madame Bonaparte. If the precise date of this marriage, observes M. Masson, is impossible to fix, since the parish registers of Mortefontaine previous to the year 1804 have not been preserved—besides which, it was an illegal contract, since no civil ceremony had preceded it, and was, therefore, unlikely to be recorded in them—of the fact there can be no possible doubt. It is attested by a note of Borghese's, unfortunately bearing no date, inviting Angiolini to accompany him, *with Lucien*, to Joseph's country-house, "where, on the same day, the marriage would take place"; and by a series of letters, in which Angiolini speaks of the happiness of the two *spouses*, "who love one another as much as man and wife are able" and "who will spend two months in the country until the termination of *their* mourning."[1]

What is the explanation of this "marriage of conscience"? The answer is no doubt to be found in the ardour of the Italian temperament and in what St. Jerome says concerning the virtue of widows. M. Masson, by the way, makes no comment on the matter, presumably being of opinion that it admits of but one explanation.

Although the marriage itself was kept a profound secret, so much so, indeed, that scarcely any one, outside those immediately concerned, ever discovered it had taken place, and that, so far as we are aware, none of the historians of the Bonapartes, with the exception of M. Masson, have even suspected its existence, the same discretion was not observed by the happy pair in their relations towards each other, and ere many

---

[1] *Napoléon et sa famille.*

days had passed, a rumour began to circulate that Borghese was the beautiful widow's lover, and people declared that it was perfectly scandalous that the First Consul should tolerate such conduct on the part of his sister. The consequence was that when the public and legal marriage took place, on the following November 6, it appears to have been the general belief that Napoleon viewed it with disfavour, and only consented to the match in order to legitimate the supposed *liaison*—a report to which his absence from the ceremony certainly gave colour.[1]

Napoleon, as a matter of fact, remained in ignorance of what had taken place until after the betrothal dinner, which he gave at the Tuileries on October 23, and his indignation at the deceit which had been practised upon him by his family may be imagined. He showed his displeasure by refusing to condone by his presence such a violation of the laws of the Republic and of his own commands; and, three days before the day fixed for the ceremony, he set out to visit the camp at Boulogne, since, had he remained in Paris, his abstention must have occasioned general surprise.

The second marriage, like the first, took place at Mortefontaine, in the presence of the whole family, with the exception of Napoleon and Jérôme—who was then in America—and a few

[1] Madame de Rémusat, *Mémoires*.

intimate friends, among whom were Bernadotte and Stanislas de Girardin. In accordance, presumably, with the First Consul's instructions, it was celebrated in the most unostentatious manner possible, and was followed by none of the usual rejoicings; while nothing beyond the mere announcement that Madame Leclerc and the Prince Borghese had been made man and wife appeared in the journals.[1]

Nevertheless, Pauline was now a princess, and her pride and delight in her new dignity was unbounded. The farewell visits to her relatives and friends, which etiquette required her to pay before leaving Paris, were for her truly delicious moments—moments when she experienced to the full the intoxication of success, the joys of gratified vanity. With her lovely face, her brilliant toilettes, her splendid jewels, and the halo of nobility which encircled her, they were one long triumphant progress.

The most important of these visits was of course that to Joséphine, who was then residing at Saint-Cloud. What joy to present herself as a princess before her detested sister-in-law, who was still only Madame Bonaparte! In a carriage

---

[1] Pauline no doubt found some consolation for being compelled to content herself with so quiet a wedding in the generosity of her husband. Borghese presented his bride with the sum of 40,000 francs to buy what she pleased—one of her purchases was *une robe d'Angleterre*, for which she paid 12,000 francs—and jewels to the value of 58,000 francs; while, at the same time, the famous Borghese diamonds were placed in her *corbeille*.

drawn by six splendid horses and preceded and followed by outriders bearing torches—a spectacle which had not been witnessed since the beginning of the Revolution—Pauline and her husband drove one evening to Saint-Cloud. "*Monseigneur le prince et Madame la princesse Borghèse!*" And she sailed into the salon, clad in a marvellous gown of green velvet and literally ablaze with diamonds: diamonds on her corsage, diamonds in her coiffure, diamonds in her ears, on her neck, on her arms, on her hands—an apparition so dazzling, so extraordinary, that the men who were present could scarce find words to express their admiration or the women their envy!

Joséphine, on her side, was not unprepared for battle. Warned by some faithless waiting-woman or *couturière's* assistant of her enemy's plans, she had chosen her ground and made her dispositions with considerable skill. She received the attack in a salon hung entirely with blue, which, it was generally conceded, greatly detracted from the effect of Pauline's wonderful green gown; while she herself was dressed in the extreme of costly simplicity, in a gown of Indian muslin,[1] caught on either shoulder by two lions' heads in gold and black enamel, and bordered with gold foil; a plain gold circlet clasped by a lion's head, similar to those on her shoulders,

---

[1] The muslin of which this gown was made cost 75 francs an ell.

for her girdle, and not a single jewel. The simplicity and good taste shown by the wife of the
First Consul formed a piquant and by no means
unfavourable contrast to the gorgeous toilette
and flashing jewels of the new princess; and
when, in her soft, measured tones, Joséphine
complimented her visitor on her dazzling appearance, the irony of the situation was not lost upon
those standing by, who could not conceal their
amusement.

A few days after this incident (November 13,
1803), Pauline and her husband set out for Italy,
their departure having been apparently hastened
by an intimation from Napoleon to his sister that
she must leave Paris before his return to the
capital. In order to mark still further his displeasure at her conduct, he declined to write the
usual letter of recommendation to the Dowager-
Princess Borghese and delegated that duty to
Joseph, and, whereas he had recently raised
Élisa's allowance from 60,000 to 120,000 francs,
he allowed Pauline's to remain at the former
figure.

Napoleon's indignation at the deceit which had
been practised upon him by Pauline was as
nothing in comparison with the fury that possessed him on learning of Lucien's second
marriage.

In May or June 1802, Lucien had met at
Méreville, at the house of his friend Laborde, a

certain Madame Jouberthou, a beautiful young woman of twenty-four, the wife of a Paris stock-jobber, who, after acquiring considerable wealth by speculation, had ended by being almost completely ruined, and had sailed with the expedition to St. Domingo, in the hope of mending his shattered fortunes. This lady rapidly acquired the most complete ascendency over Lucien's mind and senses, and the end of that summer found her installed at Plessis-Chamant, as mistress of both the house and its owner, to the intense chagrin of Élisa, who saw the influence which she had so long exercised over her brother seriously menaced.

"You know already, my amiable and excellent friend," writes Fontanes to her, under date Vendémiaire 12 (October 4), "all that I can tell you, for a single glance is sufficient to penetrate the masks; the lady is beautiful, as coquettish as she is beautiful, as greedy as she is coquettish. This reign may be long and a costly one.

"All the symptoms of a lively passion may be discerned in the countenance and conversation of the patron [Lucien]. He is discreet, mysterious; he thinks of his happiness, but it is not that to which the lady attaches importance; she desires publicity, splendour, and all the advantages which come from a properly-acknowledged connection. Her demeanour soon told us that it was she who was holding the court, and to whom we must pay it. This pride is very amusing.

"They are to play *Alzire*. It is difficult to combine less grace and more beauty. I longed

LUCIEN BONAPARTE

FROM A LITHOGRAPH BY DELPECH

to cry out that grace is more charming still than beauty ; but, while she was rehearsing her part, they pronounced your name, and that name expressed what I wished to say. However much I long to see you, I congratulate you on your refusal [to come to Plessis]. You ought not to appear to approve, by appearing here, of this choice, which makes us greatly regret the Spanish one."[1]

In expressing the opinion that the reign of Lucien's new charmer was likely to prove both a long and a costly one, Fontanes was certainly right, though not exactly in the sense which he intended to convey. In June 1802, Madame Jouberthou's husband died at Port-au-Prince, a victim no doubt to the epidemic that was ravaging St. Domingo, and on May 25, 1803, Lucien contracted a secret ecclesiastical marriage with the widow, who, on the previous day, had borne him a son, baptised by the names of Jules Laurence Lucien.

Three days after this clandestine marriage, the puppet King of Etruria died, and Napoleon, who, although he was well aware of the *liaison* between his brother and Madame Jouberthou, had not the smallest suspicion that Lucien had carried his infatuation to the point of contracting a marriage of conscience with the lady, immediately determined to arrange a match between

---

[1] The Marquesa de Santa-Cruz, the lady whom Lucien had brought from Spain, and who had now been discarded by him, in favour of Madame Jouberthou.

him and the widowed Queen.[1] Such a union
would have the double advantage of removing
Lucien from France, where he was frequently at
variance with the First Consul, and promoting
French interests both in Italy and Spain. Lucien
professed to treat the proposition as a jest,
observing that Napoleon could surely not be in
earnest in offering him a wife so destitute of all
mental and physical attractions as this royal
widow—the Infanta was ignorant and superstitious, "ugly, fat, lame, crooked, and almost a
dwarf." But, at the same time, he did not give
a definite refusal, and allowed Napoleon to think
that one day he might be brought to consent.

The wrath of the First Consul can therefore
be imagined, when, at the end of the following
October, he learned that Lucien had contracted
a civil and legal marriage with his mistress, and
recognised as his legitimate son the boy born in
the previous May. Not only had his brother
deceived him, not only had he upset his plans in
regard to Etruria, not only had he brought a lady
"distinguished for her gallantries" into the
family, not only had he provided Royalists and
Jacobins with material for any number of libellous pamphlets and ribald verses, but, failing the
birth of sons to himself or Joseph, Lucien's son
—"the fruit of a union that a tardy marriage
alone had legitimated"—would become the heir
to the future Imperial throne. What a weapon

---

[1] The Infanta Maria Luisa, daughter of Carlos IV of Spain.

to place in the hands of the enemies of the dynasty he was on the point of founding![1]

Contrary to what several writers have stated, the First Consul did not at once bring pressure to bear upon Lucien to induce him to annul his marriage, which his neglect to comply with certain formalities enjoined by the Civil Code would have rendered an easy task. He merely forbade him to permit his wife to bear his name, or to present her to the family without his authorisation. Lucien promised obedience, but his stubborn nature revolted against such orders—he held that "every man of honour ought to be the supreme pontiff of the sanctuary of his private life "—and not only did he direct his wife to assume the name of Bonaparte, but he induced his mother, Joseph and his wife, and the Baciocchi to receive her.

Matters between him and Napoleon thereupon became so unpleasant that Lucien found it necessary to withdraw for a time from France, and, at the beginning of December 1803, he set out with his wife for Italy, declaring, in a letter to Joseph, that "he departed with hatred in his heart."

Although there is no reason to suppose that

[1] The story which Lucien relates, on the authority of Murat, of the manner in which Napoleon received the news : " *Sachez que Lucien a épousé sa coquine*," arms waving like a semaphore, and so forth, is probably apocryphal, like much else in Lucien's *Mémoires*. Murat had left for Cahors on the day on which his brother-in-law's marriage took place, and, therefore, could not have assisted at the scene in question.

I.—23

Madame Bonaparte had been aware of Lucien's intentions to marry Madame Jouberthou, once the marriage was an accomplished fact, she accepted it, and there can be little doubt that the sympathy and support which he received from his mother did much to encourage Lucien in his resistance to the orders of the First Consul. During his absence, which lasted three months, Letizia espoused his cause with the utmost warmth, and some very lively discussions seem to have taken place between her and Napoleon. But all her entreaties, all her tears, failed to shake the resolution at which the First Consul had arrived. Lucien, he declared, must lose his right of succession, unless he would consent to repudiate Madame Jouberthou and lend himself to the dissolution of the marriage.

After visiting Rome, Naples, Florence, and Venice, Lucien, at the end of February 1804, returned to Paris, and had a stormy interview with the First Consul, which, he tells us, was "followed by a reconciliation due to the solicitations of mamma." What really appears to have happened, was that Napoleon proposed that his brother should repudiate his wife; that Lucien angrily refused, and that the First Consul retorted by advising him to leave France and not to return until he should be in a different frame of mind. Then Madame Bonaparte intervened, and, after vainly endeavouring to soften Napoleon, announced her intention of retiring to Italy, as a protest against what she considered his unjust treatment of her favourite son, suggested that Lucien should follow her thither, and persuaded the First Consul to cause their departure to be announced officially as journeys in search of health and pleasure.

Letizia's desire to show her sympathy towards the persecuted Lucien was not the only motive which urged her to leave France at this juncture. If Napoleon declined to allow her to dictate to him the policy which he was to pursue towards the different members of the family, he was always ready to listen to her representations, and invariably treated her with the utmost generosity and consideration. He had lately, as we have mentioned elsewhere, given her an allowance of 120,000 francs; he had also defrayed the cost of extensive improvements at her hôtel in the Rue du Mont-Blanc, and had commissioned Gérard to paint a full-length portrait of her to adorn the grand salon at Saint-Cloud. But all this did not console her for the increasing deference which she saw paid to Joséphine, and which she beheld with the bitterest mortification. At a family gathering, in the previous June, at Joseph's country-seat at Mortefontaine, a most unpleasant incident had occurred.

Wishing apparently to accustom his relatives to the sight of Joséphine taking precedence of all the ladies of the family, in their ordinary inter-course, as well as on official occasions, Napoleon directed Joseph to escort his wife into dinner and to place her on his right hand. Joseph, however, well aware of his mother's extreme sensitiveness on this point, refused, and no argument could induce him to give way. "When dinner was announced," writes Madame de Rémusat, who was present, "Joseph took his mother's hand, and Lucien escorted Joséphine. The First Consul, incensed at this opposition to his will, hurriedly crossed the room, took his wife's arm, passed out before every one, seated her beside himself, and then, turning to me, ordered me to place myself near her. The company were all greatly embarrassed, I even more so than the others, and Madame Joseph Bonaparte found herself at the bottom of the table, as though she were not one of the family. The constraint and gloom of that dinner-party can be imagined. The brothers were angry, Joséphine was wretched, and I was excessively distressed by my prominent position. During dinner, Bonaparte did not address a single member of his family." [1]

And now Joséphine was on the point of becoming Empress, of assuming a position within, as well as outside, the family circle which would no longer admit of any question. Rather than assist at the triumph of her hated daughter-in-law, the implacable matron felt that she would prefer to retire to the ends of the earth.

Lucien, in his *Mémoires*, has left us a most

[1] *Mémoires.*

pathetic account, reproduced *in extenso* by Baron
Larrey and Madame Tschudi, of his last night in
Paris. He and his wife, his mother, and Joseph
are assembled in the picture gallery of his hôtel
in the Rue Saint-Dominique ; the two ladies are
sitting by the fire, Joseph and himself are rest-
lessly pacing up and down ; the travelling-
carriages, laden with trunks and valises, stand in
the courtyard outside ; the post-horses are ordered ;
the exiles are to leave for Rome at daybreak.
Eleven o'clock strikes ; Letizia rises and approaches her sons, and, in a voice choked with
emotion, tells them it is time to bid farewell.
Joseph, however, begs her to wait until midnight,
as he is hopeful that the First Consul may yet
recall Lucien ; and Madame Bonaparte consents,
though she is but too well aware of the futility of
his hopes. Half an hour passes, and then Joseph
proposes that he shall go to the Tuileries and
make a last appeal to the First Consul. His
mother tells him that it would be useless, and, after
declaring her intention of following Lucien to
Italy, "falls back weeping and half-suffocated
into the arms of my excellent wife." The
minutes glide by ; Joseph paces the room, his
ear tuned to catch every sound ; Lucien sits on
a stool at the feet of his wife and mother. Midnight strikes ; all hope that Napoleon may relent
is at an end. Lucien, taking his wife by the
hand, kneels before his mother to receive her
blessing. "*Au revoir, au revoir ; à bientôt à*

Rome!" says Madame Bonaparte, and leaves the room to conceal her emotion.

The accuracy of the aforegoing may be judged from the fact that Madame Bonaparte's departure for Rome *preceded* that of Lucien. She left Paris on March 13, 1804, while her son remained until Easter Sunday, April 1. Nevertheless, it is of interest, if only as an example of Lucien's imaginative powers, and as showing how little reliance can be placed in many memoirs which, at first sight, appear to be of undoubted value.

Madame Bonaparte left Paris in a sumptuous travelling-carriage, the gift of the First Consul, on the repairs of which he had just expended 5,000 francs. She travelled incognito, under the name of Madame Roccoboni, and was accompanied by Madame Étienne Clary—Joseph Bonaparte's sister-in-law—Madame d'Andelarre, who occupied the post of *dame de compagnie*, her secretary Guieu, her physician Bacher, and two waiting-maids. Her incognito was strictly respected until she reached Turin, where not only a number of private persons, but several deputations, waited upon her to bid her welcome ; after which it was abandoned, and she entered Bologna amid the firing of cannon and escorted by a squadron of Polish cavalry. On entering the States of the Church, she was received with the most profound respect and lodged in the Papal palace at Loretto. Finally, on Holy Saturday (March 31), she arrived in Rome, and took up her resi-

dence with her half-brother Cardinal Fesch, at
the French Legation.

In a letter to the First Consul, the cardinal
gives an interesting account of the exceptional
honours which were being paid to his sister, who,
on her side, appears to have regarded them as
but her just due.

Your mother arrived in Rome on Germinal
10, Holy Saturday (March 31), after a journey of
eighteen days. . . .

On her arrival in Rome, his Holiness had
already given orders that a tribune should be
prepared for her at St. Peter's similar to those
occupied by the Queen of Sardinia and the
Princes of Mecklenburg, in order that she might
assist at the Easter Mass. But, since it was
only possible to place this tribune behind those
of the said persons, who had been in possession
of theirs for more than a year, she judged it
advisable to decline the honour, on the plea of
fatigue after her journey.

Yesterday, I presented her to the Pope at the
Quirinal, when she was accompanied by her
daughter [Pauline Borghese] and Madame Clary,
all in full gala dress. The Swiss Guard escorted
her as far as the first ante-chamber, where she
was received by the Masters of the Chamber,
and the Guard of Nobles presented arms. The
Pope spoke to her of his attachment to your person, and of the prayers which he offers up for
your preservation. He told her that he would
be enchanted to see her frequently, and that
he hoped she would remain as long as she
pleased. In fact, it was she herself who was

obliged to terminate the interview, after a long conversation.

The Roman nobility, without waiting for the fixed days of reception, have come to visit her. The doyen of the Sacred College instructed all the cardinals to pay their respects to her within twenty-four hours. All, even the Neapolitans, hastened to show her this attention, which is usually only accorded to royalty. She has come through all the ceremonial very well, and I believe that Rome is the very place for her. She will very willingly remain here, and I shall do everything that loving care can effect to render her happy.

The journey has done your mother a great deal of good ; she is remarkably well.[1]

Overjoyed at the new tie which he had formed with the master of the Continent, Pius VII hastened to write Napoleon a letter full of praises of Madame Bonaparte : " We know not how to tell you how pleased we have been with the conversation which we have had with her. We found her worthy of being your mother." And much more to the same purpose.

Napoleon, however, was seriously annoyed on learning that the Papal Court was under the impression that, by receiving his mother *en souveraine*, they were gratifying him. Madame Bonaparte had sided with his rebellious younger brother, received Madame Jouberthou, recognised the marriage, and, finally, exiled herself, as

---

[1] Published by Baron Larrey.

POPE PIUS VII

FROM A LITHOGRAPH BY DELPECH

a protest against what she considered his severity towards Lucien. The honours which were being paid her were calculated, in his opinion, to give her an exaggerated idea of her importance in the family, and to encourage her to oppose his will, both in regard to the marriage of Lucien and the position of Joséphine. His reply to his Holiness's effusive letter was accordingly decidedly curt, and intimated pretty plainly that he considered that the Vatican was carrying its attentions towards the mother to greater lengths than the son deemed desirable.

2 Floréal, Year XII

(April 22, 1804)

I thank your Holiness for the amiable things that you say to me in reference to the arrival of my mother in Rome. The climate of Paris is much too damp and cold for her. My first physician counselled her to settle in a warm country, more resembling her native land. Whatever resolution she takes, I shall not cease to recommend her to your Holiness.

I am with filial respect your Holiness's very devoted son,

Bonaparte

On May 6, Lucien arrived in Rome, though without his wife and children, whom he had left at the Castle of Bassano, some thirty miles from the capital, which he had rented for the summer from the Guistiniani family. He came provided with a letter of recommendation from Napoleon to the Pope, which stated that "the Senator Lucien, his brother, desired to reside at Rome, in order to devote himself to the study of antiquities and history." Lucien does not appear to have imagined that his studies would last very long; he had transgressed so many times before, only to be forgiven and received back into favour, thanks to the intercession of his mother, that he could not bring himself to believe that his disgrace could be more than temporary. On this occasion, however, he had offended, not only against Napoleon himself, but against the dynasty which he was about to establish; and all Madame Bonaparte's efforts on his behalf were to prove unavailing.

O N May 18, 1804, the curtain was rung down on the farce of republican government, and the Empire proclaimed. And, singular phenomenon! Before that Empire had been many hours in existence, one found at the new Court the same rivalries, the same jealousies, the same struggles of contending vanity, as were to be witnessed at the Courts of monarchies several centuries old.

Napoleon had experienced little difficulty in deciding as to the rank to be assumed by his brothers. The claims of Lucien and Jérôme, who, by their marriages, had placed themselves outside the pale, and who he was determined should remain there, unless they consented to repudiate

their respective wives, were altogether ignored.
But Joseph and Lucien were to be created Princes
of the Empire and to be addressed as "Imperial
Highnesses," while their wives must of course
share their new dignities. He could do no less
for them, since, in default of his having a son,
it was from their children that he must choose
his successor.[1] But it was much less easy to
determine the positions which his mother and
sisters would occupy. The elevation of his
brothers might arouse a certain amount of criticism, but they had at least some claim to the
consideration of the nation. Joseph had been
entrusted with important diplomatic missions, and
both at Lunéville and Amiens had displayed considerable ability; while Louis had fought for
France in Italy and Egypt, and, as his comrades at Castiglione and Arcola could bear witness, bravely enough. But how could he justify
the elevation of the women? According to the
old French law, a woman's social position was
determined by that of her husband; by herself
she had no legal status and could acquire none.
Even in cases where, in default of male heirs,
a duchy or a marquisate had devolved upon a
daughter, her husband had assumed the title and
exercised the privileges of the deceased noble-

[1] The *plébiscite* which established the Empire in Napoleon's
family passed over Joseph and Louis, as well as Lucien and
Jérôme, and vested the succession in the natural or adopted son of
Napoleon, and in the heirs male of Joseph or Louis.

man. Apart from the mistresses of certain kings, there was no precedent for a woman being invested with a dignity with which her husband was not associated.

On the other hand, he knew the character of his mother and sisters too well to suppose that they would be inclined to listen to reason when they beheld not only Joséphine sharing the Imperial dignity, but the wives of Joseph and Louis enjoying princely honours, by right of their husbands. It was to ask them to submit to a twofold mortification, to a double wound to their vanity, to an inferiority which must seem to those proud and jealous natures almost intolerable.

Nevertheless, it appeared to him preferable to brave their indignation, rather than to create a precedent which would be certain to provoke hostile comment, particularly among the old families of the Faubourg Saint-Germain, whom he was most anxious to reconcile to the new *régime*. He hoped, moreover, that splendid establishments, generous allowances, and the promotion of their husbands to be grandees of the State, might soothe the wounded feelings of his sisters ; and that his mother, who had hitherto limited her ambition to preserving the first place in the family, without pretending to exterior honours, might rest content with the augmentation of her allowance which he intended to give her.

Nothing then had been decided for the women

when the Empire was proclaimed. Élisa and Caroline—Madame Bonaparte and Pauline were still in Italy—had been in a condition of feverish anxiety for days past, and, though both were, as a rule, particularly skilful in dissimulating their feelings, their agitation of mind was, on this occasion, beyond their power to conceal, and aroused no small amusement. Since they did not dare to speak to Napoleon on the subject, they had recourse to Talleyrand and Fouché, whom they overwhelmed with questions concerning the Emperor's intentions with regard to the ladies of his family. The two Ministers, however, professed ignorance of their master's projects, but inclined to the belief that, though Joséphine would certainly receive the title of Empress, hers would be the only new qualification ; and Joseph and Louis, whom they also interrogated, were of the same opinion.

At length, the great day arrived. Cambacérès, the President of the Senate, came to Saint-Cloud, at the head of that body, and proclaimed the First Consul Emperor of the French, giving him, for the first time, the title of "Your Majesty," which Napoleon accepted as coolly as though he had borne it all his life. The Senate then proceeded to Joséphine's apartments, and proclaimed her Empress, in her turn.

In the evening, there was a grand dinner, to which all the members of the Imperial Family and the chief officers of State were invited. Just

NAPOLEON I

FROM AN ENGRAVING AFTER THE PAINTING BY PAUL DELAROCHE

before dinner was announced, Duroc, the Grand Marshal of the Palace, made the circuit of the room and informed each guest that the title of Prince was to be given to Joseph and Louis Bonaparte, and that of Princess to their wives.

It is easy to conceive the feelings with which Caroline and Élisa received this communication. They had schooled themselves to accept the "Majesty" of Joséphine; but they had never imagined that Julie and Hortense, who were not "of the Blood," were to receive titles which were to be denied to themselves. It was a monstrous injustice, a shame, an infamy! But, let us listen to the account which Madame de Rémusat, one of those present on this important occasion, has left us of what followed:

"Madame Baciocchi and Madame Murat appeared highly displeased at the distinction made between them and their sisters-in-law. Madame Murat, in particular, could hardly conceal her displeasure. Towards six o'clock, the Emperor appeared and began, without the least embarrassment, to salute each one present by his or her title. He was in good spirits, and, I think, enjoyed the slight confusion into which the new ceremonial threw us. The Empress was, as usual, amiable and perfectly at her ease; Joseph and Louis seemed pleased; Madame Joseph resigned to anything that might be required of her; Madame Louis, equally submissive; while Eugène de Beauharnais was simple and natural, and entirely free from ambition or discontent. This was not the case with Murat, the newly-created marshal, but his fear of his brother-in-law obliged him to restrain himself, and he maintained a sullen silence. As for Madame Murat, she was a prey to the most violent mortification, and, during dinner, was so little mistress of her feelings that, on hearing the Emperor address Madame Louis several times as ' Princess,' she could not restrain her tears. She gulped down large glasses of water in her endeavours to recover herself and to appear to be taking something, but her tears always conquered her. Every one was embarrassed, and her brother smiled maliciously. For my part, I was astonished and even shocked to see her pretty young face disfigured by emotion arising from so mean a passion as envy. . . . No one could pity her tears, and, I think, they impressed every one else as disagreeably as they impressed me.

" Madame Baciocchi, who was older and more mistress of herself, shed no tears; but she assumed a brusque and sarcastic tone, and treated the _dames du palais_ with marked hauteur. The Emperor became annoyed at last, and aggravated the ill-humour of his sisters by indirect taunts, which wounded them to the quick. All that I witnessed in the course of that memorable day gave me new notions of the effect produced by ambition on minds of a certain order. It was a spectacle of which I could have formed no previous conception."[1]

The number of persons present on this occasion, of course, prevented the indignant ladies from giving vocal expression to their sentiments; but on the following day, after dinner, there was a violent scene, in Joséphine's boudoir, between the Emperor and Caroline, whose angry voices penetrated into the adjoining salon, where the *dames du palais* were sitting. " Madame Murat burst into complaints, tears, and reproaches; she inquired why he desired to condemn her and her sisters to obscurity and contempt, while strangers were loaded with honours and dignities. Napoleon, who could not bear any criticism of his acts, replied that he was master and would distribute honours as he pleased. 'To listen to you,' he observed ironically, 'one would imagine that I had robbed you of the inheritance of the late king, our father!' The discussion ended by Madame Murat sinking to the floor in a swoon, overcome by her excessive anger and by the bitterness of her brother's reproaches." Thereupon Napoleon's wrath vanished, and when restoratives had been applied and his sister had recovered consciousness, he promised to reconsider the matter. Talleyrand and Cambacérès were sent for, and the following morning a notice inserted in the *Moniteur* informed the world that the title of Imperial Highness was to be given not only

[1] *Mémoires.*

to the Emperor's brothers and their wives, but to his Majesty's sisters also.

Having been metamorphosed into Imperial Highnesses, one would have imagined that the Emperor's sisters would have been, for a time, content, but such was far from being the case. Scarcely had the question of their own position been settled than that of their husbands demanded consideration. The regulations of the new Court, modelled on those of the old *régime*, divided the Imperial apartments at the Tuileries and Saint-Cloud into several reception-rooms. The room nearest the Emperor's cabinet was called the Salon des Princes, and to this none but the Princes and Princesses of the Blood possessed the *entrée*. One day, at Saint-Cloud, Murat attempted to enter, but was stopped by the Chamberlain, M. de Rémusat, who courteously informed him that he had not the right of admission. As this incident took place in the presence of a number of persons, some of whom, we may be sure, did not attempt to conceal their amusement at the marshal's discomfiture, Murat was highly indignant, and Caroline no less so. Both inveighed in the strongest terms against the "affront" which had been put upon them; and, although poor Rémusat was not responsible for the orders which he had received, and had executed them with scrupulous courtesy, since they were already prejudiced against both him and his wife, on account of their attachment to

Joséphine, they conceived for him, from that moment, the most implacable enmity.

Having once tested her influence over her brother, Caroline was not inclined to submit to her husband being denied a prerogative which reflected on her own importance; and, though Napoleon resisted for a time, the tyranny of tears eventually prevailed, and both Murat and Baciocchi were given the *entrée*.

As Murat had been made a marshal, it was necessary to do something for Baciocchi, in order to pacify Élisa. In 1803, Félix had been given the command of the 26th demi-brigade of light infantry, but "he had not even troubled to dissimulate his military incapacity," and had moreover neglected his duties to such an extent, that when any of his officers desired promotion or other favours, they were in the habit of writing to Paris to beg Élisa to intercede for them with her brother. To promote him to the rank of general, which was what his wife desired, was obviously out of the question; and so Napoleon caused him to be elected a Senator, with a salary of 25,000 francs, which had the two-fold advantage of pleasing Élisa and necessitating Baciocchi's retirement from the army.

Élisa and Caroline naturally did not fail to represent to Napoleon that the allowances which had been considered sufficient for the sisters of the First Consul were altogether inadequate to support the dignity of Princesses of the Blood,

and accordingly, towards the end of June, these
were raised from 120,000 francs a year to 240,000
francs; while, at the same time, the former,
whose husband was much less wealthy than
Murat, was accorded a *gratification* of an additional 240,000 francs. As for Pauline, she had,
for the present, to be content with the pleasure
her vanity derived from being a princess in her
own right, since Napoleon had not yet forgiven
her for the deceit she had practised upon him in
the previous autumn.

Of the women of the family, Madame Bonaparte alone remained to be considered, and her
case presented a problem of no little perplexity.
Although Letizia had disapproved of Napoleon
assuming the Crown, and is said to have even
endeavoured to dissuade him from such a step,
now that the Empire was an accomplished fact,
she was determined to insist upon her relationship to the new monarch receiving adequate
recognition; and her pride was deeply wounded
when she learned that her sons were princes, and
her daughters and daughters-in-law princesses,
while her name had not even been mentioned. The
flames of her discontent were fanned by Lucien,
furious at finding how completely his own claims
had been ignored, and, at length, she became so
convinced that Napoleon intended to deny her the
honours and emoluments which she considered
to be legitimately hers, that her health was

seriously affected, and even the news that the Emperor had raised her allowance from 10,000 to 15,000 francs a month afforded her but momentary relief.   At the beginning of July, she left Rome to join Pauline at Bagni di Lucca, but, before starting, she appears to have instructed Fesch, who had lately joined the office of Grand Almoner of France, with a salary of 40,000 francs, to his other dignities, to write to the Emperor and expostulate with him in regard to his treatment of his mother, although Baron Larrey is of opinion that the cardinal undertook the task on his own initiative. Any way, he addressed to Napoleon the following letter :

20 Messidor, Year XII

(July 9, 1804)

Sire,—In spite of the occupations of your Imperial Majesty, I believe it to be my duty to speak to you for a moment of your mother and her position.

Your mother has started for the waters of Lucca. Her health is undermined by moral affections, rather than by any physical indisposition.   I have remarked that her malady is aggravated every time that she sees a courier arrive without letters for her.   She was greatly distressed to learn, from the gazettes, the advent of the Empire.   She has been very much affected at not receiving any special courier during the three months she has spent at Rome.   She is under the impression that your Imperial Majesty prefers all the family to her.   These grievous reflections weaken her health and arrest all the

benefits which she ought to expect from the
journey, the climate, and the remedies which she
is taking.   I have done everything for her, and I
have neglected nothing to quiet her apprehensions and to render her stay in Rome agreeable
to her.   But all my efforts have been frustrated
by the illness of Madame Clary, who understands
so well how to influence her.

Your mother is ambitious for a title, a settled
position.   She is distressed that some persons
call her " Majesty " and " Empress Mother," and
that others only give her the title of " Imperial
Highness," which her daughters bear.   She is
impatient to learn what you have decided upon.
She no longer desires to return to Rome ; she
anticipates that your Imperial Majesty will
summon her to Paris before the end of August,
the time when she intends leaving Lucca.[1]

After reading this letter, Napoleon, who had
never had any intention of placing his mother
in an inferior position to her daughters and
daughters-in-law, and had merely postponed the
consideration of her claims owing to the difficulty
of deciding what title she ought to bear, felt that
something must be done to satisfy her without
delay.   The question, however, was most per-
plexing.   To find a situation at all analogous to
the present one—that is to say, the case of a king
of France whose mother, still living, had not
been queen—it was necessary to go back to the
time of François I and Louise of Savoy.   That,

[1] *Lettres du Cardinal Fesch*, Bibliothèque Nationale, published
by Baron Larrey.

however, sufficed to convince him of the monstrous absurdity of his mother's pretensions to be known as Empress-Mother and Majesty—for it is evident from Fesch's letter that it was upon these high-sounding titles that she had set her heart. Louise of Savoy, at the time of her son's accession, had been merely Comtesse d'Angoulême, and, notwithstanding the fact that she acted as Regent during François I's campaign in Italy and during his captivity in Madrid, she was never given the title of Queen. The only promotion she received was the erection of the county of Angoulême into a duchy, and as "Madame d'Angoulême" she lived and died.

Since, however, against his better judgment, Napoleon had invested his sisters with the titles of Princess and Imperial Highness, he could do no less for his mother. But here again a difficulty arose: Madame Bonaparte could not be called "Princess Letizia" without the risk of her being confounded with her daughters, while it would, moreover, give her a tinge of juvenility, which would be inappropriate. Accordingly, after long discussions with his Master of the Ceremonies, Napoleon determined to revive in his mother's favour the title which had been given under the Bourbons to the eldest daughter of the king and to the wife of the king's eldest brother: that of *Madame;* while, in order to avoid the necessity of a change of title in the event of the Emperor having a daughter, the designation of

"*Mère de Sa Majesté l'Empereur*" was added. Napoleon himself never spoke of his mother otherwise than as *Madame*, but at the Court, and in the country generally, it soon became customary to call her *Madame Mère*, and by that designation she is known to history.

The question of the rank she was to occupy was more easy to determine, and it was arranged that her official place should be at the Emperor's right hand, and that she should take precedence of the Princes, while the Empress was to take her position on his left hand and take precedence of the Princesses.

Finally, came the question of her allowance. At the end of the previous September—the beginning of the Republican year—this had been fixed at 10,000 francs a month, while, as we have mentioned, it had been subsequently raised to 15,000 francs a month. Napoleon now gave his mother a further increase of 10,000 francs, which brought her annual official income up to 300,000 francs, or 60,000 francs in excess of the sum enjoyed by her daughters. As her savings were very considerable, to say nothing of the sum which Lucien had settled upon her on his return from his embassy at Madrid, the Emperor fondly imagined that this would content her; but the insatiable old lady did not long permit it to remain at so low a figure.